Books, Bytes, and Bridges

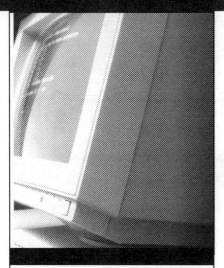

Libraries and

Computer

Centers

in Academic

Institutions

E d i t e d   b y   **Larry Hardesty**

AMERICAN LIBRARY ASSOCIATION
Chicago and London   2000

While extensive effort has gone into ensuring the reliability of information appearing in this book, the publisher makes no warranty, express or implied, on the accuracy or reliability of the information, and does not assume and hereby disclaims any liability to any person for any loss or damage caused by errors or omissions in this publication.

Project editor, Bradley A. Hannan

Text design by design solutions

Composition by the dotted i in Palatino and Helvetica Condensed using QuarkXPress 4.0 on a Macintosh platform

Printed on 50-pound white offset, a pH-neutral stock and bound in 10-pt coated cover stock by Documation

The paper used in this publication meets the minimum requirements of American National Standard for Information Sciences—Permanence of Paper for Printed Library Materials, ANSI Z39.48-1992. ∞

Library of Congress Cataloging-in-Publication Data

Books, bytes, and bridges : libraries and computer centers in academic institutions / edited by Larry Hardesty.
     p.   cm.
   Includes index.
   ISBN 0-8389-0771-7
    1. Academic libraries—United States—Data processing.   2. Universities and colleges—United States—Data processing.   3. Electronic data processing departments—United States.   I. Hardesty, Larry L.
   Z675.U5.B66   2000
   027.7′0285 21—dc21   99-040064

Printed in the United States of America

04   03   02   01   00   5 4 3 2 1

Contents

Foreword

I have waited ten years for this book. There are some excellent publications on the relations between computer centers and libraries, but Larry Hardesty's *Books, Bytes, and Bridges: Libraries and Computer Centers in Academic Institutions* is the first comprehensive book on the topic. Owing to its size, inclusiveness, and balance in topics covered, this book is a magnum opus!

When Larry Hardesty asked me to write the foreword for this book, I felt a genuine sense of honor. He has assembled an excellent group of authors for this volume. Their specialties range the full spectrum of higher education from community college to research university. Several of the authors share their real-life experiences with us. These professional experiences bring valuable insights to the understanding and appreciation of the working relationships between computing services and library services. Except for performing the act itself, there is no better way to learn what to do and what not to do than by reading about a real-life experience involving computer centers and library services. Some of the stories carried in this book reflect joy from success and disappointment from failure.

Success in one setting may not be success in another situation. Situational leadership rationalizes about how success or failure in one institution may or may not be transferred to another environment. In essence, success depends on the current situation. Thus, one should not assume that an effective working relationship between computing services and library services in one academic setting can be replicated at another environment.

There is a multitude of reasons why computer centers and libraries have consolidated, and there are a similar number of reasons why they have not. Some reasons why they have merged include expediency on the part of the institution's administration, political maneuvering, economic concerns, personalities, a good mix of service philosophies, and ignorance. Reasons for not merging the two functions include differences in management styles, content service orientation versus conduit emphasis, faculty support being greater for the library than for the computer center, preference not to place one unit at an advantage level over the other, and ignorance.

PURPOSEFULNESS

Whatever decision is made on whether to merge the two units, the decision should be based on thoughtfulness and purposefulness. Does the decision reflect the mission of the institution? Will teaching and research be better supported as a result of the decision? These and other relevant questions must be asked and answered. In common with other social structures, higher education institutions value self-perpetuation. Rather than making the change necessary for improvement in computing services and library services, administrators may choose not to bring the two units together to maintain the status quo. On the other hand, bringing the two units together without sufficient forethought may result in unnecessary commotion and worse service.

THE BEST FOR THE USERS

The choice of the organizational design for computing services and library services should be based on sound guiding principles. They should address a basic question, "What is best for the users?" Too often higher education institutions lose sight of the fundamental needs of their students, faculty, and staff. Does the existing relationship between computing services and library services serve the users in the most efficient and effective manner? If it does, then why change it? On the contrary, if it does not, then why not change it?

Has information technology lived up to our expectation? I think so. However, in *The Shaping of American Higher Education: Emergence and Growth of the Contemporary System*, Arthur M. Cohen offers the following observation:

> By no measure has information technology resulted in greater instructional productivity. For that matter few industries have enjoyed increased per capita output sufficient to justify the billions spent on it. Nevertheless, higher education has been compelled to install it because it is an essential component of student literacy. The graduates will enter a world where all forms of information technology are basic tools.[1]

CONCLUSION

Notwithstanding the cultural and other differences between computing and library personnel, the days are over when the two units can operate independently. As two separate entities or as a single unit, emphasis must be given by all parties involved to enhancing the fundamentals found in most higher education institutions' missions: learning, instruction, research, and service. The reader of this book will come away with examples of synergies realized from collaboration, models of cooperation, techniques and strategies for improving relations, and a better understanding of various topics and issues facing computer centers and libraries. Larry Hardesty has provided colleges and universities a much-needed service by editing this volume.

Donald E. Riggs

NOTE   1. Arthur M. Cohen, *The Shaping of American Higher Education: Emergence and Growth of the Contemporary System* (San Francisco: Jossey-Bass Publishers, 1998), 371-372.

Acknowledgments

My deepest appreciation to Marlene Chamberlain, Senior Acquisitions Editor of ALA Editions, for her confidence in me to edit successfully a book dealing with the complex and dynamic relationships between computer centers and libraries in academic organizations. I also want to thank Tarshel Beards, Acquisitions Editor of ALA Editions, for her assistance in editing the final version of this book.

I also greatly appreciate the role two former colleagues at Eckerd College had in the writing of this book: Jamie Hastreiter, Coordinator of Technical Services, and David Henderson, Coordinator of Public Services. Jamie and David reviewed all the contributed manuscripts in various versions and drafts. Their suggestions and comments went far beyond checking grammar and syntax and suggesting changes to enhance brevity and clarity of expression. Jamie and David offered substantive insights into the organization and content of this work. In hindsight, I should have understood earlier the significance of their contributions so their names could have rightfully joined mine as co-editors.

I want to express my appreciation to Lloyd Chapin, Vice-President and Dean of Faculty at Eckerd College, who allowed me a leave from Eckerd College during the fall of 1994 so I could do research on the relationships between computer centers and libraries at small colleges. This allowed me to have a life-shaping experience. For two months I traveled, with my wife and dog, in the eastern half of the United States, interviewing library directors and computer center directors. What a wonderful opportunity and experience! I thank my colleagues in libraries and computer centers for their hospitality as they patiently indulged my requests for their time. I also thank the Council on Library and Information Resources for funding this research.

The library staff at Austin College also deserve recognition for their patience as I completed this book. I particularly thank my able assistant, Kay Garner, for her cheerful and capable assistance in ways too numerous to list. She provided invaluable assistance through her careful monitoring of the many manuscripts as they passed through the various editing stages. I also thank John West, Associate College Librarian and Systems Librarian at Austin College. John, with his usual technological proficiency, manipulated several manuscripts, unreadable when I received them via e-mail, into readable files.

To all the contributors, I offer my fullest gratitude. We shared a mutual trust that, on my part, each would write an excellent chapter, and, on their part, that I would edit the book with high standards and would ensure that, in fact, their efforts would result in a published book. They certainly met my expectations. I hope that I have met theirs.

Finally, I thank my wife, Carol, for her usual patience, tested once again in our almost thirty years of marriage, as her husband sequestered himself away on weekends and evenings on another writing project. As the years accumulate, I increasingly appreciate the significance of never reclaiming time once past.

Introduction

When Marlene Chamberlain, Senior Acquisitions Editor of ALA Editions, first contacted me about writing a book on the relations between computer centers and libraries at academic institutions, I hesitated. Certainly this is an important issue that needs careful study and full discussion among all participants. It is capturing the attention not only of librarians and their counterparts in computing but also senior administrators and trustees. So why did I hesitate? These relationships are dynamic and evolving, and the individuals involved to date have had a wide variety of experiences—and hold an equally wide variety of opinions about these experiences. At this juncture in the evolution of computer center and library relations, understanding these relationships requires a careful examination from more than just one viewpoint. Therefore, I proposed to Marlene an edited work, which, as I wrote to potential contributors, "will provide the intended audience with a variety of perspectives."

There is no question that at most academic organizations computer centers and libraries are working more closely together than ever before. This is both desirable and necessary. What is less obvious is how to work together to achieve the best positive results and to avoid the negative ones. Numerous patterns of collaboration and cooperation between libraries and computer centers have developed within the past two decades, and no single model has emerged that all colleges and universities readily can adopt in confidence that it will fit their particular needs. This book provides a forum through which contributors share their insights into the challenges and opportunities of closer computer center and library relationships. Through this sharing, I trust the reader can better understand the complexities of the relationships between these two units and better appreciate the care needed in changing these relationships.

The reader who seeks a ready and single answer will be disappointed. Probably less satisfying to such a reader is the message of this book—there is no single path for the two units to proceed on in working successfully together! In addition, there is a corollary message—there are many perils involved in the relationships between the two units! At one end of the spectrum, an institution can do too little to facilitate positive relations and, as a result, miss important opportunities. At the other end of the spectrum, an institution can move too quickly and too far with demoralizing effects. Unfortunately, there is no convenient guidepost to tell an institution where on the spectrum it might be and how to proceed. While this book is not such a guidepost, I hope, nevertheless, readers can extrapolate how to proceed at their own institutions from the various perspectives offered.

Our present situation did not manifest itself overnight, nor has it evolved linearly. The authors of the first three chapters offer insight into the historical evolution of the discussion. Peggy Seiden and Michael Kathman trace the discussion from the early 1980s to the present. They contend that two distinct periods exist and that earlier concerns for user needs and service have been overshadowed more recently by efforts to save money and solve personnel or organizational problems. Robert S. Freeman, Scott B. Mandernack, and John Mark Tucker, through their bibliographic essay, next offer readers further insight into the historical evolution of the issues as reflected in the literature. Terrence Mech then examines the intertwining of the evolution of higher education, computers, and the library and concludes that the position of chief information officer (CIO) is a natural response to several forces coming together at this time.

Several contributors attempt to provide a conceptual framework for understanding the various issues. It is fitting that Raymond Neff contributed to this volume. He wrote an article in the mid-1980s that has helped frame the discussion ever since. Delmus Williams and Onadell Bly have written an essay in which they further define the issues through a series of questions evaluating the effectiveness of cooperation between libraries and computer centers. Paul Setze and Kimberly Jordan explore the overlapping roles of computer centers and libraries. Edward Garten and Delmus Williams review the "clashing cultures" of the two units and explore reasons and ways to bring them together.

I included results from my study of relationships at small colleges. While I found considerable evidence of cooperation, I also found many leaders of both units at these institutions concerned about moving too quickly into closer relationships. At these colleges, the emphasis is on people, not structures. Edward Meachen examines, through a series of interviews with individuals at various levels, the relationships of the two units at the eleven comprehensive universities in the University of Wisconsin system. He found a variety of situations and concludes that institutions are now seeking CIOs with a broad institutional perspective and a strong service philosophy.

Several chapters deal with specific institutions. I especially sought case studies co-authored by individuals from different backgrounds. I hope these essays fully reflect the different perspectives and, at the same time, adequately describe the results of good relationships achieved through a variety of structures. I encouraged contributors not to avoid discussing problems but, instead, to address any challenges that impeded positive relations and to describe ways they overcame these challenges.

The first several case studies deal with integrated or merged situations. Stephen Peterson and Bernard Hecker discuss the conceptual foundation for moving the library and computer center closer together and into a planned new building at Trinity College. Eugene Engeldinger provides a case study on how the service imperative brought the two units successfully together at Carthage College. Connie Dowell and Andrew White, based on their experiences at Connecticut College, contend that combining the qualities from library and computer center personnel will create a new profession that will forge an environment for success. John Olsgaard and George Terry provide an example of a merger at a large state university (the University of South Carolina). They make a case for strong administrative support and the need for a commitment from individuals to make a merger successful.

The next several chapters provide examples of computer centers and libraries working together through various organizational structures and with varying degrees of success. Rhoda Channing and James L. Dominick write of the pioneering efforts of Wake Forest University, where neither the library director nor the chief information officer reports to the chief academic officer. Through a long-term agreement with IBM, all entering students now receive a ThinkPad computer. Their success demonstrates what flexible and collegial staff can accomplish. Jennifer Cargill and Ronald Hay describe what can be achieved at not only the institutional level, but also the state level when library and computer personnel work together. Sue Samson, Kim Granath, and Vicki Pengelly offer a frontline perspective of the benefits of close working relationships.

However, the path is not always smooth. Robin Wagner provides a candid analysis of the experience of Gettysburg College when an institution moves too quickly into uncharted waters. Theresa Trawick and J. T. Hart discuss a "work in progress" in which some desirable results have been achieved, but they call for application of management theories in furthering restructuring of relationships between the two units. Adella Blain describes the challenges at a large community college to bring the two units together, and she offers several useful recommendations in completing the process.

David Lewis and Georgia Miller end this work that challenges institutions to rethink their focus on structures, hierarchies, and departments. They call for more visionary changes while still building on the traditional strengths of the university. They speculate that perhaps we have gone beyond the point where combining the library and the computer center is the most sensible solution. Lewis and Miller call for librarians and technologists to support each other in creating a new learning environment.

Where is all this leading us? I believe it is too early to predict with a high degree of accuracy. Perhaps the only thing apparent is that there are multiple paths and many pitfalls along each of them. Institutions must make a conscious decision as to which path to take, and do so only as the result of careful thought and reflection on their own particular needs, resources, and mission. Then each institution must continually monitor this decision. Holding onto tradition, adopting the most recent innovation, or trying something in between can all be appropriate or inappropriate strategies, depending on the institutional environment. No doubt all of us face some tough thinking and hard work in building and maintaining relationships across campus that will take us into the next century. I hope the efforts of the contributors to this work have made easier the challenge before us.

CHAPTER ONE

A History of the Rhetoric and Reality of Library and Computing Relationships

PEGGY SEIDEN
MICHAEL D. KATHMAN

Considerable discussion and publication occurred in the early 1980s regarding the relationship between computing centers and libraries. The dialogue centered on whether libraries and computing centers should be merged into a single organizational unit with broad responsibility for the big "I"—Information—on campus. In 1985 Raymond K. Neff wrote an article entitled, "Merging Libraries and Computer Centers: Manifest Destiny or Manifestly Deranged?" This article focused the discussion and debate that continued for the rest of the decade. It began with the sentence: "The idea of merging the university library with the university computing center is not grounded in experience—no institution has actually done it—but comes instead from trends that can be observed in both types of organizations."[1] Neff identified eight trends that demonstrated the similarities of libraries and computer centers. The increasing use libraries made of computers and electronic databases served as the basis for the similarities, resulting in an overlap and reliance, not previously existing, between libraries and computer centers.

Thirteen years later Arnold Hirshon identified more than ninety institutions in this country that had formal organizational relationships between the library and the computing center. What has happened in the intervening years to make Raymond Neff's rhetoric a reality?

The authors of this chapter believe that interest in the formalized conjoining of libraries and computing centers emerged during two very distinct periods—between 1984 and 1987 and from 1992 to the present. We believe that the unique confluence of driving forces in higher education, information technology, and libraries contributed to the waxing of interest and subsequent waning.

THE 1980S MERGER MANIA

Merger and acquisition theory suggests that structural alliances will develop when change occurs at the industry, enterprise, or institutional level.[2] Taking their cue from this theory, the authors examined the above-mentioned "driving forces" during the two historical periods to better understand why colleges and universities began to consider merging libraries and computing centers. For our purposes, we have defined the three levels at which change occurs as follows: industry level changes occur throughout higher education; enterprise level changes occur throughout academic libraries and academic computing; and institutional level changes occur within individual institutions of higher education.

Industry Level Change

During both historical periods under discussion, significant changes occurred in higher education that challenged the status quo. During the 1980s, propelled by studies such as *A Nation at Risk*,[3] which focused on K-12, and Ernest Boyer's *College: The Undergraduate Experience in America*,[4] a national imperative for achieving educational excellence arose. In particular, some leaders in higher education expressed a significant concern about the quality of undergraduate education.[5] As a response to this, universities began to reemphasize the importance of teaching. A key aspect of the educational reform of the mid-to-late 1980s focused on helping faculty members become better teachers. Technology often played a significant role in these discussions because many educational reformers viewed it as a pedagogical tool of almost unlimited promise. The new emphasis on teaching also legitimized the efforts of faculty who sought to integrate computer-based tools into their teaching, although institutions seldom rewarded these efforts in the same way as research. Traditional academic support services such as the library and media services, joined by academic computing centers, found themselves working together in efforts to enhance teaching—sometimes alone or sometimes in partnership with a "teaching center." The emphasis on the importance of undergraduate teaching enabled computing to move from being seen as something special done by researchers in the sciences to being seen as a tool for the classroom. Previously, technology in support of classroom teaching had been the purview of media centers, which were often part of libraries. Now many computer center staffs saw it as part of their purview.

At this same time, the federal government cut funds for higher education. While this had the most immediate impact on available research dollars, it also had longer-term consequences with an impact on financial aid. With the cuts in federal research dollars, educators and administrators found particularly appealing gifts and heavily discounted hardware from vendors such as IBM, Apple, and NeXT. These gifts and discounts hastened the use of technology in faculty and student research, in student work and, eventually, in teaching. They, however, resulted in a difficult financial situation four or five years later as new technology became available and many machines had to be replaced after vendors either disappeared or quit offering gifts and heavy discounting.

Enterprise Level Change

As libraries began to automate in the late 1960s and the early 1970s, libraries and computing centers often found themselves at odds with each other over the development of in-house systems. Anne Woodsworth and James Williams wrote that the library jockeying for a "stand-alone" computer and the computer center resisting this effort characterized this period. The library's desire to maintain complete control over all aspects of its services, as well as some skepticism about the responsiveness of the computer center, served as the crux of the attitude of many librarians.[6]

By the 1980s attitudes began to shift because of the high failure rate of in-house library automation systems, the costs of running these systems, the need for technical staff to maintain them, and the space and capital needed for computer rooms in libraries. As turnkey systems became the norm, libraries often brought computer centers into the contract negotiations to ensure library system capability for interfacing with other systems on campus. Compatibility issues became critical. Furthermore, while the "early adopters" of library automation often had the resources to hire and train systems staffs, as automation spread smaller libraries frequently found it necessary to look beyond their doors for support in running the hardware and software. Computing centers, particularly administrative computing centers, had the personnel and the experience to run large mainframe databases, and supporting the library's integrated system seemed a natural alliance.

At the same time, computing centers found themselves in the midst of a far more "revolutionary" change. Up until then, computing centers—where they existed—had two primary purposes: to support administrative applications like finance, the registrar, and human resources, and to support large scale number crunching for certain academic disciplines. Sciences, mathematics and, to a lesser extent, quantitative social sciences were the primary users. But with the introduction of microcomputers in the early 1980s, the user population shifted. Brian Hawkins writes, "When we moved from mainframes to micros, we certainly saw a different set of demands, a different audience. The sleeping giant of the humanists and many social scientists woke up and started to become demanding users."[7] New users now required new support structures and resources. In seeking models of service-driven organizations on campus, computing centers often looked toward libraries. Faculty and administrators seldom questioned the importance of the role of the library. Technology, on the other hand, was seen as a new kid on the block, and many in academe expressed skepticism of its value, particularly when applied to teaching. Thus, both libraries and computing centers underwent changes that encouraged them to look to each other as allies and partners.

Institutional Driving Forces

While industry-wide or enterprise-wide forces may create an environment for organizational change, alliances between libraries and computing centers will not occur unless changes at the institutional level create opportunities to rethink the relationship. These changes, unique to each institution, may be strategic, departmental, or operational.

The rapid growth of technology in colleges during this period created opportunities for strategic change. On the strategic level, many institutions struggled to discover the best organizational patterns for computing support. While administrative applications historically had centralized support, academic disciplinary computing usually had distributed support. However, distributed models created inequities, particularly when most financial support for computing came from research dollars. Where was the support for the "have-nots" to come from, particularly in the humanities and arts? When an institution decided to go with a centralized support model, it seemed to address these inequities and create an organization tied to the academic mission in much the same way as the library. Where an institution chose a centralized academic computing model, it then had to grapple with whether this new organization should be separate from administrative computing services. Libraries often found it easier to form alliances with separate academic computing organizations than with combined academic and administrative computing organizations.

Change at the department level, such as the departure of the library director or the director of computing or the hiring of new personnel, often provided the catalyst for restructuring. For example, the opportunity to hire a systems person or team often opened discussions about whether that person or team should report to the library or the computing center.

Other issues that influenced decisions to merge or not to merge dealt with the "appropriate" sort of leadership in the library or computing center. Was the library director technologically savvy? Was the computer center director service-focused?

During the 1980s many areas of mutual interest emerged from the changes occurring within libraries and computing centers. Various operational decisions also brought libraries and computing centers into each other's areas of responsibility. These included decisions to support public computing in libraries, to purchase software for circulation, to create training programs for various general applications, to allow unmediated database searching, and to develop locally maintained databases. All necessitated a closer working relationship.

In some universities and colleges, computing centers continued to work in the mainframe world, while libraries developed microcomputer clusters. In others, computing centers sought space in libraries because of the library's long hours and the increasing computer experience of many of the library staff. The trend to provide microcomputers became so significant that the Association of College and Research Libraries (ACRL) formed a group in 1984 to provide a forum for discussion of these issues. Software acquisition and support offered another area of collaboration. Sometimes these collaborations involved only baby steps, such as the library offering to catalog software documentation. Other more significant cases occurred as libraries fully integrated software support into their operations and hosted workshops on general applications such as word processing.

The Rhetoric in the 1980s

As these changes in computing, libraries, and higher education created opportunities for interaction and mutual support, members of the two professions began to examine their convergence. As libraries implemented online catalog systems, envisioning the availability, through computers, of information traditionally housed in the library did not require a great leap of imagination. Pat Molholt, then at Rensselaer Polytechnic Institute, and Pat Battin, then at Columbia University, both wrote about the coming "electronic library" and the need for a strong relationship between the computer centers and the libraries.

Pat Molholt asserted that, as more and more information became electronically available, there would be a need for an information support system made up of services from both areas.[8] She identified the various pieces of this support system that could come from the library and from the computer center. Molholt clearly believed that a logical and mutually beneficial relationship existed between computing centers and libraries that should be developed. She wrote strongly that librarians need to be proactive in coordinating and leading this new effort.[9] Pat Battin held similar views about the necessity for coordination between libraries and computing centers. She wrote:

> Scholarship will require a mixture of formats and a mixture of hardware for a very long time to come. The challenge is to provide the necessary linkages between formats, and this can only be done by reorganizing our information services—libraries and computer centers—into one coordinated information function.[10]

The Reality in the 1980s

In 1986, motivated by discussions of mergers, convergence, and the obvious need to work together to support library automation, ACRL created a Task Force on Libraries and Computing Centers "to investigate cooperative ventures between academic libraries and computing facilities and to draft guidelines for such cooperation."[11] The task force developed a list of some ninety institutions (major research libraries, state universities, and liberal arts colleges) and surveyed them to ascertain the likelihood of organizational merger. The survey results, in fact, revealed that only four institutions indicated the high likelihood of a merger, while 86 percent of the respondents thought it improbable. This is in spite of that fact that 83 percent had engaged in cooperative efforts usually involving the library's integrated system.[12]

The Task Force issued its final report in July 1988 and included the summaries of interviews with individuals at eleven institutions that had some type of merged organization or extensive cooperative programs. These institutions included Columbia, Carnegie Mellon, and Vanderbilt, precisely the same institutions from which came such library visionaries as Bill Arms, Pat Battin, and Malcolm Getz. These leaders and others from the eleven institutions represented the cutting edge of integration of technology into their libraries. The ACRL report authors recognized the very institution-specific nature of the issues. The Task Force issued fifteen guidelines to assist libraries contemplating some type of relationship with computing centers. Only the last six specifically addressed the factors that should be taken into consideration in contemplation of a merger.[13]

That same year, Anne Woodsworth suggested that the rapidly changing nature of the technology combined with rising client expectations exceeding staffing and financial abilities of both computing centers and libraries had created the need for a relationship between computing centers and libraries.[14] She believed that fear and the mistaken assumption that libraries should control their own computers provided the impetus for two of the activities the profession was involved in—the Standards for the Evaluation of University Library Performance and the ACRL Task Force on Libraries and Computing Centers.[15] Woodsworth ended her article on a positive note, however, in writing, "The combined efforts of libraries and computing centers are beginning to bear fruit on campuses where the brightest and the best from both operations combine forces. They are providing information services which, heretofore, could not be provided."[16] This acknowledgment of the unique skills that each brought to the academic enterprise was reiterated by Richard Dougherty."[17] He urged the creation of a close working relationship between the two. Wrote Dougherty, "Both have special and complementary skills that are in short supply. Working together, they should become a powerful influence in the reshaping of research and scholarship in higher education."[18]

In 1989, Pat Molholt wrote an article entitled "What Happened to the Merger Debate?" in the final issue of *Libraries and Computing Centers: Issues of Mutual Concern*. In the article she observed, "Their [computer centers and libraries] predicted merger—perhaps never comfortable to either side—has instead evolved into a kind of functional cooperation."[19] By the end of the decade, much of the discussion had subsided. Marilyn Martin, writing in 1992, summed up the end of the decade by saying:

> It [the debate about mergers] seems to have died due to lack of interest. Libraries and academic computer centers have been increasingly cooperative, as mutual benefits have become apparent, and many of the problems cited in the literature during the late 1980s have been resolved.[20]

THE 1990S REEMERGENCE

However, in the early 1990s, the debate reemerged with renewed vigor and interest. Why this reemergence of the issue? Why this change? The answers lie in the numerous forces in libraries, computing centers, and higher education that became so significant that they presaged a major paradigm shift in these organizations.

Industry-Level Driving Forces

By the early 1990s, information technology assumed a much greater role in the university as it permeated the entire higher-education enterprise. Information technology became the new "black hole" down which administrators continued to push more and more dollars without those dollars ever being enough. As old technology (legacy systems) required replacement, costs escalated. Institutions needed new phone and data switches, new administrative systems, new library systems, and new microcomputers on five-year, then four-year, then three-year replacement cycles. The vendors found themselves no longer in a position to give major hardware donations or deep discounts. They had successfully penetrated the higher education market. Institutions had built enormous hardware infrastructures that needed continual updating. Higher-education administrators struggled to deal with the technology, both financially and organizationally. The development of the college or university Chief Information Officer (CIO) position became one popular response to their concern. As noted in a HEIRAlliance background report from the University of Indiana:

> Many university presidents are countering the tendencies toward disintegration of their information resource fabric by appointing high-level administrators to coordinate and lead the evolution of their information resource environment. Approximately one third of the institutions responding to the 1992 CAUSE IT survey report having a CIO position at the present time.[21]

We must remember in 1992 that the CIO position generally referred to the Chief Information Technology person on the campus. At that time the CIO issue centered on whether both academic and administrative computing should report to the same individual.[22] Few of these CIOs had libraries that reported to them—a development that came later.

An increased demand for accountability and fiscal responsibility reflected the other major change in higher education during this period. With less federal and state aid, and "genteel poverty" no longer accepted as a perquisite of faculty rank, universities and colleges found themselves committing over two-thirds of their operating budgets to salaries and financial aid. Support services and the administrative lines provided the only places to cut costs.[23] As in business, reengineering often became the solution. Particularly at tuition-driven private institutions, strong pressure developed to reduce costs drastically in order to hold tuition increases down. Colleges without large endowments found themselves having to look at cutbacks and layoffs, outsourcing, and reengineering.

Accountability in higher education is also linked to the increased emphasis on teaching, particularly of marketable skills. Although there is no one solution, almost all colleges and universities in the past five years have struggled with the question of whether computing literacy should be a core competency required of their graduates. Discussions of computing literacy often have broadened to discussions of information literacy; and in broader campus discussions of information literacy, it has often been confused with technology literacy. Libraries and computing centers both are working on solutions to enhance students' facility with technology and information. Both want to get their foot in the door and claim this issue as their own.

Enterprise-Level Driving Forces

The widespread implementation of campus networking and the exponential growth of the Internet provided the primary driving force at the enterprise level. Efforts to integrate technology into the curriculum moved beyond the early adopters. Many more faculty members began demanding increased technical support. In the library, technology moved from the "back room," or automation of processing, to the reference desk with computer-based indexes and other resources. This move required an increased emphasis on instruction and training necessary to use technology for library research. While Molholt and Battin had predicted radical changes in the ways libraries did their business, not until the establishment of campus networking did institutions realize their visions for the transformation of scholarly information and consequent transformation of libraries and computing centers. Hirshon correctly notes that the increase in mergers corresponded directly with the advent of the World Wide Web.[24]

The formation of the Coalition for Networked Information (CNI) is symbolic of the extent to which many viewed networking as in the purview of both libraries and computing organizations. The major professional associations in higher education computing—CAUSE and EDUCOM, and the Association of Research Libraries—formed CNI. It sought to realize its mission, "to advance scholarship and intellectual productivity,"[25] through networking via the efforts of its working groups on standards, directories, teaching and learning, publication, and research projects.

Computing centers had for some time been involved in providing campus information through bulletin boards and other systems. They now quickly migrated to Gophers and subsequently to the Web. Both Gophers and the Web offered relatively simple authoring environments, so other campus units often became involved in providing information. However, computing centers almost always retained responsibility for the server. While the servers and networks fell to the computer center to support, librarians generally viewed the question of content as belonging to the library. That division seemed clearest with content in bibliographic databases. The lines soon became blurred, however, in talking about broadly defined information. The development of campus-wide information systems, the provision of access to software archives, the support of numeric data files such as the Inter-university Consortium for Political and Social Research (ICPSR), and the creation of digital libraries confounded the question of who did what.

The implementation of campus networks changed the nature of the applications that computing centers supported. While word processing and spreadsheets remained popular, communication tools and applications to support delivery of information across the network grew quickly to become the most widely used software on campuses. Both libraries and computing saw these applications as extensions of their existing responsibilities. Libraries viewed newsgroups and electronic mailing lists as part of the scholarly communication apparatus, and, to them, the content available through the Web or Gopher servers looked very much like the information libraries typically collected. The Web became a front door to a virtual library. On the other hand, the computing center viewed these as another set of applications to be supported. In fact, both librarians and information technology professionals had considerable expertise to bring to supporting users of these applications. For example, librarians brought to the problem considerable skills based on an extensive history of dealing with long-term preservation, as well as organization of knowledge and an understanding of issues of authority and authenticity. Information technology (IT) professionals understood their primary user culture, the underlying structures of these applications, and the technology to create, store, and retrieve digital information.

Buoyed by easier authoring environments such as HyperText Markup Language (HTML), the increased availability of useful digital-based resources, and intensive training programs, many faculty members moved from relying on computing simply to support largely personal productivity and research to increased reliance on computing for support for technological applications in the classroom. Continuing emphasis on educational reform and better teaching provided even more incentives to focus on pedagogy. The spread of technology placed increased pressures on already stretched computing staffs to support both standardized applications and innovation in the classroom. In some cases, librarians provided leadership in working with the faculty; in others the institutions drafted librarians because of their experience in training and instruction and their familiarity with disciplinary resources to work with faculty on curricular issues. This resulted in fruitful partnering at places like Kenyon College, Colgate University, and North Carolina State University, and some well-publicized projects like U-Wired.[26] The work of the CNI furthered these initial models of collaboration by sponsoring a series of conferences and workshops at which teams of librarians, information technology professionals, and faculty presented work accomplished through teamwork.[27]

The shift in the focus of library technology from automating processes to the provision of digital information provided a third enterprise-level change. Battin's "scholar's workstation" finally arrived on faculty and student desktops; the network provided the conduit to deliver resources as both commercial providers and scholars began to build the digital library. As technology thoroughly permeated reference services, librarians quickly became among the most skilled users of technology on campus to assist patrons adequately. Once computers found their way into the reference room, librarians also found themselves troubleshooting network and printing problems, assisting patrons with e-mail, downloading, and file transfer. Increasingly what librarians did at the reference desk and what IT professionals did at help desks overlapped each other. The idea of combining help desk and reference functions grew directly out of this dilemma of trying to parse patrons' questions.

Institutional-Level Driving Forces

Again, during the 1990s strategic changes have played a critical role in providing opportunities for mergers and other types of structural alliances. The problem of deferred maintenance necessitated renovation of many buildings, which provided an opportunity for campus-wide networking, including the networking of dormitories. In planning a new library building or expansion or renovation, senior administrators often used the opportunity to ask whether the computing center should be moved into the new or expanded or renovated building.

As accountability became an issue and costs for technology escalated, the need to plan more carefully for technology became obvious. Development of campus-wide strategic plans for technology allowed for open discussions exploring the optimal organizational structures. Even where organizational structures were not at issue, the library's new role as a key technological player opened the door for joint technology planning and paved the way for increasing collaboration.

During this period, individual institutions began to look at and adopt business models such as Total Quality Management (TQM). While reorganization seemed to be a daily fact of life in computing centers, many libraries also began to look at reengineering to streamline operations or absorb losses of positions. Libraries and computing centers experimented with team-based organizations and flattened hierarchical structures. While such structures may have more permeable boundaries and thus be more open to structural alliances, they also implied a flexibility and willingness to change on the part of members of these organizations—essential elements for any larger scale reorganization.

The Rhetoric and Reality

By 1993, the needed infrastructure had been put in place to realize the desktop delivery of information that formed the underlying rationale for Molholt's and Battin's ideas of merged organizations. To deliver the information and support users needed required strong alliances and active collaboration between the library and computing center. Hirshon's paper, issued some ten years after the ACRL Task Force's final report, cited ninety-four institutions in which significant aspects of both the computing and library operations report to the same chief information officer.[28] These he defined as integrated.

Even where the need to collaborate does not result in organizational integration, the potential overlap in responsibilities and blurring of those responsibilities can create tensions between the organizations that need to work together. Hardesty's data, gathered from 1994 to 1996, indicate few if any colleges and universities where these units work in isolation from each other.[29] In

1994, Library Solutions Press sponsored an institute for the heads of libraries and computing centers entitled "Building Partnerships." This workshop provided an opportunity to learn about successful collaborative ventures, to explore cultural stereotypes, and to develop strategies for ongoing cooperation and collaboration. In 1997, CNI began hosting regional workshops with a similar purpose. As the 1990s end, collaboration between libraries and computing centers seems to be the working model for most institutions. Formal collaboration is more often through committees than through organizational charts. Even those that have "merged" basically have two separate units that report to the same individual. Whether that individual is called a CIO, a Joint Director of Computing and Libraries, or a Vice President for Information Services, the result is a collaborative effort between the two areas. Very few institutions identified in the literature have merged the day-to-day operations of the computing center and library into one staff who handle the public services for both units.

CONCLUSION

Two distinctly different catalysts provided the impetus for mergers between libraries and computing centers for the two periods studied. During the first period, leadership within libraries and computing centers provided the catalysts. Visionaries saw a time in the not-too-distant future when the delivery of electronic information to the desktops of scholars would require a mix of skills and knowledge possessed by individuals in both libraries and computing centers. However, few actual mergers occurred. While libraries tended to be the clients—often the largest academic clients—of computing centers, true partnering between the two units remained still in its infancy.

During the 1990s two major forces coalesced: the wide-scale implementation of networks and the development of networked resources, and an adoption of streamlining support services as a strategy to control costs in higher education. As a result, there developed simultaneously an environment in which synergies could best be realized through cooperation and collaboration, and a perception by upper-level administrators that needed institutional economies could be realized through restructuring. While the largest single number of respondents (twenty out of forty-seven) to Hirshon's survey of CIOs reported the convergence of information and the technology on which it relies as the primary reason for organizational integration, Hirshon believes such formal reorganization unlikely to have happened without pressure from senior administration.[30] Hardesty also notes, "For the most part at the institutions I visited, the impetus is certainly not coming from computer center directors or library directors. I have to speculate that senior administrators are promoting the idea."[31]

The ultimate driving force should be provision of the best possible service to the patrons for the least cost. In the early years the visionaries focused primarily on the best ways to deliver the new technologies to users. The second guideline proposed by the ACRL Task Force sought to "emphasize the end users, rather than the information providers."[32] The verdict is still out on the second stage. Although there have been some interesting attempts to combine help desks and reference desks so that users can have "one-stop shopping," anticipated savings and structural considerations, as much as user needs, appear to drive this second stage. Hardesty found in his study of liberal arts colleges that much of the pressure for change came "from presidents and boards of trustees,"[33] and that neither computing center directors nor librarians had confidence in their "motives nor the supposed results."[34] Boards, presidents, and deans "wonder why there are not more positive results from all the money the institution has invested in technology."[35] Hirshon warns that one should "not integrate to save money, or to solve a particular personnel or organizational problem."[36] The need to offer this advice reveals the impact these reasons, not user needs, have on decisions to integrate. The authors recommend additional study and research to determine if creation of CIO positions and further integration of computer centers and libraries actually better meet user needs.

NOTES

1. Raymond K. Neff, "Merging Libraries and Computing Centers: Manifest Destiny or Manifestly Deranged?" *Educom Bulletin* 20 (winter 1985): 8.
2. Joseph E. McCann and Roderick Gilkey, *Joining Forces: Creating and Managing Successful Mergers and Acquisitions* (Englewood Cliffs, N. J.: Prentice-Hall, 1988); M. E. Porter, *Competitive Strategy: Techniques for Analyzing Industries and Competitors* (New York: Free Press, 1980) and many other books and articles by Porter.
3. *National Commission on Excellence in Education, A Nation at Risk: The Imperatives for Education Reform* (Washington, D. C.: G.P.O., 1983).
4. Ernest L. Boyer, *College: The Undergraduate Experience in America* (Harper, 1987).
5. Patricia K. Cross, "Improving the Quality of Instruction," in Arthur Levine, ed. *Higher Learning in America 1980-2000* (Baltimore: Johns Hopkins, 1993), 288.
6. Anne Woodsworth and James F. Williams II, "Computer Centers and Libraries: Working toward Partnership," *Library Administration and Management* (March 1988): 85.
7. Brian Hawkins and Patricia Battin, "The Changing Role of the Information Professional: A Dialogue," *Cause/Effect* 20 (spring 1997): 2. The electronic version is at http://www.cause.org/information-resources/ir-library/html/cem971.html
8. Pat Molholt, "On Converging Paths: The Computing Center and the Library," *Journal of Academic Librarianship* 11 (November 1985): 286.
9. Ibid., 288
10. Patricia Battin, "Crossing the Border: Librarianship in the Information Age," *The Harvard Librarian* 19 (September 1985): 9.
11. Richard W. Boss et al., *ACRL Task Force on Libraries and Computer Centers Final Report* (Chicago: ACRL, 1988): 1.
12. Ibid., 2-3.
13. Ibid., 16-18.
14. Anne Woodsworth, "Computing Centers and Libraries as Cohorts: Exploiting Mutual Strengths," *Journal of Library Administration* 9 (1988): 27.
15. Ibid., 27-28.
16. Ibid., 32-33.
17. Richard M. Dougherty, "Libraries and Computing Centers: A Blueprint for Collaboration," *College & Research Libraries* 48 (July 1987): 289-296.
18. Ibid., 296.
19. Pat Molholt, "What Happened to the Merger Debate?" *Libraries and Computing Centers: Issues of Mutual Concern* 13 (May 1989): 1.
20. Marilyn Martin, "Academic Libraries and Computing Centers: Opportunities for Leadership" *Library Administration and Management* 6 (spring 1992): 77-80.
21. Thomas Ehrlich, James G. Neal, and Polley Ann McClure, "What Presidents Need to Know about the Integration of Information Technologies on Campus," Background

Paper for HEIRAlliance Strategies Report *no. 1*, 1992. http://www.educause.edu/ir/library/text/HEI1030.TXT

22. Alton Brantley, Lynn DeNoia, Barbara Horgan, and Harry Reif, "The Role of the CIO in the Curriculum Change Process," paper presented at CAUSE92, December 1-4, 1992, Dallas, Tex. Available at http://www.educause.edu/ir/library/text/cnc9214.txt

23. Ron Gales, "Can Colleges Be Reengineered?" *Across the Board* (March 1994): (1-3) on Lexis-Nexis.

24. Arnold Hirshon, *Integrating Computing and Library Services: An Administrative Planning and Implementation Guide for Information Services*, CAUSE Professional Paper Series 18 (Boulder, Colo.: CAUSE, 1998), 3.

25. CNI Web site, http://www.cni.org

26. U-Wired was founded in 1994 as a collaboration of the University of Washington's Libraries, Computing and Communications, and the Office of Undergraduate Education to support the use of technology in teaching and learning. For further information, see http://www.washington.edu/uwired/about/index.html

27. For more information on similar projects see http://www.cni.org/projects/nlc for descriptions of what a large number of institutions have done.

28. Hirshon, *Integrating Computing and Library Services*, 1.

29. Larry Hardesty, "Library and Computer Relations: The Human Side," a paper presented at a conference on Information Technology sponsored by the North Carolina Center for Independent Higher Education at Wake Forest University, October 25, 1995: 28.

30. Hirshon, *Integrating Computing and Library Services*, 4.

31. Hardesty, "Library and Computer Relations," 18.

32. Boss et al., *ACRL Task Force on Libraries and Computer Centers*, 16.

33. Council on Library Resources, *Research Brief* 2 (November 1997), 3.

34. Ibid.

35. Ibid.

36. Hirshon, *Integrating Computing and Library Services*, 29.

CHAPTER TWO

An Issue in Search of a Metaphor
Readings on the Marriageability of Libraries and Computing Centers

ROBERT S. FREEMAN
SCOTT B. MANDERNACK
JOHN MARK TUCKER

The issues surrounding library and computing center relationships draw from various disciplines and perspectives. These include but are not exclusive to institutional history, organizational and leadership theory, and the sociology of higher education, as well as the structural and managerial change driven by technological developments. The literature devoted to the potential of the library and the computing center to merge ("marriageability") continues to grow and to provide increasingly useful perspectives from the past twenty years. We arranged our entries chronologically to help readers understand how this dialogue has been evolving.

We have much cause for optimism when considering how the tone has changed from our first entry in the *Journal of Library Automation* in 1979 to the assessments of Arnold Hirshon in 1998. In the interim, librarians and computing specialists each managed to claim professional authority over essential components in information technology—content for librarians and conduit for computing specialists—and to work collaboratively to create the systems and to deliver the information needed in higher education.

Throughout these years, the literatures of technology and management have enlarged the vocabularies and definitions of organizational change and communication. Thus, academics have new tools for grappling with technical and administrative issues and a fresh appreciation of the importance of definitional clarity for visions, missions, goals, and objectives. These conceptual elements must guide considerations of the structural changes that would undergird our efforts to serve user communities efficiently and cost effectively.

While the literature devoted to this topic continues to grow, we are forced into questions of how much merging actually occurs. Even though the rise of the chief information officer (CIO) served as one barometer of change in the 1980s, our highest estimates of the creation of CIOs never exceeded 200 (among institutions that number nearly 3,700 nationally). But CIOs reflect only one response among several gradations that colleges and universities have attempted. Numerous organizational structures have been explored, implemented, and revised.

And the professional literature we have access to may not reflect accurately the responses academe has made at any given point. Still, our professional literature combined with our informal dialogues becomes instructive guides and sources of encouragement for those who address the challenges of higher education. And technological development and managerial leadership will continue to shape discussions and facilitate effective decision making as long as they are successfully wedded to issues of central purpose.

"The Library and the Computer Center." *Journal of Library Automation* 12 (December 1979): 361-378.

Five brief papers edited by William D. Mathews were based on a program conducted by the Technical Standards for Library Automation Committee of the Library and Information Technology Association of ALA entitled "The Library and the Computer Center: A Marriage Made in. . . ." Ken Bierman of the Tucson Public Library entitled his remarks "The Horror Story," recalling the tale of the woman who had been married three times yet remained a virgin. She explained that her first husband died on their wedding night, her second husband was "a bit flaky" and uninterested in her, and her third husband was a computer specialist who simply sat on the edge of the bed telling her how good everything was going to be.

Hugh Standifer outlines "What the Computer Center Should Do for a Library," urging cost and service justifications on the basis of problem definition and feasibility studies. Micki Jo Young and Walt Crawford review "The Sources of Disharmony," noting that both entities are extremely serious and dedicated to their work, service-oriented, and focused on data and detail. Yet, they are fundamentally discordant due to differing patterns of professional communication, differing vocabularies, and differing priorities. In "Negotiating a Workable Compromise," Barbara Markuson underscores the need to recognize that negotiation involves risk and encourages librarians to prepare thoroughly for automation projects.

In "A Final Word," William D. Mathews offers some fascinating generalizations. Computer specialists can become instant experts while librarians can hold four degrees, read two foreign languages, and gain ten years of experience without becoming an expert on anything. Computer specialists solve problems without defining them; librarians define them without solving them. Differences such as these may be less stark today and perhaps less critical—due to our more widely distributed environments—but they bear a remarkable ring of truth, reminding all of us how challenging our roles continue to be.

Plane, Robert A. "Merging a Library and a Computing Center." *Perspectives in Computing* 2, no. 3 (October 1982): 14-21.

In the mid-1970s Clarkson College of Technology redefined its library as a service rather than a place. The college conceived of the library as a system for information support rather than a depository of information. Clarkson incorporated the Computing Center staff into the Educational Resources Center (ERC) and merged personnel from both entities into a single unit. The campus-wide computer network, operating from the ERC, supports teaching and administrative functions in addition to access to more than 150 databases in the sciences, engineering, and education.

Battin, Patricia. "The Electronic Library: A Vision for the Future." *Educom Bulletin* 19 (summer 1984): 12-17, 34.

Patricia Battin, Vice President and University Librarian at Columbia University, describes the development of information technology in light of scholarly communication and information systems and delineates her vision of the Scholarly Information Center. She contends that information technology must be integrated into the existing information system, providing invisible, coordinated access to the universe of knowledge in a way that is most conducive to users. This can be accomplished through the cooperation and centralization that runs counter to the autonomous nature of academic departments.

Identifying three generations of library computing, the author characterizes each period with its general developments and initiatives. "Library automation" focused on the application of computer and telecommunications technology to library processing functions. The second generation brought the distribution of hardware and software products to local settings via terminals connected to a mainframe in support of integrated local systems. The third generation moves these applications to the individual scholar's workstation, allowing for greater access to and manipulation of information. While the technical capabilities progress, the fragmented array of databases requires a centralized infrastructure to reduce user frustration and the costs of redundancy.

The author proposes a Scholarly Information Center, merging the library and the computer center, to "provide one-stop shopping for the university community as well as a stabilizing planning mechanism for effective and flexible response to rapidly changing technologies" (p. 17). She urges new policies for centrally subsidized information services, the involvement of scholarly societies in curbing the fee-for-service pricing structures being adopted by publishers, and careful consideration of responsibility for the costs of publishing and disseminating scholarly output. She expects her proposals to "exploit the power of new technologies in the collective interest of the community" (p. 34).

Molholt, Pat. "On Converging Paths: The Computing Center and the Library." *Journal of Academic Librarianship* 11 (November 1985): 284-288.

Recounting the development of information as a commodity, Molholt makes the claim that information, together with technological developments, is driving a series of revolutions. Earlier computer development changed the way information managers work, rather than what work they do. Growth in electronic publishing and expanding access are forcing fundamental change.

Issues of access versus acquisition, emerging management information software, and new forms of high-volume storage indicate to Molholt a vision of a system that integrates seamlessly information collection and management functions. She cites the characteristics and strengths of computing centers and the unique and complementary features of libraries as essential to such a system. She identifies five areas that require significant cooperative development: indexing to devise vocabularies that cross disciplines and offer greater depth; conversion of print sources to machine-readable files; access, including both hardware and software development; security of files and systems; and costs and pricing, including copyright issues.

Libraries & Computing Centers: Issues of Mutual Concern, issue no. 1 (March 1987), issue no. 13 (May 1989).

This newsletter appeared as an insert in the *Journal of Academic Librarianship (JAL)* in volumes 13-15. The *JAL* editors launched the newsletter with an editorial posing a series of questions that focused on whether or not libraries and computing centers were on a collision course in competition for limited resources. Richard M. Dougherty notes that librarians know more about technology and its uses than is generally credited, but that computer specialists are quite new to the library field.

Dougherty quotes the revered Jesse Hauk Shera to the effect that knowledge of books and people, of materials and their sources, and empathy with those seeking sources constitute the essential pillars of library service. Dougherty adds that the new tools of technology are increasingly essential to the librarian's ability to "collect, organize, store, retrieve, and disseminate information," and that librarians must "lay a solid foundation for cooperation and collaboration between library and computing center professionals" (*JAL* 13 [March 1987]: 3). Within two years, Pat Molholt introduced the final issue of the newsletter by noting that the growth of digital collections, local and wide area networks, and document delivery programs was bringing about a "kind of functional cooperation" (*Libraries & Computing Centers: Issues of Mutual Concern,* issue no. 13 [May 1989]: 1-2).

Dougherty, Richard M. "Libraries and Computing Centers: A Blueprint for Collaboration." *College & Research Libraries* 48 (July 1987): 289-296.

Recognition of the growing relationship between academic libraries and computing centers has become fairly well established, but uncertainty remains among professionals of both groups as to who will dominate the campus environment. Libraries and computing centers must collaborate as functions converge, but Dougherty does not conclude that organizational mergers or takeovers are the likely outcomes. He does not envision a dominant organizational structure, due to the unique history, traditions, and cultures of individual campuses. The author asserts that the guiding principle for change should be the enhancement of institutional mission, and that the focus should remain on the roles of each respective organization as information providers.

A strategy for enhancing collaboration must begin "organizational mimicry" (p. 292), as the staff of each unit learns the professional culture and technical vocabulary of the other. Dougherty suggests formal relationships through joint working groups as initial steps. He identifies several issues that a university must address: (1) An institution must invest large sums in initial capitalization as well as supplemental expenditures for succeeding generations of equipment; (2) Pricing structures will likely lean toward the provision of traditional services for free (i.e., reference, reserves, course-related computing), but charging for more specialized services; (3) Given that current copyright law presents a barrier to the manipulation and dissemination of information, librarians are encouraged to participate in developing policies on intellectual property rights that protect both the creators and the users of the information; (4) Institutions must develop campus-wide policies for acquisition, access, and dissemination of information; (5) Unifying the campus information network, through links and gateways, will enable users to navigate the different systems more effectively.

Woodsworth, Anne. "The Chief Information Officer's Role in American Research Universities." Ph.D. dissertation, University of Pittsburgh, 1987.

Woodsworth responded to the rapidly growing creation of CIOs in the mid-1980s by surveying large research libraries. She notes that in 1984 there had been fewer than twenty such positions but within the next two years more than 100 had been created. Woodsworth identified thirty-two CIOs in ninety-one research universities and, during 1986 and 1987, conducted structured interviews with twenty-eight of them. She found that the CIOs had complete or major responsibility for academic computing, major or shared responsibility for administrative systems and telecommunications, and minor responsibility for library automation. CIOs made academic computing decisions subject to administrative approval; they shared in decision making for administrative systems and telecommunications; and they advised decision makers about library automation. They reported equally to presidents, provosts, and executive vice-presidents, and typically had one or more computing center directors reporting to them. Most CIOs held a doctorate, had held their posts for less than two years, and had been promoted from within the same institution; one-third had academic backgrounds in engineering or computer science.

Hughes, Joy Reed. "A Clash of Cultures: Libraries and Computer Centers in an Information Age." Ph.D. dissertation, The Union Institute, 1989.

In 1988 Hughes, a computer scientist, led the effort to reform the library of a small university that had just received a negative report on its library from the regional accreditation association. Scarcely changed since the 1950s, the library cataloged and circulated books manually. The president of the university facilitated the retirement of the library director and appointed Hughes to head the newly created Information Services Department including the library, telecommunications, and academic and administrative computing.

Hughes based her strategies for change on the theories of Noel Tichy, Tom Peters, and Rosabeth Moss Kantor. Following Tichy's TPC model, she set out to change the technical, political, and cultural systems of the library. Applying the ideas of Kantor, she sought to reduce the barriers between organizational units so that information and resources could be shared more readily. Acknowledging Peters' principles, she planned to empower people in the lower ranks, create a sense of urgency, and arrange a few "attention getters" (p. 2.14, 2.58). She also clarified the mission and goals of the library and assessed its internal and external environments (p. 2.16-2.17). Hughes further adopted the "new role of librarians teaching information literacy" (p. 1.19).

Hughes concludes, "(1) strategic planning is an effective means of bringing about the technical, political, and cultural changes needed to effect strategic improvements in information services; and (2) reorganizing the library and computer center into one organizational unit headed by a Chief Information Officer can facilitate the attainment of strategic goals for information services" (abstract). She admits, however, that changing the cultural system of the library "was quite painful for the library staff" (p. 2.92) and regrets having neglected to empower the staff and to involve them in shaping the strategic plan.

This dissertation also surveys the condition of information services at six small private liberal arts colleges in the western Allegheny region in 1989. It reveals how the colleges differ in terms of environment, history, affiliation, curriculum, academic and demographic characteristics of faculty and students, and library, computing, and telecommunications infrastructures. Hughes finds, "(1) most are not engaged in strategic planning; (2) most do not have effective management information systems in place; (3) most do not regard the library as having strategic importance in the attainment of institutional vitality; and (4) most of their libraries and computer centers are not working cooperatively on planning for . . . improved information services" (abstract).

Creth, Sheila D. "Creating a Virtual Information Organization: Collaborative Relationships between Libraries and Computing Centers." In *Libraries as User-Centered Organizations: Imperatives for Organizational Change,* ed. by Meredith A. Butler. New York: Haworth Press, 1993, 111-132.

Creth observes that computer networking since the mid-1980s has not only made information a primary commodity but also "opened new channels of communication within organizations and across organizational boundaries . . ." (p. 112). Facing economic pressures and heightened expectations from various constituents, universities have been trying to take full advantage of the power of information technology. A 1992 paper of the Higher Education Information Resources Alliance urges university presidents "to effect the real information technology revolution, adjusting our organizational structure to accommodate and exploit what is valuable in these technological developments" (p. 113).

Creth traces the developing relationship between libraries and computer centers from the installation of library systems on mainframes beginning in the late 1970s when libraries, like any other campus unit, simply contracted with the computer center for services, to the mid 1980s when a rash of articles discussed merging the administrations of libraries and computer centers. Some of these articles "missed the point," according to Creth, "because they focused on administration structure and control . . . rather than on a process for capitalizing on the combined knowledge of both groups" (p. 114). Instead of merging administrations, which "seems to be no longer of primary concern," Creth recommends collaboration between librarians and computer professionals in a "virtual information organization" (p. 117). Her definition of collaboration, derived from Michael Schrage's *Shared Minds: The New Technologies of Collaboration* (New York: Random House, 1990), emphasizes a process between equals, an "act of shared creation," and a "process of value creation" (p. 115). A "virtual organization" is described in a 1992 *Business Week* article as a "temporary network of independent companies—suppliers, customers, even erstwhile rivals— linked by information technology . . . a group of collaborators that quickly unites to exploit a specific opportunity" (p. 116). Such an organization is non-hierarchical, flexible, and constantly changing. According to Peter Keen, the complexity of traditional hierarchical organizations makes them too "sluggish" to deal adequately with the "hyperextension of activities" that accompany advances in computer and telecommunications technologies. New organizations need to become collaborative and organized not so much "by division of labor" as "by division of knowledge" (p. 122).

To create a virtual information organization, librarians and computer professionals must understand the other's culture and values, revise their individual roles and responsibilities, and acquire a different set of abilities. Creth identifies six possible project areas where computer technologists and librarians can work together to shape this transformation: (1) in strategic planning—no longer can one group "afford to be surprised" by decisions made by the other (p. 123); (2) in creating and managing a campus information policy; (3) in building a knowledge management environment where technologists, librarians, and faculty are involved in all phases of the information transfer cycle; (4) in supporting curriculum development by providing facilities such as those at the Information Arcade at the University of Iowa where technologists, librarians, faculty, and students share electronic resources for teaching, research, and the development of instructional software; (5) in teaching information technology and information resources to students, faculty, and staff by developing computer assisted instruction (CAI) packages, or enabling users to consult technology and information specialists remotely, perhaps using "teledesk" workstations that permit interactive visual and voice connections; and (6) in supporting electronic publishing within the university.

Young, Arthur P. "Information Technology and Libraries: A Virtual Convergence." *Cause/Effect* 17 (fall 1994): 5-6, 12.

Having reviewed the literature of computing and academic libraries over the previous decade, Young describes it as (1) focusing on the differences and similarities of their respective cultures, and (2) paying special attention to issues of organizational control and structure. He observes the paucity of longitudinal reports on failures and successes or even contributions that treat the rationales for mergers. He estimates that only a few research universities and perhaps no more than twenty-five smaller institutions have brought the library and the computing center together as a single administrative unit. More significant development has occurred at the national level with the formation of a new partnership, the Coalition for Networked Information, a cooperative project of the Association of Research Libraries, CAUSE, and EDUCOM to formulate policy on network protocols and copyright and licensing issues.

Young posits that the "traditional boundaries of information and technology are more shifting and kaleidoscopic than fixed and linear" (p. 5). He adds that the exploding potential of the Internet, the creation of campus networks, and the use of client/server architecture all support the recognition that telecommunication, information management, and computing technologies are merging inexorably. The mission relatedness of computing centers and libraries forces both to transcend earlier concerns about culture and control, and highest priorities should be targeted projects linked to strategic plans.

Young proposes that we apply Michael Schrage's definition of collaboration to our rapidly changing organizational and technological settings. In *Shared Minds: The New Technologies of Collaboration* (New York: Random House, 1990), Schrage defines collaboration as shared creation. Individuals with complementary skills interact to create the shared understandings that they had not previously possessed collectively or individually. Core ingredients derived from Schrage's definition are as follows: competence; shared, understood goals; mutual respect, tolerance, and trust; creation and manipulation of shared spaces; playing with representation; clear lines of responsibility but no restrictive boundaries; decisions made collectively rather than by consensus or compromise; selective use of outside expertise; and the end of collaboration once its focus is achieved.

Allen, Bryce. "Academic Information Services: A Library Management Perspective." *Library Trends* 43 (spring 1995): 645-662.

Allen examines barriers to collaboration between libraries and computing centers within the larger context of attempts by universities to develop what Ross Atkinson called "academic information services" (AIS). Through AIS, universities would "gain control over the scholarly information transfer cycle by creating an electronic network for articles and books that are now published by commercial publishers or scholarly associations" (p. 647). Universities would become "the principal publishers and distributors" of scholarly articles, and thus enter into direct competition with commercial publishers. Although the publishers would be formidable rivals, the universities have some advantages: experts in information systems development, telecommunications and network tools, scholars who are the principal producers and consumers of scholarly publications, and libraries. Nevertheless, the success of AIS will depend on collaboration among several sectors of the university, including libraries, computing centers, university presses, and professional associations.

Allen examines three barriers to collaboration between academic libraries and other campus units: (1) clashes of organizational culture, (2) personal incompatibilities, and (3) differing approaches to change. First of all, libraries are academic units, while computing centers tend to be administrative units. Libraries are supposed to have a user-centered service orientation that is built on the idea of free access to information for all members of the community. This contrasts with the orientation of other units that serve a limited group. As Allen notes, "much of the discussion of AIS has been couched in terms of meeting the needs of faculty and researchers, and we are left to wonder at times how such systems might be adapted to meet the needs of students" (p. 650). In order that the cultural values and orientations of each unit can be shared, the boundaries between them must be made permeable. Working on technological projects, such as library automation or AIS, will in itself contribute to the breakdown of cultural and organizational barriers.

Much has been made of the differences between stereotypical personalities of librarians and computing technologists. However, research into librarian personality types by S. J. Webreck (1985), J. C. Tyson (1988), and T. A. Brimsek and D. Leach (1990), using the Myers-Briggs Type Indicator (MBTI) does not support a single stereotype; rather it indicates a variety of personality types common in other campus units. Allen suggests that library managers simply need to recognize and make use of those librarians with the types of personalities that will enable them to "work well in a collaborative environment with computer center professionals, administrators, and university press staff" (p. 654).

Different approaches to change can frustrate collaboration. Flexible organizations move faster than more conservative organizations in adopting new technology, and "differences in rates of adoption can get in the way of productive collaborative relationships" (p. 650). Some organizations, like computing centers, are supposedly flexible and able to redeploy organizational resources into adapting new technologies and supplying new services, such as support for AIS. If academic libraries were similarly flexible, they could assign staff to design access systems for networked information resources, solicit and collect electronic texts, and organize the processes of reviewing and editing the texts. But libraries tend to be conservative. They remain busy cataloging, providing access to expensive electronic and paper collections, answering numerous questions, and teaching information literacy, so it seems unlikely that they will be able to redeploy resources to AIS. Allen sees hope, however, in the idea of S. W. J. Kozlowski and B. M. Hults (1987) that organizations like university libraries, which already employ complex technological systems, tend to be able to adapt to additional technological change. Twenty years ago there were just a few "online search specialists" in libraries, yet the responsibility became more general in time. The skills required in new positions like "networked information services librarian" will eventually be shared by many librarians.

Kozlowski and Hults, however, have another idea that seems to retract the possibility of librarians becoming welcome collaborators: "Organizations typified by high levels of standardization in their procedures and means of production are less likely to have the organizational flexibility that is associated with successful adoption of technological change" (p. 656). According to Allen, MARC formats, AACR2 rules, and other standards have hindered the adoption of innovative approaches to information retrieval. "Unless ways can be found to disassociate library information systems from long-standard methods, there is reason to be pessimistic about the ability of academic libraries to make a real contribution to AIS" (p. 657). One can counter, however, that it is especially librarians' long experience with such standards that make them welcome collaborators in recent attempts to bring order to the Web.

Bly, Onadell. "Academic Libraries, Academic Computer Centers, and Information Technology." *Advances in Library Administration and Organization* 14 (Westport, Conn.: JAI Press, 1996): 207-225.

Bly provides an overview of the relationship between computing centers and libraries over the past three decades. Bly recounts the basic cultural values of each entity, noting that electronic services in the library focus on access to information generated externally while computing centers concern themselves with internally produced data. Perspectives like these result in differing organizational structures, methods of support, and philosophies of service.

Bly asserts that the library and the computing center influence more people more frequently and directly than other departments on campus. She reminds readers of the elements that both groups have in common and how each complements the other. Within this perspective, computing centers seek to establish round-the-clock access, cost-effective storage, and easily manipulatable files from remote and local sites. The library adds highly structured collections and files within uniform methods of access and a user-friendly orientation.

According to Bly, the wide variation in the implementation of CIOs suggests that it is unlikely to serve the needs of most institutions. Alternatives feature (1) those in which the librarian is especially knowledgeable about information technology (IT) and oversees the library and the computing center, (2) those in which the computer center director is knowledgeable of the library and handles both, (3) those that are separate, reporting to a senior academic official, and (4) those in which the librarian reports to the senior academic official and the computer director reports to a vice-president for fiscal affairs. Bly optimistically observes an "advanced level of interaction" that has emerged regardless of formal structures and that recognizes the interdependence of both units due to library involvement in local and wide area networks (p. 221).

Davis-Millis, Nina, and Thomas Owens. "Two Cultures: A Social History of the Distributed Libraries Initiative at MIT." In *Restructuring Academic Libraries: Organizational Development in the Wake of Technological Change*, ed. by Charles A. Schwartz, 96-107. ACRL Publications in Librarianship, no. 49. Chicago: Association of College and Research Libraries, 1997.

This article is the last of three in Schwartz's collection that discuss "Realigning Campus Computing Relationships." The first article, by Richard M. Dougherty and Lisa McClure, provides an overview of what Schwartz calls "the rise and fall of great expectations for easy mergers" and an empirical account of realignment options (p. viii). The second article, by Meredith A. Butler and Stephen E. DeLong, recounts the successes and failures of what Schwartz calls "a 'bottom up' approach to collaborative realignment" at the University of Albany (p. viii). In "Two Cultures," Davis-Millis and Owens tell the story of a "top down" approach at MIT.

The directors and associate directors of both the MIT libraries and the campus Information Services (IS) recognized by 1990 that both sides had interests in networked information and the communications infrastructure on campus. They met and built a foundation for long-term collaboration on "the respective strengths of the two organizations" (p. 98). The libraries would determine content, and IS would provide infrastructure. "[W]e sought a marriage rather than a merger—a real partnership that would allow each organization to bring its specific expertise to the problem of networked information. We wanted this partnership to grow simultaneously and organically at all staff levels—to foster a convergent understanding of goals, values, and methods on both sides" (pp. 97-98).

To maintain ongoing strategic contact between the libraries and IS, the administrators formed the Libraries/Information Systems Steering Committee, which decided that the project to bring electronic library services to the MIT community and the world, the Digital Library Initiative (DLI), "would be guided—but not driven—by specific, current projects" (p. 98). In 1991 technical staffs from both the libraries and IS got together to talk about the IS computing network, MARC records, and the history of library automation. This group, the Electronic Library Developers (ELIBDEV), began working on a few small projects. As the number of such projects increased, the administrators of IS and the libraries established a second formal group, the Digital Library Initiative Coordinating Committee (DLICC), which also included the Intellectual Property Counsel and a representative from the Laboratory for Computer Science. In 1993 a DLI vision statement and a general schedule of network development were finally published. Also another formal group, the Network User Team (NUT), was created. "NUT manages new releases of existing applications, develops access to new resources, and coordinates technical support of applications and hardware with functional support of content and training" (p. 100). New projects have continued to create less formal ad hoc groups.

Davis-Millis and Owens identify two key elements in the success of the Digital Library Initiative: (1) "the active participation of upper-level administrators from both units in setting goals and priorities, concurrent with the participation of frontline staff in the actual design and delivery of services;" and (2) the awareness of cultural differences and similarities, "together with the decision to invest staff time in exploring them . . ." (p. 102). They repeat Creth's explication of the differences between the cultures of the two groups, but also echo Kristin McDonough's recognition of "'subcultures' and 'vested interests' within and between both professions." "There used to be talk," McDonough recalls, "of separate 'cultures' within our own profession, as exemplified by public services and technical services librarians. [There is also] the competition that has existed on some campuses between administrative and academic computing" (p. 103). Davis-Millis and Owens suggest social factors "are as important as operational, technical, and economic factors" to the success of collaborative technology projects (p. 105). A focus group consisting of participants in DLI collaborative projects confirmed that most of the people from IS and the libraries enjoyed their collaboration and learned to appreciate the other profession. Nevertheless, the members of one subculture, the library systems personnel, had "a sense of being caught between two cultures, each with a clearly defined area of expertise." Their experience was "distinctly more ambivalent" (p. 105).

Hardesty, Larry. "Computer Center-Library Relations at Small Institutions: A Look from Both Sides." *Cause/Effect* 21, no. 1 (spring 1998): 35-41.

Hardesty summarizes and elaborates on two previous publications, "Library and Computer Center Relations at Small Academic Institutions," *Library Issues: Briefings for Faculty and Administrators* 18 (September 1997): 1-4, and "Relationships between Libraries and Computer Centers at Liberal Arts Colleges," *Council on Library and Information Resources Research Briefs,* issue no. 2 (November 1997): 1-4. All three report on interviews of forty computer center administrators and fifty-one librarians at fifty-one small colleges throughout the United States. Conducted during the period of January 1994 through October 1996, Hardesty's survey represents the first and likely only substantial field report on this topic from liberal arts colleges.

He finds that a number of authors from the 1980s had predicted mergers but that by the end of the decade, the movement had lost momentum. Early in the 1990s, however, mergers regained momentum with a number of colleges creating formal structures that would bring libraries and computing centers closer together. Institutions in this category include Berea, Bucknell, Carthage, Coe, Connecticut, Eckerd, Kalamazoo, Lake Forest, Macalester, Mount Holyoke, and Wellesley. The nature of the library-computing center relationships among these models varies greatly. One highly visible example, Gettysburg College, brought the library and computing center together both administratively and in shared spaces as the Division of Strategic Information Resources. This experiment proved unworkable and Gettysburg split the library and the computing center into separate units effective 1 August 1997 (see chapter 17, "The Gettysburg Experience" by Robin Wagner).

Hardesty's findings corroborate much of the literature from the 1980s, that the two entities have different professional backgrounds and patterns of academic socialization. Stereotyping of the two cultures continues with the full recognition that such perceptions—however ill-founded—drive professional behavior. It seems axiomatic that librarians tend to test a service before delivery and that computing staff are more experimental and willing to attempt projects not fully developed.

Most of Hardesty's respondents concur that effective organization depends not on structure but on the people involved. Most expect the two entities to continue evolving and working together more closely. Librarians acknowledge the need for greater technical knowledge; computing center staff acknowledge the need for better organizational and communication skills. (One respondent ex-plained, for example, that in hiring a computer center director, his institution would seek someone with softer skills than in the past, someone with the attrib-utes of vision and leadership. His college wanted someone compatible with "fac-ulty mission and a mindset about what education is all about" [p. 40]). Many interviewees shared the sentiments of one computer center director that mergers with libraries would simply create new problems to solve. "Creating CIOs and mergers may be like getting married and having a spouse help you with prob-lems you would not have if you had not gotten married" (p. 41).

"Is Merging IT with the Library a Good Idea?" *EDUTECH Report: The Education Technology Newsletter for Faculty and Administrators* 14 (November 1998): 1, 4-5, 7.

Newsletter editors have assembled their version of the current wisdom on this topic. First among these is that libraries are using electronic technologies and adapting them much more rapidly than anyone anticipated. Moreover, such technologies have become essential to core activities and libraries are questioning the extent to which they control those technologies. Librarians have new levels of comfortability with new technology and are learning how to ask tough questions about it. Computer specialists have only recently come to understand the seriousness of librarian concerns about accessibility and conti-nuity. A crisis in confidence attaches to computing/network specialists due to high costs and lags in timetables for implementation.

Only a few institutions have created a fully merged unit with staff substan-tially altering roles and providing new and improved services. However, admin-istrators ask the merger question "almost everywhere" a vacancy occurs in a computing or library directorship (p. 5). Additionally, numerous colleges engage in both project-driven and structural collaboration that ranges in tone from gen-uine cooperative work to "uneasy alliance or even jealous mistrust" (p. 4).

The editors identify four good reasons to merge and four bad reasons. The former include (1) that the institution is looking toward the future, (2) that li-brarians and computing staff have complementary knowledge about faculty and students, (3) that the leadership to make change is in place, and (4) that the campus is ready for change. The bad reasons are (1) that the institution wants to solve deep problems with dramatic change, (2) that cultural differences be-tween the library and computing center—one being service-oriented and the other not—are given too much weight, (3) that change is determined behind closed doors, (4) that the merger is like a "shotgun wedding."

Hirshon, Arnold. *Integrating Computing and Library Services: An Administrative Planning and Implementation Guide for Information Resources.* CAUSE Pro-fessional Paper Series 18. Boulder, Colo.: CAUSE, 1998.

Hirshon, formerly Vice President for Information Resources at Lehigh University, offers a thorough and pragmatic approach to the integration of com-puting and library services. Acknowledging that organizational integration is a relatively recent phenomenon, Hirshon notes that resurgence occurred simulta-neously with the introduction and expansion of the World Wide Web. He does not advocate organizational integration, but provides an objective guide and key steps in decision making about the issue.

The author explores the causes of organizational integration, the desirable conditions, alternatives, and initial steps for institutional consideration. Hirshon urges a clearly defined vision of institutional mission, goals, and objectives. Integration should not be an objective unto itself, but rather a tool to achieve organizational vision. Strategic planning emphasizes the importance of vision for both the information content and the technology infrastructure.

Hirshon describes the role of the CIO in the context of reporting relationships, position titles, recruitment, and hiring issues. An appendix contains advertisements of successful CIO searches. He presents organizational structures but notes that most institutions retain relatively traditional substructures of distinct library and computing center lineage. He provides sample organization charts for integrated organizations and asserts that human resource considerations in restructuring an organization must consider staff reassignments, position descriptions and titles, salary determinations, and distinct organizational cultures.

The author concludes that successful integration "requires forethought, planning, and a sustained commitment and faith in the direction taken" and believes that "with . . . continuous effort to improve the organization, integration can yield significant improvements in the quality of services . . ." (p. 30). Hirshon's seasoned advice should guide institutions through the process of organizational integration and, together with readings from his extensive bibliography, provide a firm basis for addressing the complexity of issues. Hirshon's bibliography complements and expands on that of Denise J. Johnson in "Merging? Converging? A Survey of Research and Reports on Academic Library Reorganization and the Recent Rash of Marriage between Academic Libraries and University Computing Centers," *Illinois Libraries* 79 (spring 1997): 61-63.

CHAPTER THREE

The Organizational and Historical Context of the Chief Information Officer's Position

TERRENCE F. MECH

The chief information officer (CIO), the newest administrative position on many college organizational charts, is part of American higher education's continuous adaptation to its environments. The CIO's position is an institutional response to the convergence of several related developments, including the widespread adoption of new technologies, changes in the fortunes of American higher education, and changes in the library and the role of librarians. The purpose of this chapter is to place the CIO's position in its larger organizational and historical context.

Successful organizations design their administrative structures to match the environments in which they operate.[1] Institutions create new positions and change old organizational structures depending upon significant changes in their roles, their environments, and the constituencies they serve. Organizations do not change easily. Nor do they change for the sake of change. Like biological organisms "existing in a wider environment," organizations are born, grow, and develop. They adapt to changes in their environments or they decline and die.[2] American colleges have been evolving and responding to changes in their environments since their beginnings in the early 1600s. Evidence of these adaptations is found in their administrative structures, and the CIO is the latest in a series of administrative evolutions that began during the late 1800s.

HISTORICAL BACKGROUND

The CIO's position did not appear overnight; rather it emerged from the rich history of American higher education, libraries, and computing centers. Before the Civil War, the typical self-contained American college enrolled less than 100 male students. These very fragile organizations with their rigid classical curriculum failed more often than not.[3] After the Civil War, the "university movement" emerged to modernize higher education by creating new secular academic organizations with graduate education and professional schools, undergraduate specialization, access to new kinds of knowledge, and practical career preparation.[4]

By the 1920s, America's first era of mass education, the organization of the modern American university was established.[5] With undergraduate curriculum providing several scientific courses of study taught by "professional" faculty, enrollments grew as the expanding middle class sent its children to college. Faculty with Ph.D.'s felt a greater loyalty to their discipline than they did to their employers and measured their productivity by their publications.[6] With faculty professionalization and the development of new disciplines came new scholarly associations and journals to support this specialization. This transformation of American higher education directly affected libraries and the shape of university administration.

As universities competed for top faculty, the quality of their libraries became a presidential concern. With growing enrollments, universities had the finances to invest in libraries. In 1876, only Harvard had a collection of over 100,000 volumes. By 1920, Harvard had over two million volumes and many universities had over 100,000 volumes. By the mid-1920s the circulation of books to students had become a major activity in academic libraries.[7] Reference service, however, did not assume an important role at liberal arts colleges until the 1940s and did not become a "major activity" before the 1960s.[8]

The evolution of the librarian's position from an adjunct duty to a distinct specialization progressed slowly.[9] If university presidents wanted full-time librarians to build their library collections, they also wanted individuals with administrative talent who shared the concerns of scholars. The evolution of this new position took many years, and a shortage of librarians existed until the early 1970's.[10]

The supposed financially "golden age" of American higher education of the late 1950s and 1960s came to an end in the 1970s. Many colleges and universities had difficulty adjusting. A decline in federal and foundation support followed a wave of national reports during the 1980s, calling for curricular reforms. In the face of growing unemployment, other reports questioned the value and rising costs of higher education. With a declining college age population, sharply diminished financial resources, and a rising public demand for alternative education services, active "market forces" shaped higher education in the early 1990s.[11] Many institutions now realized they would have to change. In many cases, senior administrators looked to technology and organizational realignment as part of the solution.

HIGHER EDUCATION'S ORGANIZATIONAL STRUCTURE

Academe's creation of a position to address technology issues is not without precedence. Higher education, like other organizations, responds to significant organizational issues by creating new positions or expanding the responsibilities of existing positions. The modern American university and the modern business enterprise are large organizations that developed in tandem during the late 1800s and early 1900s. America's transformation from an agrarian and rural economy to an industrial and urban economy produced revolutionary changes in the conduct of business and in the structures of organizations.[12] Beginning in the 1890s, after a wave of empire building, industrialists faced the challenge of designing the structures essential for the efficient administration of large organizations. Full-time managers would emerge to administer large organizations.[13]

By the 1890s, the full measure of college administration was developing.[14] American higher education underwent a period of rapid growth from 1890 to 1930. More students meant more professors, more facilities and equipment, and more problems. The president had increasing responsibilities for securing support and for managing the internal complexities. Initially, a few professors assisted the president by serving as part-time registrars, bursars, and librarians. However, by 1900, such part-time staffs proved insufficient.

To manage the growth of universities and deal with their complexities, academe's organizational structures emerged quickly with little variation. Small at first, administrative structures grew in size and complexity. In 1870, Harvard appointed the first "dean." "His main task, apart from teaching, was to take the burden of discipline off the president's shoulders."[15] In 1890, Harvard split its deanship into the academic dean and the dean of students. This pattern was well established by the early 1900s.[16]

By the 1950s, the academic dean assumed authority for all operations in the president's absence. The position has changed significantly since the 1950s, with the vice president for academic affairs exercising an ever-widening scope of authority. By the 1980s, provosts had the daily managerial responsibility for the entire campus, formerly exercised by the president. Chief academic officers who taught full-time and did a little administrative work have been replaced with full-time administrators with little time to teach.[17]

Many factors transformed universities into complex administrative systems. Implementing an intricate system for student admissions and an educational accounting system for electives and majors gave rise to registrars and a full-time administrative bureaucracy. In 1880, less than 10 percent of colleges had registrars; by 1910, almost half did. Administration evolved in roughly the following sequence: librarian, secretary of the faculty, registrar, business officer, academic dean, and dean of students. The librarian's position was among the first to become full-time.[18]

LIBRARIES AND TECHNOLOGY

In a relatively short time librarians have introduced many technology-related changes that have gradually but significantly reshaped libraries. Library online computer operations appeared during the 1960s. By the early 1970s, several university libraries had developed online circulation applications. Creation of the machine-readable cataloging (MARC) record made online catalogs possible. With the advent of commercial "turnkey" systems in the mid-1970s, libraries could purchase an automated module "off-the-shelf." By the 1980s the integrated system appeared. These events, coupled with advances in computing technology and marketplace price competition, made it possible for libraries of all sizes to think about automating.[19]

COMPUTING CENTERS

The increasing enrollments after World War II and the organizational complexities of many universities led to an interest in some of the developing "scientific management" practices. Seeking ways to use their limited resources more efficiently, many institutions adopted modern management techniques and tools, including the computer. Like business, higher education eagerly adopted computers. In 1956, fewer than five universities had computers. By 1964, over five hundred universities had computers for administrative uses.[20]

By the 1960s, computing centers appeared as separate administrative departments. Because of their expense and size, these early mainframe computers found homes in centralized air-conditioned computer facilities, responsible to the chief financial officer. At the time, a medium-sized computer cost a quarter of a million dollars and required highly trained personnel to keep it running.[21] Early data processing centers employed legions of programmers to write the code necessary to create and maintain these "homegrown" administrative systems. Until the advent of vendor supplied software in the early 1980s, many colleges could not afford to operate an integrated administrative computing system.

During the 1980s, computing hardware became more powerful, physically smaller, and less expensive. The personal computer along with rapid developments in word processing, spreadsheet, and database applications sent ripples through institutions. Departments could purchase personal computers, and computers became no longer the sole domain of the computing center. At the same time, computing centers had growing demands for administrative and academic computing. Many computing centers entered this new era unprepared to meet these new support demands from personal computer users. On some campuses mainframe computing center staffs considered the early personal computer a novelty and not a serious computer. Such views made it easy for an entrepreneurial media service or library to see its entrance into "computing" as an extension of its mission. On several campuses, this move led to confusion as more academic departments viewed the computer and its use in the curriculum through the lens of their particular agenda.

THE EMERGENCE OF THE CORPORATE CIO

By their nature, academic institutions are resistant to change. However, as universities developed closer ties with the larger community, academe became less isolated. Higher education administrators observed that business and academe suffered from similar organizational problems, such as how to accommodate the growing use of technology and become more efficient. The concept of the CIO, formulated in 1981,[22] emerged from changes during the mid-1970s in how organizations viewed information resources. A senior officer needed to guide the evolving concept of information resource management. The CIO needed to provide the vision and "maximize the company's investment in information systems and technology for long-term competitive advantage."[23]

As the United States shifted from an industrial to an information economy, information took on increased economic importance. Information management evolved from a simple concern for the computer and the physical control of the data (pre-1950) to a focus on how the information could be helpful to the organization. Before 1980, few organizations made strategic use of their information systems to serve the organization's mission. As information systems grew more complicated, the required capital investments grew larger. Company presidents saw the management of information and the supporting technologies as too important a strategic resource to be left to data processing personnel.[24]

By 1989, 26 percent of the Fortune 500 companies had CIOs who reported to the CEO. Companies with an information technology strategy as a key element in their profit plan often had CIOs.[25] For corporate CIOs, the emphasis centered on their ability to contribute to the company's profitability, not on their technical expertise. They are technology generalists who bridge the gap between management and technology specialists to apply technology and information resources to solve business problems and gain competitive advantage.[26] As a change agent, the CIO must manage information resources as a vital corporate asset and facilitate the use of those resources to the company's advantage and profitability.[27]

CIOs IN HIGHER EDUCATION

The issues leading to the creation of CIOs in higher education did not originate suddenly. They emerged slowly. Gradually, universities responded to growing pressures in their environments. At first, colleges responded to environmental changes by expanding their organizational structures and creating new administrative offices. At first, libraries and colleges used technology to help them cope with the volume of work and the demands for improved services. As time went on, their expanded use of technology eventually produced additional pressures and challenges for organizations. Historically, higher education and business have used similar strategies to respond to similar changes in their environments, business being the first to respond.

In the late 1970s, academe's libraries and computing centers functioned as separate entities. Several events would change this relationship. The breakup of AT&T required organizations to reexamine their telephone systems. Improved information systems forced universities to reassess their computing resources. The long-term institutional commitment for technology became increasingly expensive.[28] The computing center vied with the library to be the "bottomless pit" into which money disappeared.[29]

As discussed by Kathman and Seiden in their earlier chapter, by the mid-1980s some librarians and computing professionals concluded that libraries and computing centers had become increasingly alike. Both provided access to information resources and services, stored, organized, and distributed information, and had become increasingly more costly.[30] While others described the trends intertwining libraries and computing centers,[31] some library, computing center, media service directors and others, anticipating a "shake out," jockeyed for position in the competition for influence and resources. Perceiving their competitor's alleged political advantages, perhaps more than one player saw the potential partnership as a "deadly embrace" with each partner "leveraging resources from the other while retaining complete control."[32]

Presidents, facing declining enrollments, tougher competition for students, and pressures to be more accountable, cost effective, and affordable, envisioned the benefits of a comprehensive technology plan and a different set of library and computing center relationships. The advantage of a coordinated technology policy and the potential for better management information systems looked very attractive. Just as the quality of libraries became a faculty recruitment issue at the end of the nineteenth century, technology became a student recruitment issue at the end of the twentieth century for many schools.

Instead of measuring institutional quality by the size of the library, people now perceive institutional quality by how "wired" the college is.

Among the first institutions to restructure their library and computing center operations were Columbia University, Vanderbilt University, Rutgers University, Stanford University, Oregon State University, Virginia Commonwealth University, Rice University, and Carnegie Mellon University. However, no clear organizational model of the CIO's responsibilities developed from these ventures.[33] At Columbia University, the library director became the CIO. At Carnegie Mellon University, the computing center director became the CIO, while at Stanford University, the two directors shared responsibilities. However, subsequent "organizational reforms reestablished much of the former units' independence" at many of these universities.[34] But by the late 1980s, integrated library and computing center operations under a single college officer responsible for technology remained very much the exception.

One more reason exists for this lack of integration. Organizations had to be ready for the changes. Academic institutions are inherently conservative organizations not given to sudden bursts of sustained innovation. This type of action requires support from throughout the institution. Faculty and staff may not view the institutional challenges in the same light as do administrators.

Others noted the "cultural differences" between libraries and computing centers.[35] Librarians have similar career paths and socialization experiences as well as a history of shared standards, philosophies, and a service orientation that drives their many cooperative ventures. Computing personnel do not have a common career path or shared history. They possess a technical orientation that fosters creativity and individual action and fires the entrepreneurial spirit. Computing personnel may be more accustomed to rapid technological change than are librarians. Perhaps most members of each group did not fully understand the other's environment and what it took to do their job.

While most libraries and computing centers did not merge during the 1980s, they did begin to work together as their common interests emerged. By the late 1980s, personal computers and spreadsheet and word processing software had moved several mainframe computer applications to users' desktops. With this, computing centers changed their focus from the centralized processing of data to providing network communications between the growing numbers of desktop computers. By 1990, many universities had or had plans for a campus network to provide Internet access and electronic mail.

Also by the early 1990s, automation and the expansion of digital information services out into campuses caused a number of changes within libraries.[36] The large-scale adoption of technologies by libraries increased their visibility on campuses. A library's use of technology to provide better information services frequently caused a shift in institutional power structures and relationships.[37] Besides working with the administration to fund the expense, librarians had to work with many different offices to deliver new digital information services. The potential of these technologies stirred the imagination of faculty and administrators, and their use caused librarians to rethink a number of issues.[38]

A few librarians noted the increasing difficulty of the director's job in this new environment.[39] At the same time, senior administrators, faced with increased pressures to control costs and develop new programs to attract students, looked for new sources of ideas and managerial talent. They sought individuals with experience working with several campus constituencies and managing technology and change. Presidents looked for an institutional per-spective, an understanding of higher education's environment, leadership, communication and executive skills, and the ability to function as part of a team. They sought individuals with an understanding of technology and a vi-sion of how it might support the mission of their institutions.[40]

The need for fiscal control over expensive technology and a plan for its implementation often drove the decision to establish a CIO position. Many be-lieved centralized control, at a level higher than the computing center director, necessary to build a comprehensive information and technological infrastruc-ture and to ensure the collaboration necessary to produce the envisioned results and efficiencies. Several presidents found the idea of a senior level technology advisor with an institutional vision more attractive than several mid-level tech-nology managers with different philosophies and institutional views. Many in-dividuals hoped that, besides the economic benefits, the shared expertise would bring some innovations.[41]

By 1986, thirty-two of the ninety-one Association of Research Libraries member universities had established a CIO's position, and another ten univer-sities were in the process of establishing the position. Of the CIO positions, only four had been in place four years or more.[42] Using 1988 information, Penrod, Dolence, and Douglas found one hundred thirty-nine CIOs in higher education, mostly at larger research and comprehensive institutions. These CIOs had been in their positions an average of 3.6 years.[43] By 1997, CIOs could be found at smaller institutions. In that year Cain found 35 percent of the CIOs at doctoral institutions, 30 percent at comprehensive, 23 percent at baccalaureate, and 8 percent at two-year institutions. He also found that only 25 percent of the CIOs had responsibility for both library and computing-related operations.[44]

Since 1992 there has been an increase in the number of four-year academic institutions integrating their library and computing operations and creating a CIO position. Of the ninety colleges identified by Hirshon as having integrated library and computing center operations, 82 percent had integrated their oper-ations since 1993.[45] Sixty percent of the CIOs came from within their institu-tions. Of those promoted from within, 61 percent were librarians, 32 percent had computing backgrounds, and 7 percent were faculty or other administra-tors. Of the 40 percent of the CIOs who came from outside the institution, 53 percent had computing and 47 percent had library backgrounds.[46] Hirshon's data on the CIOs' backgrounds indicate librarians compete successfully for these new leadership positions.

The increase since 1990 in library and computing operations reporting to a common administrator occurred particularly at smaller comprehensive and liberal arts institutions. Not until the promise of the technology became a real-ity at the smaller institutions did these institutions begin to consider the CIO position. At these small institutions, a change in how faculty and administrators viewed technology provided the impetus for the creation of the CIO position and the reorganization of information and technology operations. When ad-ministrators and faculty began to perceive that affordable technology could en-hance a student's educational experience, increase administrative efficiencies, and advance the institution's mission, some at smaller schools no longer con-sidered the CIO and technology as only "big" school issues. No doubt parents of prospective students asking technology-related questions during campus visits helped bring the "technology issue" to the attention of many senior level administrators at tuition-driven colleges. To remain competitive, many at these colleges believed they had to "get a better handle on technology." Although technology served as the focal point in these CIO discussions, other administrative reorganization and efficiency agendas became interwoven with them.

CIO PATTERNS

Although the concept of a CIO is commonly understood, the position is not uniform. The CIO's position is still being shaped, particularly at smaller institutions. An examination of the organizational charts collected by Hirshon reveals several different approaches.[47] Organizational adaptation to local need results in many variations. For example, colleges needing to build their technology infrastructure or purchase new information systems may look for a different type of CIO and organizational structure than a college wanting to adopt technology to enhance student learning. Presidential preferences and expectations, the degree of faculty autonomy, "the relative strength of the collegial and hierarchical management systems, and changes in the roles" of the various information managers all affect the scope and influence of the CIO's position.[48] As institutions enhance technology infrastructures, as users develop increased technological sophistication, and as CIOs change jobs, institutions will review and craft a CIO's position that meets their organizational needs.

Despite the numerous variations, Woodsworth identified the more common versions of the CIO's position.[49] In "The Total CIO" model, the CIO reports to the president and has complete responsibility for academic and administrative computing, telecommunications, the library, instructional services, graphics, printing, copying, and mail services. There are few working examples of this perhaps more theoretical model. In the "Almost Complete CIO" model, the most common and most fluid model, the CIO is responsible for academic and administrative computing and telecommunications. A variety of other responsibilities complete the "Almost Complete" CIO's portfolio. Missing from these responsibilities are one or more of the following: the library, printing, copying, or mail services. The boundaries and reporting lines for the excluded areas may be firm or blurry. In some early cases, only the library's technology operations fell under the CIO's oversight. This oversight, but not operational, responsibility creates dual reporting lines for some library personnel. This cumbersome model may be a transitional model until the institution decides on the library's reporting structure.

LIBRARIANS AS CIOs

At smaller institutions, often an internal candidate is appointed CIO, and frequently the library director is appointed to this position.[50] Whether this is an enduring model or a temporary expedient solution remains to be seen. Appointing the librarian or other internal candidates is a safe choice for a smaller organization unsure of the type of individual it might hire from outside the institution. The internally appointed CIO is known and knows the college. Some liberal arts colleges may appoint a librarian as the CIO in an effort to maintain its academic self-image. Appointing a technologist as the CIO might send an undesirable message to the faculty that the institution is more interested in the technology than in how the technology can serve the college's mission and curriculum. Nor are there heightened expectations for sweeping changes or significantly increased spending that often accompany the appointment of an external candidate with a mandate. The changes are more likely to be incremental with an internal appointment.

A library director's past performance, reputation with faculty and administrators, and appropriate "academic credentials" may enhance his or her selection as the CIO. Often at small institutions candidates from the computing center with these qualifications do not exist. Nor is there a large pool of current or potential CIOs ready to relocate. Even when willing to consider external candidates, more than one college in the early 1990s used an executive search firm to find their CIO candidates.

Perhaps on occasion a library director is appointed because he or she is viewed as a neutral party between two "warring factions." Or, perhaps, some at smaller institutions may not recognize the need for a full-time CIO. More likely, the appointment of the library director as CIO while retaining operational responsibilities for the library allows the institution to avoid the politically and economically unwelcome expense of another full-time administrator. Many college presidents, wanting to control costs and sensitive to faculty pressure, are reluctant to create another administrative position. By increasing the duties of an existing position there is no immediate net gain to the organizational census. However, without the right support, this is a difficult situation. Holding two jobs requires the incumbent to maintain a delicate balance between responsibilities. The nature of the CIO's position is still very fluid.

THE CIO POSITION AND ITS FUTURE

Many believe limiting the number of separate technology-related departments provides the benefits of resource sharing, economies of scale, and collaboration. However, there may be no right or wrong answer because of varying local situations. Therefore, creating the CIO position does not guarantee its organizational success or its incumbent's personal success. Drawing a box and lines on an organizational chart belies the organizational complexities of a new position whose influence must extend beyond its formal authority if it is to be effective.

With the creation of a senior administrative position, new working relationships have to be developed. The previous relationships among the senior administrators are altered with creation of the CIO position. The new CIO will need to establish the position's identity and create new working relationships with these and other administrators. Some of these administrators may have been or still are competitors. Collaboration with academic administrators may prove vital as the concept of the provost emerges on smaller campuses. Because the CIO has to facilitate projects across divisional boundaries, the ability to influence actions may be more helpful than the use of formal authority. Political and communication skills rather than technical skills are more useful for CIOs in facilitating the institutional changes expected. The large number of CIOs at smaller institutions reporting to the chief academic officer means the CIO's ability to be successful may depend on the abilities, power, influence, and vision of the chief academic officer, or on the CIO's ability to influence the chief academic officer.

Often in establishing the CIO's position, different organizational units have their reporting lines redrawn. Each of these departments has its own history, agenda, anxieties, and allegiances. The cultural and philosophical differences among the different units reporting to the CIO present their own challenges. In many organizations veteran middle managers may hold the CIO's fate in their hands. The incumbent's ability to maneuver among them and the maze of "subterranean" personnel issues help determine the position's organizational stability and success. Another factor, frequently overlooked, that contributes to the organizational success of the CIO's position is the incumbent's ability to make the personal transition from middle to senior level manager. Being a successful middle manager does not necessarily mean an incumbent can navigate the currents in the senior end of the swamp. As individuals they are in unfamiliar waters swimming with different fish, subject to more forces than they would like to admit, making choices they sometimes would rather not make. How well they do as individuals has organizational consequences for the position and its future.

CONCLUDING OBSERVATIONS

Although academe's CIO position is relatively new, the challenges that fomented its emergence have longer roots than the 1980s. The CIO's arrival is part of American higher education's continuous adaptation to its environments. Just as the quality of libraries became a presidential concern in the 1890s, technology has become an issue of the 1990s. The reasons are essentially the same: costs and the issue's influence on an institution's capability to compete in its marketplaces.

As other administrative positions before it, the CIO position debuted at larger universities before developing at smaller institutions. As with the college presidency and deanship, institutional need, the local situation, and the position's early occupants will shape the position. Organizationally and historically, as institutional needs evolve in response to environmental changes and market forces, so too evolves the nature of the positions. The CIO position is no different. The issues that created the CIO position will continue to evolve. Pioneering CIOs will leave their marks. As institutions work through their needs, a more common set of expectations and pattern of responsibilities will develop for the CIO position. As institutions finish building their campus infrastructure, they will turn their focus more towards how this investment can further the institution's mission. This change of focus should influence what an institution expects from its CIO and the preferred qualifications it seeks. The CIO must be able to facilitate change within the organization to enable the college or university to respond continually to its environment.

NOTES

1. Henry Mintzberg, *The Structure of Organizations: A Synthesis of the Research* (Englewood Cliffs, N.J.: Prentice Hall, 1979), 219-220.
2. Gareth Morgan, *Images of Organizations* (Beverly Hills, Calif.: Sage Publications, 1986), 14, 39-40.
3. Frederick Rudolph, *Curriculum: A History of the American Undergraduate Course of Study since 1636* (San Francisco: Jossey Bass, 1989), 101-115.
4. Roger L. Geiger, *To Advance Knowledge: The Growth of American Research Universities, 1900-1940* (New York: Oxford Univ. Pr., 1986), 4.
5. Laurence R. Veysey, *The Emergence of the American University* (Chicago: Univ. of Chicago Pr., 1965).

6. Martin J. Finkelstein, *The American Academic Profession: A Synthesis of Social Scientific Inquiry since World War II* (Columbus, Ohio: Ohio State Univ. Pr., 1984), 7-31.
7. Orvin Lee Shiflett, *Origins of American Academic Librarianship* (Norwood, N.J.: Ablex, 1981), 126, 133, 144-145.
8. Arthur T. Hamlin, *The University Library in the United States: Its Origins and Development* (Philadelphia: Univ. of Pennsylvania Pr., 1981), 137, 142; Richard E. Miller, "The Tradition of Reference Service in the Liberal Arts College Library," *RQ* 25 (summer 1986): 460-467.
9. Shiflett, *Origins of American Academic Librarianship,* 135.
10. Hamlin, *University Library,* 76.
11. James Martin and James E. Samels, "First among Equals: The Current Roles of the Chief Academic Officer," in James Martin and James E. Samels, eds., *First among Equals: The Role of the Chief Academic Officer* (Baltimore: Johns Hopkins Univ. Pr., 1997), 3-20, 207-209.
12. Alfred Dupont Chandler, *The Visible Hand: The Managerial Revolution in American Business* (Cambridge, Mass.: Harvard Univ. Pr., 1977).
13. Alfred Dupont Chandler, *Strategy and Structure: Chapters in the History of Industrial Enterprise* (Cambridge, Mass.: MIT Pr., 1962), 19, 24.
14. Veysey, *Emergence of the American University,* 305-306.
15. John S. Brubacher and Willis Rudy, *Higher Education in Transition: An American History: 1636-1956* (New York: Harper, 1958), 322.
16. Ibid.
17. Martin and Samels, "First among Equals," 4-5, 10.
18. Jay A. Halfond, "The History of Higher Education and the Registrar's Changing Role," *College and University* 59, no. 4 (1984): 351-356; Earl James McGrath, *The Evolution of Administrative Offices in Institutions of Higher Education in the United States from 1860 to 1933* (Ph.D. dissertation, Univ. of Chicago, 1938).
19. Barbara B. Moran, *Academic Libraries: The Changing Knowledge Centers of Colleges and Universities* (Washington, D.C.: Association for the Study of Higher Education, 1984), 7-8.
20. Francis E. Rourke and Glenn E. Brooks, *The Managerial Revolution in Higher Education* (Baltimore: Johns Hopkins Univ. Pr., 1966), 17, 20, 22.
21. Ibid., 35.
22. William R. Synnott and William H. Gruber, *Information Resource Management: Opportunities and Strategies for the 1980s* (New York: Wiley, 1981).
23. William R. Synott, *The Information Weapon: Winning Customers and Markets with Technology* (New York: Wiley, 1987), 23.
24. James I. Penrod, Michael G. Dolence, and Judith V. Douglas, *The Chief Information Officer in Higher Education* (Boulder, Colo.: CAUSE, 1990), 1, 5.
25. Ibid., 2.
26. Synott, *Information Weapon,* 23-25.
27. Ibid., 19, 13, 11.
28. Anne Woodsworth, "Libraries and the Chief Information Officer: Implications and Trends," *Library Hi Tech* 6 (January-March 1988): 37-44.
29. Larry Hardesty, "The Bottomless Pit Revisited," *College & Research Libraries* 52 (May 1991): 225.
30. Richard M. Dougherty and Lisa McClure, "Repositioning Campus Information Units for the Era of Digital Libraries," in Charles A. Schwartz, ed., *Restructuring Academic Libraries: Organizational Development in the Wake of Technological Change* (Chicago: American Library Assn., 1997), 70.
31. Patricia Battin, "The Electronic Library: A Vision for the Future," *Educom Bulletin* 19 (summer 1984): 12-17, 34; Raymond K. Neff, "Merging Libraries and Computer Centers: Manifest Destiny or Manifestly Deranged? An Academic Services Perspective," *Educom Bulletin* 20 (winter 1985): 8-12, 16; Pat Molholt, "On Converging Paths: The

Computing Center and the Library," *Journal of Academic Librarianship* 11 (Nov. 1985): 284-288.

32. Nina Davis-Millis and Thomas Owens, "Two Cultures: A Social History of the Distributed Library Initiative at MIT," in Charles A. Schwartz, ed., *Restructuring Academic Libraries: Organizational Development in the Wake of Technological Change* (Chicago: American Library Assn., 1977), 104.

33. Woodsworth, "Libraries and the CIO," 40.

34. Dougherty and McClure, "Repositioning Campus Information Units," 70-71.

35. David C. Weber, "University Libraries and Campus Information Technology Organizations: Who Is in Charge Here?" *Journal of Library Administration* 9, no. 4 (1988): 5-19; Sheila D. Creth, "Creating a Virtual Information Organization: Collaborative Relationships between Libraries and Computing Centers," *Journal of Library Administration* 19, no. 3-4 (1993): 111-132.

36. Barbara B. Moran, "The Unintended Revolution in Academic Libraries: 1939 to 1989 and Beyond," *College & Research Libraries* 50 (Jan. 1989): 25-41.

37. Gregory A. Crawford and Ronald E. Rice, "Technology, Power, and Structure: Developing a Model of the Effects of Automation on Liberal Arts College Libraries," *Library & Information Science Research* 19, no. 3 (1997): 265-300.

38. Moran, "Unintended Revolution."

39. Anne Woodsworth, "Getting Off the Library Merry-Go-Round: McAnally and Downs Revisited," *Library Journal* 114 (May 1, 1989a): 35-38.

40. Woodsworth, "Libraries and the CIO," 43.

41. Ibid., 38.

42. Anne Woodsworth, *Patterns and Options for Managing Information Technology on Campus* (Chicago: American Library Assn., 1991), 23.

43. Penrod, Dolence, and Douglas, *CIO*, 13.

44. Mark Cain, Note to CAUSE electronic discussion group, April 15, 1997.

45. Arnold Hirshon, *Integrating Computing and Library Services: An Administrative Planning and Implementation Guide for Information Resources*, CAUSE Professional Paper Series 18 (Boulder, Colo.: CAUSE, 1998), 3.

46. Ibid., 10-11.

47. Ibid., 38-47.

48. Anne Woodsworth, D. Kaye Gapen, and Kenneth Pollock, "Chief Information Officers on Campus," *Educom Bulletin* 22 (summer 1987): 2-4.

49. Woodsworth, *Patterns and Options*, 43-47.

50. Terrence F. Mech, "Small College Library Directors of the Midwest," *Journal of Academic Librarianship* 11 (March 1985): 12; Terrence F. Mech, "The Managerial Roles of Chief Academic Officers," *Journal of Higher Education* 68 (May/June 1997): 288.

CHAPTER FOUR

Merging the Library and the Computer Center
Indications and Contraindications

RAYMOND K. NEFF

During the 1980s, many colleges and universities reconsidered the organization of the library and the computer center. Early in the discussion of this reconsideration, I wrote an article that has helped to frame a debate that has gone on ever since.[1] Some institutions decided to merge the two units, and they remain together today. Others decided that the two units should remain separate. Yet a third group tried a merger and, after some time, decided to undo it. Unions and separations of libraries and computer centers continue to occur across the spectrum of higher education. My purpose in this chapter is to reflect on reasons for considering a union and some contraindications. Not all campuses would be better off with a merged academic services organization, and caution is important in changing the status quo. From the years the merger question has been before us, at least three things have become clear: nearly every campus is embracing information technology (there is no retreat on this front); academic libraries are increasingly dependent on information technology; and intercampus networking is providing a basis for consortial sharing of both library resources and computing services on a scale only dreamed about just a few years ago.

One matter of terminology that we need to settle at the outset is just what is the "computer center." On many of our campuses the computer center, including its equipment and staff, has evolved from being a solitary "glass house" to being distributed across several service units. In its distributed form, the computer center has generally evolved into a central office of information technology (IT) with equipment and consulting services located in schools and departments close to the faculty, students, and staff who use them. In this chapter, the computer center and the centrally managed IT organization are considered synonymous.

Many factors today drive organizational change on our campuses. These include changing personnel, ongoing integration of technology into the academic fabric, and evolving expectations for academic services. The tempo of society has speeded up, and users now expect more from both the library and the IT organization. With more networking on our campuses, including residence halls, classrooms, laboratories, libraries, and offices, and with a great many students and faculty members having their own personal computers, the empowerment of campus citizenry continues. Unmediated services from the library and the computer center are replacing those that once required expertise and experience as necessary prerequisites. As user interfaces to network-based information resources became simpler and more interchangeable, a wider audience for digital information has been created, and this audience now needs to be served.

One of the driving forces pushing mergers of libraries and computer centers has been the creation of digital learning environments, and one of the factors driving this creation has been the development of new student markets for distance education. Once an on-campus learning environment has been transformed into a digital learning environment, extending it to serve remote students is relatively straightforward. When library services are integrated into a digital learning environment, the services can be extended to serve remote students.

Organizational change occurs in response to clearly perceived trends. Let us consider some recent trends that are reshaping campus-based libraries and computer centers.

1. Users in ever-increasing numbers prefer using information resources and full-text scholarly works offering immediate delivery over those that must be shipped through interlibrary loan, requiring several days or weeks for delivery.

2. Campus networks have become as crucial to librarians as they are to students, teachers, and scholars.

3. The technological skill-sets of librarians are growing but the technological knowledge, experience, and expertise continue to reside in the staff of the computer center. This makes the library dependent on a close working relationship with the computer center.

4. Training requirements of library users presuppose skills set forth by computer center staff for accessing networks, e-mail, OPACs, Web sites, multimedia repositories, and databases.

5. Distributed computer resources and distributed digital libraries are being linked together using a common type of communications networking.

6. Conversion of traditional paper-based information resources to digital formats is continuing to accelerate.

7. New consortia are being created, and existing ones continue to expand, to share scholarly materials that are becoming increasingly expensive.

8. Internet-2, which is currently under development, will be the next step in network access and information delivery and will enable delivery of high-quality, streaming audio and video media.

9. Libraries and IT both require substantial capital outlays and ever-larger operating budgets for staff, equipment, and library materials. IT staff are increasingly costly and scarce. Since universities and colleges cannot afford to have duplication of staff, integration of technical staffs has become inevitable.

Organizational structures continue to evolve in academic institutions as new opportunities, as well as new stresses, present themselves. These reflect both internal needs and external stimuli. When a new person with extraordinary talents and insights is introduced into the picture, frequently that person becomes the point of origin for organizational change. Sometimes the publicly stated reason for organizational change is only a convenient excuse for one that lies below the surface. My purpose here is not to weigh the import of any particular reason for changing the organizational structure or the relationships among campus academic services units; these depend significantly on the context that exists at a particular campus and are not readily generalizable. Rather, as noted earlier, we will simply consider some important indications for bringing the campus library and the campus computer center together. A companion section on contraindications for organizational mergers will follow.

INDICATIONS

Why merge the library and the computer center? Some possible indications for merger are as follows:

1. The desire to develop, implement, and sustain one vision for the future is a natural reason for merging two separate organizations. A new, merged organizational structure would follow a new mission for a combined information services unit. Indeed, the most important indication for merging the information technology unit and the library is that members of the institution see great value in their joining. In my experience, value is derived from the adoption of a common vision. Thus, the shared vision for the two units is the primary indicator of the need to merge. Many campuses are, in fact, developing new visions for learning environments, visions that take advantage of information technology. A brief listing of the elements of a digital learning environment is given in the appendix. The vision for this environment, which includes both on-campus and off-campus educational offerings, is based on naturally intertwined roles for the library and the computer center.

2. Merger may be based on a recognition of overlapping missions and strategies for the library and the IT organization in areas of information access, delivery, storage and retrieval, training and education, reference and help desk services, and consulting and user services. This indication recognizes the convergence of interests and roles. Reference and help desks share many common features of service and methodology. They may be combined to serve the campus better, especially in providing a common user interface as well as a common problem tracking system. Training and education services for the library and the computer center are based increasingly on common threads and infrastructure. Training in use of new types of delivery services, new tools for searching the digital library, and new sources of research-based information, including finding aids, has become essential. The library continues to carry a substantial burden in its effort to train users on the new tools of scholarship. The computing organization likewise has a substantial training burden brought about by developments in networking, the Internet, new browsers, new techniques for accessing databases, new ways to construct personal Web sites, and new methods and techniques for working with multimedia. Without training, faculty cannot use these new techniques effectively, and without instruction, students have "hit-or-miss" experiences with computers.

3. A desire to create a library of the future, one that will depend on information technology, is another indication for merger. This was the dominant reason for merging IT and the University Library at Case Western Reserve University. More generally, consider a campus that has developed a new vision for the library and adopts a library of the future strategy that envisions an expanded mission for the library. Naturally, information technology will play a central role. It is my experience that libraries generally do not have personnel

with the expertise to handle all of the necessary information technologies including networking, Web site maintenance, OPAC maintenance, increasing the power of bibliographic tools, digitization, creating and maintaining servers for file sharing, printing, and media streaming. Thus, the library either needs to have a steady campus partner in the computer center, duplicate the essence of the computer center, or merge with the computer center as part of a strategic solution to providing the service offerings that campus users require. Experience shows that such a critical organizational dependency is difficult to manage in a mere partnership of equals. Organizational merger is the surest way to meet this requirement.

We have found also numerous campuses where neither the library nor the computer center had a critical mass of technical staff to build and operate the technology infrastructure for the campus. Merging the two units with some degree of reorganization may provide the technical resources to meet campus needs while staying within budgetary limits.

4. External forces may bring the library and the computer center together to satisfy a need to improve academic services and access to information services. Both the library and the computer center are being subjected to greater forces of change than ever before. These forces of change are coming first from students and their parents who expect that institutions of higher education will embrace IT for learning and research. They also resonate from legislators, boards of trustees, other funders of higher education, and administrative officers who have to manage the rapid growth rates in expectation with the smaller growth rate in tuition. Interestingly, faculty members, for the most part, are not leaders in seeking change, perhaps because they have little control over academic service organizations and their budgets. Although we may not want to admit it, a need to reduce the combined budgetary share of campus resources is an important indicator. When we have to do more with less, a merged organization can often redistribute funds to add services and expand offerings. Thus, merger can be a valid response to forces of change for improving academic services and increasing the expectation level for access to information resources.

A related indication to merge is the desire to achieve efficiencies based on a common infrastructure for communications and digitization (using bits instead of atoms). For example, it is an indication to consider a merger if both the library and the computer center use the same campus network (Intranet, Internet, Internet-2), base their families of services upon the same campus standards for personal computers, and provide instructional programs with the same basic software suite of personal productivity tools. Compatibility, ubiquity, and universality of campus academic services would be an indication that a merger could achieve efficiencies. Thus, a merger may be a consequence of the development of campus-wide standards and the reliance on a common campus information architecture for IT and the library.

It may be an indication for a merger when the campus has embarked on a large-scale distance learning initiative. On many campuses, the IT organization is taking on or is being encouraged to embrace distance learning initiatives. At the present time, few libraries are in a position to support students at a distance with the same library services they supply to on-campus students. The distance learning effort becomes one more dimension of organizational alignment.

5. A desire to increase the organization's effectiveness and efficiency is a reason to consider merging the library with IT. Mergers can reduce organizational

bloat and flatten organizational hierarchies. The trend toward increased use of digital formats produces an overlap in technologies and personnel as common ground is increased. In my experience, a merger of the library and the computer center can produce a substantially strengthened organization. Sometimes, as a consequence, the new information services organization has more campus influence. The elimination of redundant staff can free up resources, which, in turn, allow investments and programmatic improvements to be made. In larger academic libraries one may find as many as five or more levels in the organization. In contrast, computer centers rarely have more than four levels; three are most common. Merging to eliminate redundant layers of management and overhead is becoming a somewhat more common occurrence in academe. Indeed, perhaps the most compelling reason to merge the library and the computer center is to achieve a single point of executive-level responsibility and eliminate dual responsibility hierarchies. Redundant management structures in the library and the computer center often produce organizational confusion. Missions overlap, visions are confused and contradictory, and strategies conflict, especially with respect to the control of a critical campus resource, such as a building site, or with respect to responsibilities, such as fund-raising. With the financial pressures being exerted on all of our campuses to do more with less, often an imperative requires an institution to seize the opportunity to consolidate and resize the group to fit the institution's needs and resources.

Merger of the library with the computing organization is a more common occurrence when the administration creates an executive-level position to provide both vision and direction to these two units. Ordinarily, the provost or vice president for academic affairs would play this executive role, but as the demands of IT and the library become greater and the chief academic officer becomes more stretched, it may be in the best interest of the institution to create the executive position of chief information officer (CIO) to coordinate both IT and the library. A merger becomes a possibility whenever a CIO is appointed. The corollary also seems to occur with some frequency: the indications for a merger discussed above are frequently precursors to the creation of the CIO position.

6. A decision to physically distribute the computer center across campus is another indication for a merger. On some campuses, the traditional mission of the computer center becomes irrelevant as computing resources become distributed at departmental and workgroup levels. Yet the residual functions of the computer center need an organizational home, and because of its common orientation to servicing the whole campus, the library is a natural place in which to consolidate them. This has occurred most frequently in smaller research-oriented universities.

CONTRAINDICATIONS

Logically, a contraindication is the negation of an indication. Thus, a list of each indication discussed above with the word "not" inserted before the action verb would constitute a list of contraindications. I will leave the reader with the exercise of constructing a negative for each indication and examining its validity. In this section, we will consider a number of contraindications that are more profound than these simple negations.

1. It is a contraindication for union when the library has its own computing unit. When the library's automation system is directly under its control, it does not need the IT organization.

2. It is also a contraindication when there is little value to be gained by having a campus-wide network. Typically this situation occurs at institutions where the student population is largely nonresident, and faculty and staff are also largely nonresident or have been drawn from a great many allied organizations that have their own networks. In such a case, the campus citizenry can rely mainly on a local Internet service provider or the regional telephone company for dial-in services to either a small collection of on-campus servers or to services provided on an outsourced basis. Such arrangements might be found in community colleges that use, for example, America Online for e-mail, newsgroups, Web hosting, and a general assortment of Internet access services.

3. It is a contraindication to merge if the library is a satisfied customer of a separate IT organization. "If it ain't broke, don't fix it." It is not difficult to determine if the library personnel are happy with the campus's networking services or the OPAC and related automation systems that the computer center provides to the library. If the library is pleased with the strategic direction of information technology on campus and the leadership in IT, why merge? In my experience, though, deficiencies in one or more of these areas are sufficient cause for the library to seek control of the direction of IT. One of the ways in which this can occur is through the appointment of the library director as the campus CIO.

4. It is a contraindication for a merger when the costs of reorganizing are too high. Libraries are traditionally funded from campus operating budgets, which include tuition revenues and indirect charges or "overhead" from research grants. With the changes in research funding patterns over the past decade, especially at the federal level, computer centers are generally funded from a mixture of direct charges to users, a student technology fee, and assessments to administrative offices and academic centers and departments. The computer center is, thus, dependent on recovering some of its costs directly from its users. If the merged organization would have to give up its revenue from charging users and, as a consequence, its entire budget would have to be shifted to a line item in the campus's operating budget, a merger might be contraindicated because of this impracticality. If the computer center already uses a library-like financing model of not charging for specific computer services, then a merger from a budgetary perspective would be much simpler. According to the library model of financing computer centers, use of the computer center is open to all without the need to pay just as use of the library is free to all campus citizens.

5. It is a contraindication for a merger if separate IT and library organizations are well developed and servicing the campus adequately. For example, it might be a contraindication for a merger when the computer center has a strong user base in the quantitative disciplines, such as chemistry, engineering, physics, and astronomy. The demands of these users for cutting-edge technology services to support their research and instructional activities are substantial. When the computer center has a large customer base in the disciplines or the administrative offices, the library becomes just another customer. In my experience, the merger of the library with an IT organization having large and important campus customers is not a recipe for organizational success. It is

generally too much for a merged organization to balance out the demands of its large customers with those of the library organization itself.

6. If the library culture is not easily reconciled with that of the computer center, the contraindication can go either way. I have seen situations in which the organizational values of the library and the computer center were so similar that the two groups worked together easily and valued each other's work interchangeably. In such situations, progress occurred without great disruption. I believe the explanation of this phenomenon was their overwhelming identification with the campus's culture, rather than that of each organization. On other campuses, the computer center culture is so different from that of the library that it is difficult to get representatives of the two organizations to adopt a common point of view or pursue common goals or share a vision or set of strategies. The computer center has its ways of meeting the needs of its users, and the library has its different ways; there is little tolerance for the views of the other. Sometimes the two are so separate that they can hardly abide the presence of the other. There is little trust, little respect, and few shared experiences. Each unit operates with a parallel or divergent organizational point of view.

CONCLUSION

When all is said and done, it is information technology that will unlock the strategic power of the library. Thus, the library and the computer center should always be close partners in serving the world of education. The library is both a point of service (as an intellectual commons servicing all) and a conservator of knowledge (maintaining a repository that is a core collection plus in-depth collections in selected scholarly domains). The computer center is a service point and a concentration of ever-changing technological expertise. When they work together, whether through a merged structure or not, the entire institution benefits. Careful consideration should be given to the indicators and contraindicators to determine which structure would work best in any particular situation.

APPENDIX Elements of a Digital Learning Environment

There are six basic elements of technology that make up the infrastructure of a digital learning environment:

> Personal microcomputers for students and faculty—the portal into the world of information
>
> Multimedia classrooms with high performance displays and some with individual computer interfaces
>
> Digital libraries' repositories of software, electronic journals, and multimedia
>
> Campus-wide information system based on the World Wide Web technology
>
> Specialized shared servers—including high-speed laser printers
>
> Ubiquitous and continuous networking; the network is the utility of the future; it is at the core of much of how things get done

We say that it is an environment because the system is

Universal (the same everywhere)

Ubiquitous (is available in student residences, libraries, laboratories, classrooms, and faculty offices)

Comprehensive (it handles coursework in all disciplines, administrative chores, and "edu-tainment")

Integrated (we do not just buy hardware and software and hope for the best; instead, we acquire just the equipment we need and make the pieces work together)

NOTE

1. Raymond K. Neff, "Merging Libraries and Computer Centers: Manifest Destiny or Manifestly Deranged?" *Educom Bulletin* 20 (winter 1985): 8-16.

CHAPTER FIVE

Does the Scholarly Information Center Work?

Evaluating Library-Computer Center Cooperation

DELMUS E. WILLIAMS
ONADELL BLY

The idea that computer centers, audiovisual service and production units, telecommunications agencies, and libraries must learn to work together has become axiomatic over the last fifteen years. When Patricia Battin first proposed the idea that the best elements of each of these units be combined into a "scholarly information center," computer use had already become a mainstay on campus.[1] Academic futurists had been speculating for more than a decade about how the advent of the computer age might affect library operations. The scarcity and expense of the computers of that era encouraged these discussions. The development of software for libraries gave computer specialists sufficient reason to buy the machines that they wanted, and few libraries could afford stand-alone equipment to drive their automation projects. Cooperation offered a solution for both groups. At first these discussions often seemed like a competition as to who would or should have center stage as the primary information provider on campus.

Battin's view, and the view of those who came after her, reflected a growing understanding that competition needed to be replaced by arrangements that would encourage cooperation among those associated with the production and distribution of information for the campus. These discussions about cooperation continue to this day. As sophisticated computing equipment becomes increasingly ubiquitous and as the dependence of the campus and its libraries on computing grows, universities and colleges have begun to implement programs designed to encourage collaboration among information providers and to create integrated organizations that include various elements of the information infrastructure.

The current literature on the management of computer centers and library operations is full of articles about strategies for integrating various information services. Virtually all of these seem to be predicated upon an underlying assumption that integration will be more efficient and lead to more effective service. Arguments are made about the importance of cooperation and cases are presented that describe the implementation of programs. Intuitively, we have come to believe that interagency cooperation is good. However, there is not much evidence that the impact of these organizational changes is being measured in any effective way. In our haste to move towards integration, it appears that we have neglected to develop anything that can pass for measures of success for joint enterprises. Sooner or later we need to develop a set of measures to evaluate the organizations we are attempting to create. Are information organizations headed by a Chief Information Officer who oversees the operations of all information providers on campus effective? Is coordinating these activities through committees worth the time and energy it consumes? Are mergers warranted? Coordination is expensive, and we must develop measures that can be used to justify that expense.

We have written this chapter to assist in the development of evaluation tools by offering questions that should be addressed as institutions of higher education implement new structures. We will offer several criteria designed to help determine whether efforts to build appropriate structures are accomplishing what we want. The criteria will also help us identify new opportunities that can expand these cooperatives. They are also intended to help institutions decide how to get the most out of the resources they are pouring into libraries, classroom support, networking, computing services, and other campus information resources.

THE BACKGROUND OF THE DISCUSSION

All of the groups that make up the information infrastructure of the campus bring resources to the table that can increase administrative and research productivity, improve teaching, and support the efforts of researchers and administrators. At the same time, all have limitations that constrain their capacity to serve their publics. Computer center personnel bring to the mix an understanding of the mechanics and economics of computing and of the electronic components that are available to support information systems, but they are not always known for their "customer relations" skills. They are strong planners who sometimes have difficulty communicating with naive users.

Telecommunications staff are rapidly expanding their responsibilities from telephone systems to providing expertise on the architecture of the campus network and other elements of the communications infrastructure. Networks that accommodate everything from satellite feeds to communications from the World Wide Web, to video streams, to full-text journal articles are quickly becoming a necessity. As campus communications systems are being upgraded to transmit data and images as well as voice, these professionals are being asked to expand their infrastructures and develop the capacity to handle high-speed connections on campus and between the campus and the rest of the world. Telephone personnel are being asked to shift from a reactive to a proactive role and assume a major responsibility for anticipating future needs for campus infrastructure.

Audiovisual services staff bring to the table an understanding of audio and video production and of the equipment required to distribute and use networked information from the network in the classroom. They are now also being asked to provide the kind of aesthetic design support necessary to present data in attractive and useful formats on the World Wide Web. Audiovisual service programs are also expected to incorporate functions like programming for the Web and document scanning into their activities and to add an ever broadening array of equipment to support expansions of their program.

Librarians bring to the table an understanding of content and a service ethic that connects end users with the information they need. To be effective, many librarians have been required to embrace the technologies that they had previously looked upon with suspicion. Meeting the challenge of a modern library program has required them to show more flexibility, allowing them to consider and act upon new sets of possibilities in a timely fashion.[2]

Discussions about working together for a common good center on the idea that campus information needs can only be met effectively at an affordable cost if all of the people in the information infrastructure cooperate to optimize their strengths. Such discussions are taking place on virtually every campus in the United States and abroad. As early as 1988, David Weber described the wide range of information support structures then existing on campuses. At one extreme, were instances in which the library and the computer center reported to different vice presidents within the university with little effort to cooperate. At the other, there were situations in which both organizations reported to either the head of the campus library or the head of the computer center.[3] By the time Weber was considering the problem, most campuses had already begun to consider structures that might facilitate a more integrated approach to providing information services.

Today the emphasis seems to be on developing a higher level of coordination among these activities. This is, in part, because there is a belief that information resources are a utility that provides "power" to a broad spectrum of the campus community. Additionally, the advent of distributed processing, the increase in technical sophistication of the library staff, and the library's increasing reliance on computers have created a need for a higher level of coordination and cooperation. Finally, the centrality of the network in all aspects of information transfer on campus has demanded better, more widespread planning.[4] In his recent study of Chief Information Officers, Arnold Hirshon indicated that, while coordinating efforts are becoming ubiquitous on campus, the degree to which information services are integrated on various campuses still range along a continuum. At one end are organizations that have fully integrated operations with a single service program and no real distinction between what had previously been part of the library and what had been part of the computer center. At the other end are organizations in which the library, the computer center, and other information providers remain as distinct as ever. The place that these organizations fall along this continuum related directly to local conditions, and no two organizations that he described were the same. Hirshon's study did not include any discussion of other information providers on campus (except to the degree that they were already part of either the library or the computer center) or of universities that have kept traditional organizations and coordinate their information resources informally. Even so, he found that there was little uniformity from campus to campus, even in the subset that he considered.[5]

PARAMETERS FOR AN EVALUATION PROGRAM

More often than not, efforts to coordinate information resources on campus began with a desire to control costs as administrators tried to cope with new information technologies.[6] In recent years, however, the movement toward integration has taken place more because of a perceived need to understand the nature of the information present and to plan for an information future. As a result of these efforts, administrators are beginning to understand that the support required to make this future a reality is expensive. The situation is further complicated by the fact that technology is changing at a dizzying speed. Few campuses can attract and keep enough people with the expertise required to understand the possibilities and use the technology to best advantage. In libraries, the ever more complex array of formats available, the use of external databases, and the increasing variety of equipment that we use are making it difficult for both librarians and lay people to understand the environment in which we operate. This level of complexity has forced campuses to reexamine the premises upon which past decisions about services were based and to develop more flexible operations.

Any tools that are developed to evaluate the effectiveness of an information services program must, therefore, be designed to help people with differing sets of expertise understand the current status of technology on the campus, what new directions information services need to take, and how the program might get to where it needs to be. It must take into account that information programs differ widely from institution to institution. This tendency to tailor programs to meet local needs is a double-edged sword. On the one hand, tailoring lets the institution take full advantage of local expertise and cover those areas where it is less strong in effective, though sometimes inelegant, ways. On the other hand, tailoring makes it more difficult to find and transplant effective models used in other institutions. It requires more planning and management oversight as the organization monitors the solutions it has chosen and continuously modifies them as the need arises.

The evaluation of a tailored organization requires a more creative consideration of programmatic outcomes. It cannot rely simply on comparisons of the local organization to the inputs associated with standards and the "normal" organizational models employed by peer institutions if its structure is markedly different from those institutions. As a result, the measures of a successful coordination effort should address what the institution wants to accomplish rather than focus on an ideal bureaucratic structure. The measures must focus on the value of changes that are effected to make the organization more efficient and effective. Success is measured in terms of the capacity of organizational changes to solve real problems, and the restructuring should aim first at doing no harm. "If it ain't broke, don't fix it" becomes the maxim of the day.

THE LITERATURE

Perhaps the best way to begin a discussion of the value added to the organization by cooperation among information providers is to look at the literature in an attempt to determine why proponents of cooperative or integrated operations advocate this change and what benefits they see from these new arrangements. In a 1993 article on the promise of the electronic library, Hannah King laid out several benefits that might just as easily fit here. King said that electronic libraries could be expected to provide increased access to more information, economic gains from decreased costs, increased productivity, and increased institutional competitiveness. They should also revitalize the educational process, enhance the research capability, and increase the status and prestige for information services within the university.[7] As one implements programs of this sort, it is important to know that these expectations are being met.

In 1995, Maxine Brodie and Neil McLean made a case for reengineering academic libraries that also provided some guidance as to why organizational change can be useful. They contended that academic library structures required dramatic changes. Librarians were being asked to expand their service programs despite a decline in the resources available to them. They were also being expected to cope with new ways of doing things without dispensing with the old and to shift resources quickly from one program to another with little time for planning. Librarians faced a chronic underinvestment in technology while being asked to reexamine or change existing practices without appropriate training and education. They also were expected to support organizational structures that were resistant to change. Brodie and McLean also noted that many libraries seemed to encourage those who worked within them to accept insularity and to see themselves as victims of circumstances they cannot control, further complicating the situation.[8] While these symptoms justify reengineering libraries, they also provide good reasons for restructuring any kind of organization that is related to the creation and distribution of information across campus or for any effort to coordinate these activities.

Robert Heterick and William H. Sanders offered additional reasons for coordination. In a discussion of the need for an "information czar" on campus, Heterick and Sanders said that this person should serve as the keeper of the vision for educational technology on campus. The czar they envisioned should be expected to provide special attention to its relationship to the institutional mission and its implications for the administration, the organization, and its clientele. They also suggested that the czar might encourage planning across organizational boundaries, support experimentation, promote consensus on standards, and effect rapid reorganization when necessary. In short, this person would be in a position to raise issues relating to information services at higher levels on campus than might otherwise be possible, and help develop consensus in terms of needs and priorities. The czar would then be expected to work with those charged with delivering services to develop programs that could be implemented in a decentralized way while reflecting a unified vision of desired outcomes and priorities.[9]

On a more functional level, Martha Sharrow suggested nine areas that offered challenges to those developing library/IT collaborations. She identified them as priority setting, funding, staffing, turf, mutual respect, levels of authority, communication, personalities, trust and respect, and the effects of campus climate and politics.[10] While all of these reflect process rather than outcomes measures, they clearly provide indicators as to how successful the collaboration is and is likely to be.

To this we might add several advantages of a more integrated approach that Hirshon identified in his recent study of Chief Information Officers. Hirshon found that these organizations tended to develop as a response to a set of local needs. For instance, the campus suddenly had to cope with the convergence of information technologies. Or those who administered the institution sought to expand efforts to integrate these technologies into the teaching, learning, and research processes. Or the campus needed to remediate organizational weaknesses, and new technologies offered opportunities to coordinate campus services by provided additional information in useful formats. Or a precipitating event occurred that led to the introduction of the CIO to campus, such as the planning of a new building, administrative failures, financial or staffing concerns, or a need to reevaluate information resources as part of a planning process. Hirshon also found that CIOs saw the benefits in terms of increased services, improved visibility on campus, greater organizational flexibility, increased cooperation, and more equitable compensation for employees.[11]

A variety of other people offer additional reasons for a more integrated approach. David Weber suggested that integration might address concerns about recruiting sufficient numbers of people with the expertise required to solve technical problems.[12] While he suggested this for libraries, the wisdom of his suggestion for other areas becomes apparent as computer centers cope with the World Wide Web, as network services and telecommunications offices find themselves under increasing pressure to be responsive to end users, and as audiovisual services units are being drawn into the design and operation of local and wide area networks. Anne Woodsworth noted the use of integration as a tool for rationalizing and sustaining the campus infrastructure so that it can support all users and coordinate the provision of information to students, faculty, and administrators working throughout the campus.[13] Pat Molholt saw this as a way to develop a consistent service program across organizational boundaries,[14] and Dennis Aebersold and Gordon A. Haaland summed up by noting that a successful integration of these units will help develop a top quality organization that is consistent with customer needs.[15] These are all qualities to be encouraged in a successful organization, and, as such, they provide operational measures against which the organization can be judged.

QUESTIONS THAT MIGHT BE ASKED WHEN ASSESSING EFFECTIVENESS

But what kind of guidance do these authors provide regarding the questions that should be addressed as campuses seek a structure that will add value to the institution's information services? We can best summarize in a catechism that can provide some direction in planning and evaluating these organizations and the discussions of what information service organizations might accomplish when performing at peak efficiency to meet the initiators' expectations. We do not propose the following as an exhaustive list of the questions that one might ask. In fact, local tailoring makes it impossible to develop such a list. But these questions do offer a beginning. When combined with questions of local interest and embroidered by experience, these questions can provide a useful tool for planning and implementation.

> *Structural Issues.*　　Is information services properly placed within the university structure? Does it report to the right place or places? Will the new information services structure encourage discussions at a level that includes those who make key budgetary and personnel decisions

about providing technical support and initiating innovations in the classroom? Are those who are charged with addressing the needs of researchers and administrative services included regularly in discussions about computer and library resources?

Planning.   Will the new organization encourage planning for information services on campus? Will it enhance the capacity of the campus to transcend turf battles, personalities, and the kind of insularity that can make those who work in the organization see themselves as the victims of a situation over which they have little control? Does everyone feel that they share the vision of the new organization? Does the organizational structure enhance the institution's capacity to forge consensus about the priorities and needs of the information services program?

Capacity to Make Necessary Changes.   Will the new organization encourage flexibility, enabling it to break down structures that resist change and replace them with an organization that enhances its capacity to experiment? Does it enhance the institution's capacity to develop programs that can serve the institution and its capacity to make additional changes as the need arises? Does it have the capacity to effect reorganization or retasking when required to facilitate the implementation of new ideas or the use of new technologies?

Organizational Climate and Personnel Issues.   Will the new organization encourage cooperation among all those who generate, transmit, and use information within the organization? Will it help create a cohesive culture that encourages mutual respect among those who work within it? Will it encourage optimal utilization of scarce talents and resources and exhibit an appropriate prioritization of needs? Will it assist in developing rational compensation plans that ensure that people doing similar work are paid the same? Will the structure provide an appropriate standing for information professionals within both the organization and the university? Will it create a sense of community that encourages interaction and professional growth through the exchange of ideas? Will it make the university a more attractive place for people to work? Does it encourage loyalty and enhance the capacity of the institution to attract and retain people with scarce talents?

Access to Resources.   Will the new organization be able to acquire the resource base needed to ensure that the institution invests appropriately in both its technology infrastructure and in peripherals? Will it help libraries, computer center personnel, and others cope with a rapidly changing environment, continuously dealing with the present and planning for the future while coping with legacy systems from the past? Will it provide economic benefit through decreased costs and increased productivity?

Service Program.   Will the organization that emerges offer an efficient structure that can provide excellent services tailored to fit the needs of the institution and other users? Will it provide more effective access to more information in more places?

Evaluation.   Will the new structure enhance the capacity of the university to generate sufficient management information to evaluate its programs and meet the challenges offered in an environment of rapid change? Will it address, in a reasonable and constructive way, the problems or situations that spawned it?

CONCLUSION

We create structures to coordinate information resources so that we might adjust more readily to changes in information technology, encourage efficiency, and continuously improve the institution's capacity to meet the needs and expectations of its clients. To accomplish this purpose, we must develop criteria that will allow us to evaluate the success of that structure and fine-tune the organization we put in place. The implementation of new organizational structures is only justified if it makes the information services program better. We can ensure that this will happen only by defining early what we want from the structures and then determining the degree to which new structures meet those expectations. We hope that this chapter can serve as a beginning in that process.

NOTES

1. Patricia Battin, "The Electronic Library: A Vision for the Future," *Educom Bulletin* 19 (summer 1984): 34.
2. Maurice Mitchell and Laverna M. Sanders, "The Virtual Library: An Agenda for the 1990s," *Computers in Libraries* 11 (April 1991): 8-11.
3. David C. Weber, "University Libraries and Campus Information Technology Organizations: Who Is in Charge Here?" *Journal of Library Administration* 9 (1988): 5-19.
4. Anne Woodsworth, D. Kaye Gapen, and K. Pollock, "Chief Information Officers on Campus," *Educom Bulletin* 22 (summer 1987): 2-4.
5. Arnold Hirshon, *Integrating Computing and Library Services: An Administrative Planning and Implementation Guide for Information Resources,* CAUSE Professional Paper Series 18 (Boulder, Colo.: CAUSE, 1998).
6. Nancy Nelson, "Electronic Libraries: Vision and Implementation," *Computers in Libraries* 10 (February 1990): 6-13.
7. Hannah King, "Walls around the Electronic Library," *Electronic Library* 11 (June 1993): 165-174.
8. Maxine Brodie and Neil McLean, "Process Reengineering in Academic Libraries: Shifting to Client-Centered Resource Provision," *Cause/Effect* 18 (summer 1995): 40-46.
9. Robert C. Heterick and William H. Sanders, "From Plutocracy to Pluralism: Managing the Emerging Technologies," *Educom Review* 28, no. 5 (September 1993): 22-28.
10. Martha J. Sharrow, "Library and IT Collaboration Projects: Nine Challenges," *Cause/Effect* 18 (winter 1995): 55-56.
11. Hirshon, "Integrating Computing."
12. Weber, "University Libraries."
13. Anne Woodsworth, "Computing Centers and Libraries as Cohorts: Exploiting Mutual Strengths," *Journal of Library Administration* 9 (1988): 21-34.
14. Pat Molholt, "On Converging Paths: The Computing Center and the Library," *Journal of Academic Librarianship* 11 (November 1985): 284-288.
15. Dennis Aebersold and Gordon A. Haaland, "Strategic Information Resources: A New Organization," *CAUSE 94: New Opportunities for Partnering: Proceedings of the 1994 CAUSE Annual Conference November 29-December 2, 1994, Orlando, Fla.* (Boulder, Colo.: CAUSE, 1995), III-2-1.

CHAPTER SIX

Evolving Relationships

The Intersecting and Nonintersecting Roles of the Small College Library and Computer Center

PAUL J. SETZE

KIMBERLY A. JORDAN

In this article, we examine the evolving and often stormy relationship between the library and computer centers at small colleges in the United States. We first identify and examine similarities and differences of the two organizations. We argue that, regardless of reporting structure, there are different yet overlapping pressures on the two organizations, which result in the two organizations responding differently to similar pressures. Furthermore, both organizations face many challenges in the near future, and they often find themselves competing against each other for scarce resources.

Finding common ground for discussion is difficult yet important if the two organizations are to serve the academic enterprise. We present data collected and analyzed by one of the coauthors (Jordan) that suggest that there are areas of agreement on which to base discussions of how to best serve the needs of faculty members and students. Lastly, we propose a structure to foster communication and the exchange of information and to provide for input and guidance from faculty and students.

SERVICE AND SUPPORT IS THE PRIMARY MISSION

The roots and primary purpose of libraries and computer centers are very different. The primary role for the library at a small college is always, without question, to support academic programs. Before the advent of electronic information sources, supporting the academic programs meant developing collections that supported the curriculum, having staff that worked well with undergraduates, and having good interlibrary loan programs.

Computing centers, on the other hand, are relatively new to small colleges, having existed for only two or three decades. In the early days of computing, small college computer centers existed primarily to support the business functions of the college. Faculty might have been able to get some time on the administrative system for research or for students in a class, but these early computer centers had not been put in place to support the academic program. As computing became less expensive and began to play a more significant role in some academic disciplines, a need arose for some sort of "academic computing" as opposed simply to administrative computing.

Academic computing, however, served very specific purposes and faculty members and students often found gaining access to computing resources a laborious process that required significant effort and justification. More often than not, upon completion of a project faculty members and students no longer had access to the computer resources because of the need to ration an expensive and scarce resource.

Two developments occurred in the early 1980s that radically changed computing at small colleges: networking and personal computing. These developments had significant repercussions for the small college library, faculty, and students. Access to information resources expanded and became decentralized. Over time, access to computing for faculty and students became ubiquitous. Expansion has resulted in more people having access to a wider range of resources without limitations on the time of day or week. Decentralization has resulted in a loss of control over the resources to which faculty members or students have access. This loss of control, however, does not lessen the faculty or student demand for top-quality assistance. The ubiquitous nature of computing and high-speed networking has made expansion and decentralization possible and has resulted in libraries and computing centers finding themselves having constantly to react to ever-changing environments, regardless of how well they plan. Pressures on budgets and staff continue to mount. In short, we are constantly coping with the changes that wide-area networking and computing have brought to the campus. We can be assured that the future will bring even more changes.

Academic libraries have a long history of service and a well-defined mission. Academic computing centers are a recent creation: They are usually an ad hoc response to a very real need, and academic computing centers do not fit very well within any existing organization. Academic computing, therefore, does not have a long history and often has a vaguely defined mission of supporting computing for faculty and students, whatever that may mean. Furthermore, unlike librarians, most academic computing professionals do not have professional identities, though they may have master's and doctoral degrees.

Library and computing organizations want to provide the best level of service possible. At their core, libraries and computer centers are service providers, and both provide service to the same individuals. However, if you define their constituencies by the services they request, you find that the services provided by the two organizations may overlap considerably, and these overlaps center around electronically based information resources—how to find them, how to access them, and, to a lesser extent, how to use them. Which organization is used by any given person often depends on individual relationships, previous experience with a given organization, and the degree of cooperation between the two organizations, and not on whether one or the other organization is "charged" with providing support in a particular area. When it comes to electronic information, the boundary is sometimes blurred or, in some cases, nonexistent.

THE PRESSURES

Few members of the campus community are able to get through the day without at least indirect use of electronic information resources. Online public access catalogs, CD-ROMs, electronic databases, and World Wide Web pages are all routinely accessed. Few other campus resources impact the productivity of so many people every day.[1] In addition to the ever-increasing number of electronic information sources available, college students are arriving on campus having had more experience with electronic information resources. Parents and incoming students expect that a variety of electronic information resources be available. Although the availability of information resources is not likely to be the sole reason for attending a particular institution, the absence of these resources may be a reason not to attend.[2]

While colleges do what they can to provide the electronic resources parents and prospective students require, faculty members and students continue to look for assistance wherever they can find it. The result stretches library and academic computing services to the breaking point. Librarians faced with dramatic increases in the cost of paper-based materials must now purchase CD-ROMs and provide access to Internet accessible databases with little or no increase in their budgets for such materials. Further, library staffs may have had little or no training or experience with these new resources. Often, additional training is not available nor are there resources for the hiring of new staff with experience and expertise. Of no small concern is the need to assess the value of information resources supporting the academic mission. When students can access resources located anywhere at anytime, someone needs to be able to identify those information sources that are likely to be most valuable in support of the academic program.

Academic computing staff face mounting pressures as well. Everyone wants a networked computer on his or her desk or in his or her residence hall room. Networks, servers, electronic mail, remote dial-in access, and Internet availability must be reliable and accessible all day, every day. Naturally, all of these resources must be as easy to use as a toaster, and if they are not, support staff must be available to answer any imaginable question (and even some that cannot be imagined) at any time. To compound these challenges, technology tends to become obsolete quickly and the need to update equipment and software and to introduce new technologies adds to the difficulties of planning, budgeting, and support.

Staffing is a significant challenge for academic computing directors as well. Unlike librarians, who must obtain an MLS degree, there is no specific advanced degree for academic computing professionals. Some academic computing professionals may have credibility within an academic institution due to an advanced degree (Master's or Ph.D.) in an academic discipline. However, even with an advanced degree, they are generally not considered for faculty status unless they have a joint appointment with an academic department. Further, there is no defined career path for academic computing professionals, and people often leave the field for other areas with more clearly defined advancement opportunities. No small challenge is the retention and motivation of qualified staff in a tight labor market where private sector salaries outpace nonprofit salaries. These staffing challenges complicate the goal of delivering consistent and reliable service.

Faculty and students are often confused about where particular questions should be directed, and service providers themselves often find it difficult to determine which questions fall into their purview and which ones are best referred elsewhere. Roles are blurring between the library and computer center.[3] As service organizations, providing assistance is a priority, but staffs are finding it harder to satisfy the needs of their constituencies. Thus, we find librarians becoming more technically competent and academic computing professionals learning more about directing faculty and students to information resources. These responses are commendable, but as the complexity and vastness of information resources increase, service providers find it difficult to keep up. There is just too much information to keep abreast competently. Occupational trends now require more specialization, and this points to a need for more collaborative efforts.[4]

To collaborate, organizations need to speak the same language; unfortunately, librarians and academic computing professionals do not always do so.[5] A striking example of the difference in language involves the word librarians and computing professionals use for the groups of people they serve. Librarians traditionally use the word "patron," whereas computing professionals prefer the term "user." The Massachusetts Institute of Technology, as part of a computing and library collaboration, has decided to use "our faculty, students, and staff" in place of any other terms adopted by one group or the other.[6] Adopting a term that reflects the person's relationship to the larger organization (i.e., the college or university), rather than the person's relationship to the service provider, may indeed be best.

Today, libraries and computer centers face many, often external, pressures. Expectations are high, financial resources are tight (and getting tighter), and good employees are hard to find and keep. Little or nothing can be done to change these pressures. They are just part of the larger environment. Nonetheless, to identify and be aware of these external constraints and be honest about their origins are important. For example, one organization getting a budget increase or decrease is not necessarily due to the other organization's ability to argue a better case (although a better argued case probably helps!). The computer center may get a budget increase because of a residence hall networking project and the subsequent support that is required. Marketing and recruiting needs may drive the timing of the project, and the project may not even be a high priority for the computer center. There are cultural differences as well. The very language used by the two organizations reflects these differences. Over this last point, the two organizations have more control.

SERVICE ATTITUDES

Some observers have suggested that the primary difference between library and computer center approaches to serving their constituencies is that libraries have always had a service focus whereas computer centers have had a technology focus.[7] In 1997, Hardesty reported a similar conclusion from his interviews of library and computer center directors at small colleges.[8] Although impressions are important, we need to determine if a difference truly exists in the way these two organizations approach service.

In 1996, Jordan conducted a survey of fifty-seven small liberal arts colleges in the United States.[9] She employed an adaptation of the "Becoming a Customer

Service Star" inventory.[10] The study focused on the persons directly involved in providing information services to students. Forty-seven of one hundred academic computing professionals surveyed and twenty-eight of one hundred librarians responded to the questionnaire. Although the sample surveyed does not represent a random sample of the population of academic computing professionals and librarians, the results seem to contradict conventional wisdom.

Jordan found little difference between the two groups of professionals in terms of "feeling positively towards the customer," in terms of who was "most likely to respond to customer problems," and in terms of "seeking to exceed customer expectations." However, academic computing professionals were more likely to "encourage customer feedback" and attempt to develop "repeat relationships." These differences, however, may be because librarians have well defined and tested service methodologies, whereas computing professionals, responding to an ever-changing environment, require constant feedback to determine whether they are meeting user needs.

Nevertheless, this study suggests a significant common ground exists between librarians and academic computing professionals. Instead of concentrating on their perceived differences, perhaps these two groups should seek more strenuously to identify their common ground and to develop relationships that focus on their strengths and on how they complement each other. They also need to recognize that for the foreseeable future there will be an overlap in the services provided by the two organizations, and that this overlap is likely to be fluid.

MAKING IT ALL WORK

The overlap between the two organizations is likely to be fluid because the environment is itself fluid. Technology changes. Faculty members' and students' familiarity with and use of technology are constantly increasing. The integration of technology into the fabric of the college becomes tighter and tighter with each passing year: teaching, communicating, and access to information rely more and more on technological underpinnings. New services become available. Obsolete services, although often difficult to terminate, eventually die. How can we develop a concrete method to make it all work when it is nearly impossible to predict the operational environment from year to year?

Discussions about library and academic computing relationships tend to focus on organizational structures and are based on the assumption that the "correct" structure will solve most of the "problems" associated with the support of electronic information services. Although organizational issues are important, they are far less important than the overall structure that defines how the two organizations relate to one another. How the organizations relate to one another, to their constituencies, and to the senior administration of the college are far more important than to whom they report.

RECOMMENDATIONS

Both libraries and computer centers need to understand better than they typically do now the types of services the other offers. Academic computing professionals must know and understand how a library is organized, why it is organized the way it is, what services the library offers to students and faculty, what type of direct support the library needs from academic computing professionals, and what the major challenges for the library are. Librarians should encourage academic computing professionals to learn more about the library. Furthermore, library professionals must know and understand how the academic computing staff is organized and why, what services are offered to faculty and students by academic computing, what services academic computing can directly provide to the library and vice versa, and what the major challenges for the academic computing organization are. In other words, an ongoing dialogue and exchange of knowledge and information must take place if both organizations are going to be successful and fulfill their missions.

But dialogue alone is not enough. There needs to be a framework for dialogue. Certainly, one framework is the administrative organization. There needs to be strong leadership from the president of the institution and the senior leadership team. If the library and academic computing have distinct reporting lines, it is imperative that the vice presidents at the head of these reporting lines insist on cooperation and not competition. Library and academic computing planning needs to take place within the context of the institutional strategic plan. The two organizations should work closely together and coordinate their planning processes.

While important, administrative structures are not sufficient in themselves to ensure an ongoing working dialogue between the two organizations. Administrative structures do not necessarily represent or respond adequately to student and faculty needs—particularly when these needs are constantly changing. Administrative structures are often slow to even change in a rapidly changing environment. Therefore, the creation of a set of permanent advisory committees with balanced representation from the faculty and student body is critically important. These committees should be actively involved in the dialogue regarding service issues, along with the other matters typically addressed by advisory committees. The college librarian should be at least an ex officio member of the committee advising academic computing, and the head of academic computing (or the head of the entire computing organization) should be at least an ex officio member of the committee advising the library. Such cross representation would reduce the chances for misperception and increase the chances for constructive dialogue. These committees not only provide opportunities for formal and direct feedback from faculty and students, but also they can often identify potential problem areas before administrators become aware of them.

CONCLUSION

As stated earlier, the library and academic computer center are service organizations. Both organizations face many challenges and have enough common ground to assist each other in becoming better service providers. Nevertheless, common ground and an organizational structure, while necessary, are not sufficient to guarantee success. Besides leadership from the president of an institution and the senior leadership team, the library director and the individual responsible for academic computing must provide leadership within their respective organizations. No one should feel threatened that someone is encroaching on his or her turf. No one should ever tell someone seeking assistance that it is not his or her job to help the individual with that question. No one should ever blame the other organization for a particular problem and absolve himself or herself of all responsibility. Every challenge posed and every question asked is an opportunity for us to learn, and we need to understand that what we learn will allow us to better serve students and faculty.

NOTES

1. Linda H. Fleit, *Self-Assessment for Campus Information Technology Services,* CAUSE Professional Paper Series 12 (Boulder, Colo.: CAUSE, 1994).
2. Martin Ringle and David Smallen, "Can Small Colleges Be Information Technology Leaders?" *Cause/Effect* 19 (summer 1996): 18-25.
3. Anne Woodsworth and Theresa Maylone, *Reinvesting in the Information Job Family: Context, Changes, New Jobs, and Models for Evaluation and Compensation,* CAUSE Professional Paper Series 11 (Boulder, Colo.: CAUSE, 1993).
4. Terence T. Huwe, "Information Specialists and the Cooperative Workplace: Challenges and Opportunities," in *Advances in Librarianship,* ed. Irene P. Godden, vol. 17 (San Diego, Calif.: Academic Press, 1993): 1-31.
5. Woodsworth and Maylone, *Reinvesting in the Information Job Family* and Marilyn McMillan and Gregory Anderson, "The Prototype Tank at MIT: 'Come On In, the Water's Fine,'" *Cause/Effect* 17 (spring 1994): 51-54.
6. McMillan and Anderson, "The Prototype Tank at MIT."
7. Marilyn J. Martin, "Academic Libraries and Computing Centers: Opportunities for Leadership," *Library Administration and Management* 6 (spring 1992): 77-81, and Sarah Fine, "Reference and Resources: The Human Side," *Journal of Academic Librarianship* 21 (January 1995): 17-20.
8. Larry Hardesty, "Library and Computer Center Relations at Smaller Academic Institutions," *Library Issues* 18 (September 1997).
9. Kimberly Jordan, " A Comparison of the Service Orientation of Reference Librarians and Academic Computing Professionals" (Master's thesis, Univ. of Oregon, 1996).
10. Bruce R. Matza, *Becoming a Customer Service Star* (King of Prussia, Penn.: Organization Design and Development, Inc., 1993).

CHAPTER SEVEN

Clashing Cultures
Cohabitation of Libraries and Computing Centers in Information Abundance

EDWARD D. GARTEN
DELMUS E. WILLIAMS

But it is not only that there are too many books; they are being produced every day in torrential abundance. Many of them are useless and stupid; their existence and their conservation is a dead weight upon humanity which is already bent low under other loads.[1]

—Jose Ortega y Gasset, 1934

For many years, academic libraries and computer centers have seen themselves as very separate organizations with very different roles. This perspective is changing as technologies converge. As these organizations seek a common ground to meet new realities, they are finding that old differences cause them to look quite differently at emerging issues relating to information services. Library organizations and computer centers have been structured in contrasting fashions, and the organizational cultures that they have developed reflect very different philosophies of service. As information professionals in both of these settings find themselves under increasing external pressure to work together, they must come to terms with these differences and appreciate the perspectives of their counterparts. In this chapter we will define some of these cultural differences and look at ways in which they might be addressed. We conclude by asking the question of "what fundamentally separates us" and then consider "whether it really matters."

LIBRARIES AND COMPUTER CENTERS COMPARED

First it may be useful to look at the evolution of libraries and computer centers within the context of higher education to see where they have been. Libraries have always been a part of the campus, but until about a hundred years ago, they served more as museums than as service organizations. Until about 1870, a junior faculty member usually administered the library as an added responsibility. With the advent of the German concept of the research university in the last quarter of the nineteenth century, the modern library began to take shape, and its administration became a professional responsibility that required specialized training. In relative terms, libraries are old organizations based on old and appreciated technologies, i.e., the printed page. Between 1876 and 1920, pioneers of the profession conceptually framed the current structure of the modern academic library, the form of its services, the primary organizational tools upon which it is based, library education, and the principles that undergird the profession. While librarians have refined their programs since that time and now rely on media that might have been the subject of science fiction in the 1920s, much of the literature of librarianship produced in the first two decades of the twentieth century reflects the principles upon which the profession continues to operate.

On the other hand, computer science is a much newer profession, stemming from, among other innovations, automated artillery range-finders and code-breakers developed during World War II and the civilian applications to which those machines were put after the war. While some discussions that "thinking machines" based on binary codes could have widespread application occurred as far back as the early 1940s, real applications within academic contexts did not transpire until much later. Even then, users limited applications for some time to administrative functions or to esoteric research in the sciences and engineering. Even in the mid-1970s, computing in many colleges and universities operated under the supervision of small groups of committed faculty members trained in a variety of traditional disciplines. Many of these individuals either found the computer a tool to advance their research or simply developed an interest in its potential capabilities. Not until the 1980s did computing gain status in academic life as a separate professional track and computer science curricula begin to take hold as a separate discipline. Even now, many computer center directors are individuals originally schooled in mathematics, engineering, physics, or other related disciplines who came to computing first as an avocation and then later adopted it as their primary professional focus. In fact, many of these people built the first computer services organizations on their campus or have only recently taken the reins from earlier pioneers. As a result, the philosophy of these early innovators is still much in evidence in the field. In some instances, this philosophy is operationalized as the prevailing wisdom in computer operations. In others, it is viewed as a "negative" to which those inside and outside of the computer center react.

What are the attributes that make libraries and those who work in them different from computer centers and their personnel? The answer to that question requires some historical analysis, none of which may be particularly new to the reader. Librarianship on academic campuses developed first as a "helping" profession, dedicated to assisting students and researchers complete their work. Like other similar professions, academic librarianship has been, until the last twenty-five years or so, a profession with three very distinct tiers. Often, male librarians had a fast track to leadership positions, sometimes with little preparation in the basics of library operations. Female graduates of library schools often provided most of the basic services, generally spending their entire careers in low level positions doing the basic work of the profession. And, finally, a third class of employees was made up of the clerical or paraprofessional workers. While generally well educated, they had little specialized training or opportunity for upward mobility. With the important exceptions of librarians with professional backgrounds in science and business, most librarians and other library workers have, over the years, come out of the humanities and social sciences. As a result, librarianship naturally has been grounded in a commitment to acquire and control printed materials and their derivatives—clearly older but still important technologies. Librarianship's special affinity to the printed and visual record is best exhibited by its penchant for describing all materials as if they were variants of the book.

Library stocks have expanded to include everything from archival collections to sound recordings to films to data files, and librarianship is shifting its emphasis away from the warehousing of materials toward a focus on providing access to materials. Clearly, in the last twenty years, the image of the stereotypical librarians, described by Lipow and Creth as passive-aggressive individuals with little understanding of technology[2] and by Hawkins and Battin as rule-bound people bent on warehousing and protecting information rather than using it,[3] has even less validity than in years past. However, enough truth may exist in the old stereotypes to make them appear credible to some observers.

Being steeped in tradition, libraries often approached automation with caution. Many early attempts to automate libraries began in computer centers rather than in the library. Nevertheless, as early as the 1970s librarians began to realize that they needed to understand computing and its applications to maintain the relevancy of their profession. They began to seek out additional training, develop specialties, and pursue partnerships with computer professionals who could facilitate the application of computers to an environment that sometimes neither felt comfortable with technology nor exhibited an inclination to take risks. Allen Veaner, in his 1974 article on political and fiscal factors limiting the uses of computers in libraries, wrote eloquently of the need for those individuals charged with the oversight of library and computer center operations to work together. Veaner concluded that computing offered a fine example of a cooperative application of a scarce resource that could be emulated in the library and elsewhere on campus.[4] In 1979, when Joe B. Wyatt wrote, "Every librarian should be computer literate—to be able to read and write computer programs for a variety of information applications," he reflected the sentiments of many of the leadership in the profession at the time.[5]

Automation and systems applications developed slowly at first but increased speed as librarians and their patrons began to understand the potential of computers. With improved and easier-to-use technology, librarians developed the skills required to apply and maintain equipment and software. However, planning for computerization in libraries has emphasized content rather than technology and has operated with an eye toward developing tools for novice users and the minimization of risk.[6] The essential functions of the library have not changed materially. To quote Richard De Gennaro, "The role of the librarians, in the future as in the past, will be to carry out the library function, i.e., to decide what information to collect and preserve, how to organize it and how to make it freely available to those who need it."[7] Librarianship and its services focus on providing access to externally generated databases and the information contained within them.[8] In dealing with technology, libraries have built their niche in dealing with problems relating to the rapid retrieval of information from large text databases. Until recently, these files often strained the capacities of the computers affordable to colleges and universities. In manipulating these files, administrators often judged the cost of mistakes as high, and, consequently, change has been slow. Librarians have often tended to place less emphasis on technology per se in favor of the application of technology to solve specific problems. Consequently, technologists have often found the pace at which automation has evolved in libraries to be frustrating. While the discomfort some librarians have with technology has put them at a disadvantage, this discomfort has forced other librarians to build the kind of expertise that allows them to approach new opportunities with the eye of a critical consumer and as a translator for novice users.

The development of academic libraries has evolved as those who work in them have tried to rationalize the organization of knowledge and translate that organization into a useful form that can be understood by students and faculty. Contributors to library literature over the years have continually tried to identify the unique professional characteristics of librarianship. But the conclusion reached seems to be that libraries are most successful when they amalgamate techniques developed elsewhere and apply them to the specific problems arising from the organization of knowledge and its presentation. The original professionals in the library had responsibility for managing a warehouse of information that had taken shape prior to the existence of the profession, and, while the warehouse has changed, the function remains.[9] Librarians have always been encouraged to take the long view of their work. They have had the good sense to recognize that the contents of the warehouse gradually grow in value over time and, that, while some of the information it contains is physically or intellectually perishable, much will retain its value or even become more useful as time passes. Indeed, many printed materials take on added value as they in and of themselves become historical artifacts. While librarianship has never viewed itself as an overly prescriptive profession, it has been one that has encouraged collaboration. For example, librarians placed an early emphasis on the establishment of consortia and networks (something that still largely eludes computing centers outside of the occasional governmental collaboration or, in recent years, the networking afforded by CAUSE). The primary mission of librarianship remains to make its work seem transparent to the user. The job of the library is to connect people to information so that they can complete their research with as little effort as possible. Librarians are expected to be "aggressively helpful" to users so that the consumers of information will have time to think about what they have found.[10] Accordingly, librarians have not generally defined themselves as experts. Rather, they tend to view themselves mostly as generalists who facilitate the work of others.

Over the years, academic librarians have come to be defined as faculty within their colleges and universities. Consequently, they have separated themselves to some degree from others working in the library who do not hold professional academic degrees. This definition and separation offered librarians the status they sought within the academy, and, in part, offered them the capacity to move freely among those they considered to be their colleagues on campus—scholars and researchers. The result has been that on most campuses, libraries are organized into units that are hybrids, combining elements of the academic department with the model more often associated with the bureaucracy. In virtually all cases, however, librarians identify themselves as professionals closely oriented to the academic enterprise, a distinct class of professionals with unique credentials.

More often than not, librarians have been compelled to earn and maintain their faculty status through involvement on campus academic and governance committees and through teaching and publication. These alignments, in turn, have offered them the opportunity to interact with teaching faculty on a regular basis. Librarians thus have developed an understanding of the issues and struggles faced by faculty and academic administrators who support the work of faculty. Librarians have long maintained that they, more than most units on campus, have a holistic view of the academy based largely on the extensive campus connections and relatively discipline-free objectivity they have developed over time.

Librarians, like teaching faculty, have preferred decision making that is deliberate and that emphasizes consensus building. Given this posture, they are often more conservative when approaching change than is altogether helpful. But librarians do tend to pursue global solutions that can be applied over and over again when situations reoccur, rather than addressing the specific unique problems at hand.

Salary issues have often divided librarians from computer professionals, both literally and emotionally. While historically integrated within the academy, unlike those who work in computing centers, library jobs often are not as highly valued monetarily as those of other information professionals. Salaries paid to librarians typically are found clustered with those paid to teaching faculty in the liberal arts.[11] The message "you're important to what we do," but "we'll only pay you this" has long created ambivalence for academic librarians. This has been especially true when great differences have existed between the salaries paid to librarians and information technologists.

Computer center managers and their professional employees often are viewed by those within the academy as a different breed from librarians. The professionals who work in computing operations are part of a newer field, led by people who, as noted earlier, often came to their profession through the back door. As one computer center director put it, "we are a ragtag group of folks who are doing interesting things . . . quite professional, but we do not belong to a profession."[12] Many are faculty members who left the classroom to pursue their love for the technology and who started their programs by dividing their time between teaching, programming, soldering wires, and administering operations.

Computer operations often evolved because individuals became enchanted with these machines and began looking for applications for the technology on campus or because administrators become convinced of the necessity of computers as a tool in managing their affairs. More often than not, individuals conceptualized the specific applications that developed in detail only after purchasing equipment and hiring people.[13] Most campus computing organizations began as relatively small administrative units, processing payroll and supporting personnel systems, generating transcripts, issuing grades, and the like. Until recently, the primary function of these agencies remained the processing of data and the generation of information, at first for administrative processes and then, more recently, in support of teaching and research.[14]

While the emphasis on campus computing is shifting away from these administrative applications at an ever faster rate, researchers using computing tools have generally been people who bring some level of technological sophistication (or at least a curiosity about technology) to the process. As a result, observers tend to view computer centers as expert organizations providing systematic solutions to administrators. When it has come to customer service, computing experts typically are most comfortable dealing with those users who enjoy the challenge of writing computer programs, applying software pack-ages, or configuring equipment to meet specific needs. And, while librarians may too often assume that their patrons are helpless, computer center person-nel often come to the table believing that, to be worthy of their assistance, users ought to bring to the discussion a certain threshold of interest, knowledge, and experience. Indeed, one still encounters two distinct attitudes toward work among those employed within academic computer centers. There are individu-als whose primary aim is to create an elegant solution, whether or not that so-lution is user-friendly, and there are those who orchestrate the "quick-fix" to meet the user's needs. While both postures may have their place, when domi-nant these attitudes can produce unpredictable and unsupportable results that impose barriers to a more healthy perception of computer center professionals by user communities.

Defining the kind of preparation required for people who work in con-temporary computing environments is much more difficult than defining the preparation for librarianship. While the book and its variants are predictable and stable technologies, the computer is not. Developing a coherent discipline within the framework of tools whose capacities and applications are changing both rapidly and in unpredictable ways is difficult. As noted earlier, curricula in the computer sciences are relatively new, and the need to apply rapidly chang-ing technologies to real problems tends to drive the field more than any com-mitment to an overarching philosophical base.

Computer center personnel frequently relate more easily to off-campus people doing similar work in business or in not-for-profit organizations than they do to people on campus not primarily and regularly working with com-puters. This should not be surprising, since most of the off-campus contacts they cultivate (vendors and outsourcers) are, themselves, business persons. They typically focus on the work rather than the environment. Credentials often take a back seat to applied expertise. Evaluating the vitae of computer center staff often requires a certain flexibility. While librarianship finds itself overburdened by attempts to intellectualize and document its activities, com-puter services seems more governed by a "try it and see if it works" attitude. At its best, this pragmatism produces a flexibility that enhances the capacity of computing centers to adapt quickly to rapidly changing needs. At its worst, it leads to an organization whose service is not predictable and has difficulty fo-cusing its attention and resources on specific missions.

We must remember that the pioneers who first brought to campus com-puters, when still expensive and considered somewhat esoteric, often still head campus computing operations. Those they supervised were recruited at various times during which computer operations changed functions. The computer center went from a protected main frame environment that focused on business applications to a time when minicomputers became popular. Then it experi-enced the introduction and maturation of microcomputing and moved into the current environment in which networking and distributed processing have made computers a pervasive force in all aspects of the university. Accordingly, many computer centers include some people who constantly retool to address contemporary requirements; some people wedded to outdated technologies who resist change; and some people who can only see the future and become impatient with the need to generate practical, user-friendly solutions in the pres-ent tense. Computer operations often support some elements outsourced to private vendors, legacy systems developed years earlier that remain in service, and a whole array of new applications under constant development to replace or upgrade failing systems. To their credit, most computer center professionals have the best intentions as they apply computing applications to new demands on campus. Staff members in computing centers perceive themselves as highly committed to the application of technology to the work of the university, and, as futurists, they try their best to predict where the next turn will come in their pursuit of an automated future.

This stated, however, even within the computer center, the perspective from which computer center personnel view the future differs radically. As their field grows and as those working in it age, a more cautious approach has replaced some of the adventurous spirit of their ideology. It is small wonder that Onadell Bly in 1996 noted that some characterize computer center personnel as people with no common set of values and no common approach to defining the computing environment.[15] This is not altogether bad. At a midwestern university in the early 1980s, a debate raged in developing its computer science program about whether COBOL should continue to be taught, given the emergence of more sophisticated languages. COBOL has been declared dead many times since. However, anyone involved with computer problems related to the advent of the new millennium must have a strong COBOL background to work with legacy systems. In a field where practice drives theory, pragmatism is not only advantageous, it is required.

THE NEW REALITY—LESS AND LESS CONTROL

The problem both computer centers and libraries now confront is that neither can fully control either the technology that is driving them or the sources of information content that their clients wish to use. At the same time, they are being asked to share the arena with new professionals focused on information delivery and newer and faster tools mass marketed to novices and usable by people with little background in either computing or librarianship. The coming of the microcomputer has limited the capacity of computer professionals to exert control over campus computing and over the equipment needed to support teaching and learning. Simultaneously, the advent of the computer network, the Internet and the World Wide Web has loosened the grip librarians once held on the physical artifacts of scholarship.[16]

To some extent, the library and the computer center have emerged as nodes in an information network populated by users and suppliers of information freely exchanging their wares. But, at the same time, the complexity of these tools and their applications are increasing the importance of the skills that both of these organizations bring to campus. Computer professionals are being called upon to design the networks, to keep the equipment functioning, and to size switching systems, transmission lines, and computer servers to allow for sufficient growth while containing costs. Librarians are being called upon to become ever more sophisticated users of the complex information systems that require support from the campus network. Librarians are also attempting to function as information brokers, who retain their niche by organizing channels of access to information, whether it be on the Web, in locally created data files, or in local print collections. User constituencies, often exhibiting increasingly varied levels of expertise in using both information resources and the tools required to produce and to use them, press both groups. No one of these information professionals can any longer claim control of the information environment.

The development of a second problem requires the attention of both librarians and computer center personnel. As academic institutions try to deal with both the glut of information descending upon them and the technology required to deliver this information to the user, new skills, as well as combinations of old skills, are needed to fully exploit new technologies. Some of these skills are currently available elsewhere on campus. Most universities have support units that provide audiovisual materials to classrooms and employ graphics designers or instructional designers, telecommunications specialists, photographers, videographers, and the like. But the disbursement of these skills in offices throughout the campus limits development of a cohesive approach to support information transfer. The level of interest shown by individuals working in these positions, the understanding of those who supervise them, and the capacity of someone in the administrative structure of the campus to develop and negotiate a shared vision of what technology can and should do determine the capacity of the campus to meet faculty and student expectations. The changes in information technology pose immense organizational challenges. Redundancies confront organizations large and small as different offices build expertise to accomplish remarkably similar tasks. In many cases the different offices with an organization even compete for the same people to do that work. The inadequate definition and scarcity of skills required to complete the task at hand compound the challenge.

Some redundancy is useful and necessary. Few libraries are now willing to rely on other campus agencies to provide all of their systems support, and most employ, in addition to a systems staff, many people who have a working knowledge of various aspects of computing. At the same time, Web designers are often assigned to various campus offices (often in the person of a faculty member or student) with some central coordination in the office of a campus Web master. This allows for the "bottom up" development upon which the Web depends. Inexpensive technology, distributed processing environments, and the ubiquitous nature of the skills required to exploit them will continue to emphasize decentralized service, and we will see the amount of redundancy increase.

While administrators may find it difficult to accept this environment, it also facilitates responsiveness not replicated in any other way. At the same time, however, librarians, computer center personnel, and other information professionals on campus must develop a common approach for their services, one that will allow for the nurturing of serendipitous development on campus. Users will increasingly demand operations like the Media Arcade at the University of Iowa, aimed at making available a single interface through which users can approach the universe of campus technology. These facilities make technology accessible to second and third tier adopters of technology. In that capacity, they take the technology developed by futurists to the rest of the campus, and make yesterday's "golly gee whiz" tools the standard for the campus.

Collaboration can either develop as an organizational structure that combines various functions under a single chief information officer, or it can develop on an informal basis between the offices that have traditionally been responsible for these activities (library deans, computer center directors, and academic technology administrators). These collaborations can result from a consensus among information professionals or between professionals and their clients, or they may result (sometimes disastrously) from an executive decision. In any case, an effective structure helps participants agree on priorities, determine adequate funding, balance the traditional role of librarians in selecting content with the role of information technologists delivering that content, and identify and deal effectively with "turf" issues. The latter implies the assignment of responsibility to someone or some group for defining clear lines of authority for projects, communicating constantly during joint project development, and dealing with personalities, all the while remaining sensitive to the campus client.[17] The success of any organizational model will depend on its capacity to combine the interpersonal skills and relationships that libraries have traditionally had with teaching faculty with the technical expertise of the computer center.

At the same time, both organizations must willingly develop flexible organizations that can provide different skill sets required for user needs in an integrated information environment. Both organizations must recruit talented people, give them appropriate status, and compensate them for their work rather than for their credentials. The process of scanning the horizon for appropriate projects, developing a coherent mission, identifying the resources available to support changes in the information environment, and augmenting resources in a way that makes operational sense are all critical. Combining skill sets to meet operational requirements, while rationally dealing with measures of status and developing sensible financial reward structures, is also critical to focusing the operation on accomplishing the tasks at hand. Maintaining this balance may be the most difficult challenge of all.

WHAT FUNDAMENTALLY SEPARATES US, AND DOES IT MATTER?

Those who manage academic libraries and those who manage computer centers cohabit a common information universe. But cohabitation is just that—cohabitation—not marriage. In Europe one finds many hotel rooms with separate single beds that may be pushed together to form one large bed or, alternately, moved apart to function as separate beds in close proximity to one another. It may be useful to think of libraries and academic computing centers in this way. Each area will continue to nurture and sustain its own bed, its own comfort zone. Yet individuals managing academic libraries and campus computing centers will likely be required to identify many points of convergence of interest in the future. As managers of information technologies "we both have an opportunity to provide leadership by recognizing that information technology services organizations on our campuses can benefit from planning together and cooperating in the provision of services. While the organizations may remain separate, they need to have a common planning focus."[18] Clearly strong, open administrative leadership is needed to nurture healthy collaboration.

Where the value of collaboration and the rapidity of technological change are both considered, librarianship will remain fundamentally about the conservation of ideas; computer operations management will remain fundamentally about the successful application of technical skill and the refinement of process. Given its historical position within the academy, as well as its philosophical underpinnings and humanistic bent, librarianship has always emphasized its cultural role and will likely continue to do so. Librarians' thoughts at some point always turn toward the essential notions of intellectual freedom and the protections that guarantee free access to information. Moreover, librarians will likely continue viewing their libraries as places of common ground, as intellectual commons. The best libraries—as physical places—have always been places of welcome that bring people of differing intellectual interests together. Much popular support and goodwill has always accrued to both academic libraries and the people who run them, ranging from the formal support of hundreds of Friends of Libraries groups to individuals simply walking in off the street and donating money or interesting collections.

Coming out of a utility and business base and background, computer center managers until recently have seen little reason to understand the academy or the community it serves. The resulting lack of understanding, especially the perceived lack of concern for human interactions, has made it more difficult for them to gain friends and advocates. Librarians have been working to redefine and update their role for over twenty years. But, for the most part, those who manage computer resources have only recently come to realize that their focus must expand to include more emphasis on human relations skills. Hawkins and Battin observed recently that "for years the library was the scapegoat—scorned by the purveyors of the new 'paperless society' and labeled as the 'black hole' of budget deficits. Now the honors for the 'bad seed' have passed to information technology divisions."[19] Today, computer centers are plagued "by anguished cries for more speed, more accessibility, more reliability and howls of dismay over the ceaselessly spiraling costs."[20]

As Paul Metz has noted, academic libraries

> will continue to manage programmatic subsidies, to negotiate site licenses, and to help information users navigate through the glut. While the successful electronification of academic information may have to depend on the success in the commercial world, academic information will always be different and will appeal to highly sectored and in many cases small audiences.[21]

This highly sectored (discipline-oriented) world will continue to require both preservation and mediation. In the same information-rich environment in which staff are being asked to develop new client-centered orientations and are being drawn into the movement toward a more learner-centric campus model, librarians will continue to apply their historically tested expertise in information discovery and retrieval. Their experience with the organization of knowledge, their history of collection building and archiving, and their strong client service orientation will continue to be valuable. As Ortega y Gasset eloquently observed in 1934 in his now classic address to the International Congress of Bibliographers and Librarians:

> Today people read too much. The condition of receiving without much effort, or even without any effort, the innumerable ideas contained in books and periodicals [and we might add to Ortega, the Internet!] has accustomed the common man to do no thinking on his own account; and he does not think over what he has read, the only method of making it truly his own. . . . ordinary minds are thus stuffed with pseudo-ideas. In this aspect of his profession, I imagine the librarian of the future to be a filter interposed between man and the torrent of books.[22]

While fundamental differences will continue to exist between those charged with administering academic libraries and computing centers, both groups must start—if they have not already—to ask, "What is it that faculty and students really need? What is it that the academy needs?" These questions will be asked in a time when we all seem to be both mesmerized by and floundering in the information glut. Can we cease the turf battles long enough to raise common questions about the meaning of information and knowledge, to step back and together creatively imagine what we can evolve and develop during this time of "torrential abundance"? While there is clearly a "right" answer to these questions, the answer that will be given in most universities is still very much in doubt. Librarians and computer center professionals, coming out of different cultures, must come together to position themselves to handle the remarkable opportunities to serve the emerging forms of higher education that lie ahead. The question remains, will they?

NOTES

1. Jose Ortega y Gasset, "The Mission of the Librarian," translated from the French by James Lewis and Ray Carpenter, *Antioch Review* 21 (summer 1991): 154.
2. A. G. Lipow and Sheila D. Creth, eds., "Building Partnerships: Computing and Library Professionals," *Proceedings of the Library Solutions Institute, number 3, Chicago Illinois, May 12-14, 1994* (Berkeley, Calif.: Library Solutions Press, 1995).
3. Brian L. Hawkins and Patricia Battin, "The Changing Role of the Information Resources Professional: A Dialogue," *Cause/Effect* 20 (spring 1997): 22-30.
4. Allen B. Veaner, "Institutional Political and Fiscal Factors in the Development of Library Automation, 1967-71," *Journal of Library Automation* 7 (March 1974): 5-26.
5. Joe B. Wyatt, "Technology and the Library," *College & Research Libraries* 40 (March 1979): 124.
6. Onadell Bly, "Academic Libraries, Academic Computer Centers, and Information Technology," *Advances in Library Administration and Organization* 14 (Westport, Conn.: JAI Press, 1996).
7. Richard De Gennaro, " Shifting Gears: Information Technology and the Academic Library," *Library Journal* 109 (July 15, 1984): 1204.
8. Diane J. Cimbala, "The Scholarly Information Center: An Organizational Model," *College & Research Libraries* 48 (September 1987): 393-398.
9. Arnold Hirshon, *Integrating Computing and Library Services: An Administrative Planning and Implementation Guide for Information Resources,* CAUSE Professional Paper Series 18 (Boulder, Colo.: CAUSE, 1998).
10. Larry Hardesty, "Computer Center-Library Relations at Small Institutions: A Look from Both Sides," *Cause/Effect* 21, no. 1 (spring 1998): 35-41.
11. Anne Woodsworth and Theresa Maylone, *Reinvesting in the Information Job Family: Context, Changes, New Jobs, and Models for Evaluation and Compensation* (Boulder, Colo.: CAUSE, 1993).
12. Hardesty, "Computer Center-Library Relations," p. 37.
13. Bly, "Academic Libraries."
14. Cimbala, "The Scholarly Information Center."
15. Bly, "Academic Libraries," p. 214.
16. Maurice Mitchell and Laverna M. Saunders, "The Virtual Library: An Agenda for the 1990s," *Computers in Libraries* 11 (April 1991): 8-11.
17. Hirshon, *Integrating Computing,* p. 8.
18. Jane N. Ryland and David L. Smallen, "Cooperation on Campus Calls for Leadership," *Cause/Effect* 12 (summer 1989): 9.

19. Hawkins and Battin, "The Changing Role," p. 22.
20. Ibid.
21. Paul Metz, "Revolutionary Change in Scholarly and Scientific Communication: The View from a University Library," *Change* 27 (January-February, 1995): 33.
22. Ortega y Gasset, "Mission," p. 154.

CHAPTER EIGHT

Computer Center and Library Relations among Small Colleges

LARRY HARDESTY

No one will dispute that the computer has had a profound effect on academic libraries over the past twenty-five years. So pronounced is this influence that on many campuses discussions relating to the library and computers now focus on the fundamental nature of the organizational structure and the reporting relationships between the library and the computer center. Should the institution merge the library with the computer center or should both units report to a chief information officer (CIO)?

Increasing interest among library directors at small colleges in answer to these and related questions prompted me to conduct a study of the changing roles and relationships between the two units. With the financial support of the Council on Library and Information Resources, I interviewed forty computer center administrators and fifty-one librarians (forty-nine library directors) at fifty-one small colleges throughout the United States between January 1994 and October 1996, the results of which I report in this chapter.[1]

BACKGROUND

In the early 1980s, many observers predicted the convergence, even the merger, of libraries and computer centers.[2] Such interest existed that Richard Dougherty, then dean of libraries at the University of Michigan, founded a publication, *Libraries and Computing Centers: Issues of Mutual Concern,* to explore library and computer center relations. By the late 1980s, this movement seemed to have lost its momentum. In 1988 an Association of College and Research (ACRL) Task Force found, "Nearly all of the libraries (90 percent) reported no change in the reporting relations at either director level (computing or library) is under active consideration."[3] Dougherty discontinued his publication in 1989, and in the last issue, Pat Moholt reported, "Predicted merger [of libraries and computer centers] . . . has evolved into a kind of functional cooperation."[4]

By the mid-1990s, however, the movement had regained momentum. Among small colleges, Gettysburg College provided the most notable example of an effort to completely integrate the library and the computer center into one unit (see Robin Wagner's chapter). Other colleges, such as Augustana (Illinois), Berea, Bucknell, Carthage, Coe, Connecticut, Eckerd, Kalamazoo, Kenyon, Lake Forest, Macalester, Mount Holyoke, and Wellesley, created formal organizational structures to bring the library and computer center closer together.

Many questions, however, remain unanswered. Are these colleges on the leading edge of a paradigm shift? Does integration of the two units clearly and readily bring advantages not achievable through separate units? Or will most libraries retain their traditional organizational structures and reporting relationships?

FINDINGS

I found most computer centers and libraries at small colleges have neither merged nor closely converged. Few CIO positions with responsibilities for the computer center and the library exist at these institutions. In addition, very few of the directors of either unit support the concept of a merged organizational structure or the CIO position, and even fewer think it a good idea for their own institution. The increasing reliance of libraries on computers has indeed brought them closer to the computer center, but to varying degrees this is true of almost every unit on campus. Despite a closer relationship between the two units, the library directors and computer center administrators almost universally reported in the survey that they had not moved so closely together that they engaged in long-range planning or strategic planning with their counterparts.

Differences

While it may be an overstatement to write that librarians and computer center personnel come from different cultures, the library directors and computer center directors interviewed generally came from dissimilar backgrounds. While the library directors all had the same graduate degree—the master's degree in library science—computer center administrators did not have a common degree. Undergraduate and graduate degrees in the social sciences and the humanities predominated among the library directors, while undergraduate and graduate degrees in mathematics and the sciences (both almost nonexistent among degrees of the library directors) predominated among the computer center administrators. A few computer center directors did not have any advanced degrees—something not found among the library directors.

Unlike the educational path to becoming a library director, no formal educational path exists for an individual to become a computer center director. Those few computer center directors with computer science degrees typically observed that it did not prepare them to become computer center administrators. One computer center director did have a degree in information studies, which he considered helpful in preparing him for his responsibilities.

Many computer center administrators had been classroom faculty members who became interested in technology. Not atypically, one such administrator commented, "Computer services started here with me. I did everything.

That meant I cut the wires, I soldered the wires, I planned the budget." Now, ten to fifteen years later, such individuals find themselves overseeing complex and rapidly evolving organizations that challenge even the best prepared managers. As one library director observed of his counterparts in the computer center, "It is a newer field, and the people who were fixing the engines in the biplane are still at the stage of becoming presidents of the company."

Stereotypes, of course, can do a disservice to members of both units. Nevertheless, directors of both expressed an awareness of dissimilarities. One computer center administrator, with tongue in cheek, described stereotypical images of the two groups: "There is the view of computer center people as being bearded, long-haired, wearing flannel shirts, sitting in a room at 1 A.M., and playing with computers, and librarians as being stiff, prim, and proper, and keeping everything down to the finest detail."

Library directors referred frequently to their responsibilities for collecting information resources and helping users find and make use of information. They often employed the expression "content versus conduit" to describe differences between the responsibilities of the library and the computer center. The library directors often used the word "service" in describing their responsibilities. They also emphasized the need to evaluate information. With some exasperation, a library director reported on a recent discussion with computer center personnel, "While I was trying to get at content and evaluation and the material that is there, they were not interested in that at all. . . . The documents themselves had no intrinsic interest for them." Reflecting the view of many other computer center directors, one computer center director observed, "My staff and my strength will never be in saying, 'This is good information.'" This feeling led one well-respected midwestern college librarian to comment, "This may appear smug, but I see librarians more as educators and computer people more as technologists."

Arguably, librarians have most of the trappings of a profession.[5] Computer center personnel do not. As one computer center director (educated as a sociologist) observed, "Librarians represent a profession in which you have an accepted degree. You have an organization—a library association that makes you a profession—and we are not. We all came to computing by the back door—almost all of us. We are just a ragtag group of folks who are doing some interesting things." He added, "I think we are quite professional, but we do not belong to a profession." Without an academic socialization process similar to that of librarians, computer center administrators may lack ready networking opportunities made possible though sharing common experiences. The lack of a common academic socialization process may inhibit the development and reinforcement of widely shared values among computer center administrators.

This is not to imply that many computer center administrators are not service-minded or that all library directors are. Nevertheless, responses by some computer center administrators tend to support the view that the service orientation of the two groups differs. Most computer center directors accepted the "content versus conduit" dichotomy between the two groups, although a few thought the term "too simplistic." Commenting on the differences, one computer center director observed, "My gut instinct is that the techniques for handling information electronically have developed in the computer centers and a sensitivity to the uses and substance of the information has developed in the libraries." One computer center director observed, "The library has taken an attitude of being aggressively helpful, and I have taken an attitude 'If you ask me, I will help.'" Another computer center administrator remarked, "There is a tendency I see in my staff to pass on the responsibility for seeking [information] to the client. 'Here is a tool; try it. Here are a bunch of good sites. Go play with them and discover all that you can.'" Yet another computer center director remarked, "I would say that our concern is much more with getting access, and we do not fret about the uses." In fact, some computer center administrators viewed the assertive service orientation of librarians as unnecessary. A computer center director observed, "While our views are extremely charitable toward the users, theirs [the librarians] are overly compensatory." He added, "There is almost the presumption of the user being lost: 'You cannot do without us.'"

Remarkably, despite lack of formal arrangements, administrators of both units seldom mention tensions between the two units. For example, administrators of both units seldom mention tensions over salary, in part because at these private colleges few in one unit have any idea about the salaries in the other. Status, on the other hand, becomes an issue when the two units move closer together. Typically librarians have some type of faculty status and there is a clear demarcation between librarians and support staff. Computer center personnel seldom have faculty status, and the distinctions among levels of personnel are often not very clear. Perhaps one computer center director was referring to these issues in merged situations when he observed, "We will not make good bedfellows if we snuggle too closely together."

Many individuals from both sides referred to the differences as strengths instead of weaknesses. One computer center director observed, "You need the computer folks to be leavening and say 'let us try this,' and you need the library folks to have some reservations and say 'have you thought about. . .?'" Another concluded, "We are seeing more and more overlap. The problem with libraries and computer centers is that librarians are trying to be 'techies' and computer center people are trying to be librarians."

To be sure, some tensions do exist between computer centers and libraries at these liberal arts colleges. Issues of turf occasionally came up. One library director observed, "It is not easy to avoid the turf question because there is a fuzziness about who is responsible for what." Several computer center directors referred to the stress caused by the heavy workload borne by the computer center. Most library directors expressed awareness of the demands on the computer center, and a few stated they had supported the institution providing additional staff for the computer center.

Several computer center directors commented on tensions created by the rate of change in their areas. One computer center director colorfully described the mode in his area as "slash and burn." He explained, "We move over and chop down the trees, plant a crop, and, if we are lucky, we stay long enough to get the first yield." Another computer center administrator commented, "We shed yesterday's stuff for today's stuff very readily." From this perspective, librarians who want "to see things settled and tied up and permanent and regulated" sound like they are saying "no." The computer center director who just wants "to be able to provide access if people want it" sees himself as saying "yes" to user needs. The difference in the perspective, of course, relates to the question of how much training and guidance the user will need and how much ongoing support the hardware and software will require.

Most computer center directors and library directors seldom think they compete head to head, or believe that resources for one unit came directly at the expense of the other. At most of the colleges, the budgets of both the computer center and the library go through the chief academic officer, and most directors of both units expressed strong confidence in the process at their colleges. Despite occasional references by administrators to the library as the "bottomless pit" and the computer center as the "black hole," there are other bigger competitors for the finite resources at these colleges. One senior college administrator responsible for both the computer center and the library commented, "What is eating our lunch budgetarily is financial aid. That is the opponent of the library. That is the opponent of computer services." Nevertheless, some directors from both units realize there is a degree of competition, however unseen it may be to them. As one computer center director put it, "When anybody wants to do anything, it takes away from something else." A library director responded in a similar vein, "You cannot help but be competitors. The pie is only so big."

Working through Differences

The differences, areas of overlap, and uncertainty about the future have created some uncertainty among directors of both units. One library director observed:

> I think that my counterpart in computing and I both feel uneasy about the other's aspirations and what responsibilities will be left for us in the future, but we have not talked about this very explicitly. I have a feeling that, in the end, one or the other of us will lose out. We are like repeating species and the ecology cannot sustain both of us.

Nevertheless, despite the frequent mention of different philosophies (and occasional frustrations) many of the individuals interviewed emphasized a high degree of cooperation between the two units. They often mentioned the commonly understood missions of these small colleges. From the library side, a director remarked, "I think we are all together in the same direction. There is certainly no real disagreement about what we want to accomplish here." From the computer center side, a director observed, "I think we both feel that we have the same mission. Any time I get into discussions of this with the library staff, I feel I am preaching to the converted."

Several individuals pointed out that just because there may be personality and even cultural differences between members of the two units, such differences do not mean they cannot work together. A library director articulated a most sensible approach when observing, "The only way to avoid unhealthy competition is to make sure that the working relationship is strong and that it is open and honest. That is why the advantage of reporting to an academic dean is so significant. The more people we get pulling from the academic side the better. We protect each other." One computer center director bluntly put it, "You do not avoid tensions. You work through them."

Frequently individuals interviewed described joint ventures, such as newsletters, regularly scheduled meals and meetings together, and other efforts to establish and maintain good communications between the two units. While formal committees and task forces occasionally exist, most of the day-to-day relations between the two units are conducted through an informal continuing dialogue. Most interviewees considered this an adequate means of maintaining good relations. Commented one computer center director, "If everyone is headed in the same direction, if there is consensus at the informational level, you can accomplish a lot more than you can in a committee that is built from twenty different groups that is representing the campus."

When it comes to budgets, cooperation appears to be a key word. "We have found it is easier to get money for something if we go to the administration jointly on projects," observed a library director. Another library director explained the importance of understanding the taking of turns. He commented, "There will be times when you are rewarded and then there are times when you have to go to the back of the class."

Many library and computer center directors at these small colleges reported personal friendships with their counterparts. In fact, in many cases, the good relationships between two units are based on personal friendships. This led one library director to comment, "It kind of worries me that 80 percent of our cooperation is based on the fact that [the computer center director] and I are friends."

In the end, most problems between the two units are resolved by, as one library director put it, "just by talking it over. I do not see any other way." Another long-time library director observed, "The point is how to get people to do things, not how to make them mad." These comments probably reflect the nature of most small colleges where there are many opportunities for face-to-face informal communications.

ORGANIZATIONAL STRUCTURES AND REPORTING RELATIONSHIPS

The Chief Information Officer (CIO)

When asked about the need for or their response to dramatic changes in their organizational structures and reporting relationships, most library and computer center directors are ambivalent about it or oppose it. Reflecting a frequently expressed ambivalence about the CIO position, one computer center director responded, "Well, I toyed around with that and catch me one day and I'll say one thing, another day I'll say another." Others more emphatically considered the concept flawed and out of date. Again a computer center director observed, "Even in corporations the CIO thing was probably a five years ago thing. . . . I think when the corporation brought in the CIO it was because they were in a mess. They did not get out of the mess and the concept got discredited."

A computer center director at a wealthy northeastern college reported that to attract an individual with the necessary skills, "They may have to talk about the $100,000 and up price range [in 1994]." Others referred to the resistance among faculty members for the addition of another high level administrator. In particular, many library directors expressed strong thoughts about the library remaining in the "academic camp" and reporting to the chief academic officer.

To be sure, some individuals interviewed support the CIO position. They tend to be neither library directors nor computer center directors, but individuals at the associate provost or equivalent level. Generally, they had neither technical nor library backgrounds and had only general oversight responsibilities for the computer center. When combined, these factors may provide them with the time and broad perspective needed to reflect on the future of the two units without being preoccupied by (or sensitive to—depending on one's viewpoint) day-to-day operational demands.

Some of the small colleges have avoided the additional costs of creating a new position by simply putting either the current computer center administrator or, more frequently among these institutions, the library director in the CIO position. However, the CIO typically retains day-to-day operational responsibility for his or her old unit in addition to taking on new responsibilities. As one library director-turned-CIO put it, she was "doing a job that previously they were paying one and two-thirds people to do."

Another problem is that a CIO from one unit may be viewed as biased toward that unit. One library director/CIO commented, "My vocabulary is so library-driven that it is hard sometimes not to seem partisan." Placing the head of one unit in charge of both can result in that person being viewed as an interloper in one location and as negligent in fulfilling previously held responsibilities in the other. In addition, as management skills become more diffused, a previously well led unit may languish while the former director concentrates on the other unit.

Those interviewees in charge of day-to-day operational demands seem less confident of their abilities to manage the second unit. A computer center director commented, "I don't know how someone like me could be director of a joint operation when I don't know anything about libraries." Similarly, a library director responded, "Clearly, I do not have the expertise to do [the computer center director's] job and he does not have the expertise to do mine. I am fairly clear about that."

Mergers of Libraries and Computer Centers

A small minority of those interviewed thought mergers the wave of the future. However, most of these individuals spoke of it as occurring in the distant future. "If we run this out twenty years, I think the librarians and the information processing types are going to come together," observed a computer center director. Several interviewees looked for guidance from the experience of the Gettysburg College merger.[6] Some directors expressed support for mergers, but quickly added, "If (the name of their unit) was in charge of it." This, of course, is not an unimportant detail.

In general, however, most individuals interviewed did not support a complete merger of the two units and did not foresee it happening at their own colleges. A computer center director responded, "Taking two people with different training and stuffing them together in the same organization, is that going to change anything at all?" Personalities may be particularly important at small colleges. As one computer center director observed, "If the personalities and styles of operation do not fit, then no matter how good it looks on paper, it will not work." Many from both units agreed with the library director who stated, "I think a lot of energy, effort, and time, and, therefore, dollars, go into that kind of organization [mergers], and I am not convinced that there are sufficient benefits to do that."

Source of Change

From the interviews, one can conclude that the impetus for mergers and CIO positions comes from neither library director nor computer center administrators. In fact, in some cases, as one library director/CIO admitted, "I think we are being somewhat coerced." However, this individual also expressed the feelings of others in similar positions when she added, "On the other hand, it is one of those opportunities that you cannot let go."

Many see the pressure for such change as coming from presidents and boards of trustees, and they have no confidence in either the motives or the supposed results. A library director elaborated:

> My perception is that board members and very often presidents are making reference to the experiences of other organizations, such as private corporations, and imagining how those solutions may be visited on higher education, with the general notice that higher education is going to be conservative or slow to respond and needs to be whipped into shape. A solution is kind of crammed down higher education's throat without reference to the real goal, which is what information should be best available to the students.

Again and again, directors of both units came back to the people involved. Echoing this view, a library director commented about existing mergers, "The examples that I know about so far are very dependent on a certain set of people being in place." Finally, as one computer center director expressed his attitude about mergers, "You can make all the beautiful speeches you want, but it will take a lot to make it successful."

If the impetus is coming from boards of trustees, presidents, and other senior administrators, they appear to have more confidence in their vision of the future than most library directors and computer center directors. When asked about the organizational structures and reporting relationships, one library director carefully articulated his response:

> My answer is that I do not have clear enough vision of the future to want to shape all my actions in the direction of that vision because I think it could lead us down a path that ends up being wrong for us. What I would much rather do is start with the things that we can agree upon and do together, and take those steps we might want to take beyond that. And if that leads to a full merger, then by the time we get there, then we will know that it is the right step. But the future is too cloudy for me, at this point, to look down there and say that is where we are headed.

CONCLUSIONS

Is there a paradigm shift in the organizational structure and reporting relationships of academic libraries and computer centers at small colleges? To paraphrase a statement attributed to Yogi Berra, it is hard to make predictions, particularly about the future. Computer centers are a recent phenomenon. At the small colleges I visited, I found among the computer centers a wide variety of organizational structures and reporting relationships. Libraries, on the other hand, have a long history. Certain functions, such as acquisitions, cataloguing, circulation, and to a lesser degree, reference, have a long history. The computer, of course, has changed these functions in recent years, and libraries and the library profession have continued to evolve. Nevertheless, I find it difficult to conclude that large numbers of academic libraries will make sudden and radical changes in their organization structures and reporting relationships. Academia seldom moves this quickly.

Advocates of mergers and the CIO position can point to an impressive list of integrated library and computer operations.[7] Achievements of some integrated operations are reported elsewhere in this book, and there is no reason to doubt the reports. Integration can work well in certain situations. It can strengthen both units. The individual in charge of both usually holds a senior administrative appointment, reporting directly to the president and serving on the senior administrative council. This position can enhance visibility, attract resources, and bring added benefits to both units and their staffs.

Nevertheless, the results of my interviews suggest the need for integration is seldom obvious to a majority of the staff of both units. Most efforts to bring together the library and the computer center originate from the top down. In the mid-1980s, Ray Neff wrote an article asking if it was manifest destiny that computer centers and libraries would merge.[8] The adoption-of-innovation literature suggests that an adopter must perceive an innovation as better than the idea it supersedes.[9] To many observers, the advantages of integrated organizations are neither readily apparent nor easily achievable. Clifford Lynch, Executive Director of the Coalition for Networked Information, wrote in Arnold Hirshon's *Integrating Computing and Library Services,* "Merging the functions is an expensive, complex, risky investment under the best of circumstances, and is a terrible way to try to repair an environment in which effective collaboration isn't happening, or to shore up one or more dysfunctional organizations."[10] Without a clear advantage there is no imperative to integrate the two units.

While there is a growing list of institutions with integrated library and computer operations, they remain a small minority. In fact, in some colleges, integration exists more in name than in practice. There are also a growing number of institutions that have attempted some form of integration only to revert to a more traditional structure.[11] Integration can work, but the experiences of many of the authors of other chapters in this book demonstrate that more traditional structures can also work. As one library director interviewed succinctly put it, "The one thing I discovered is that structure does not mean a tinker's damn. If people have a good attitude and can communicate, structure does not matter."

NOTES

1. Results of this study have also been published in the following: Larry Hardesty, "Library and Computer Center Relations at Smaller Academic Institutions," *Library Issues* 18 (September 1997): 1-4; Larry Hardesty, "Computer Center-Library Relations at Small Institutions: A Look from Both Sides," *Cause/Effect* 21, no. 1 (spring 1998): 35-41; and Council on Library and Information Resources, "Relationships between Libraries and Computer Centers at Liberal Arts Colleges," *Research Briefs* 2 (November 1997).

2. Patricia Battin headed at Columbia University in the early 1980s probably the first merger between a library and a computer center. She wrote about it in "The Electronic Library: A Vision of the Future," *Educom Bulletin* 19 (summer 1984): 12-17, 34; even earlier Robert Plane, the president of Clarkson College of Technology, wrote about merging the two units in "Merging a Library and a Computer Center, " *Perspectives in Computing* 2 (October 1981): 14-21. Numerous articles, many of which are included in the "Bibliography" elsewhere in this monograph, followed during the 1980s.

3. ACRL Task Force on Libraries and Computer Centers, "Final Report" (Chicago: ACRL, 1988), 4.

4. Pat Molholt, "What Happened to the Merger Debate?" *Libraries and Computing Centers: Issues of Mutual Concern* 13 (May 1989): 1.

5. Harold L. Wilensky, "The Professionalization of Everyone?" *American Journal of Sociology* 70 (September 1964): 137-158.
6. At the time of most of the interviews, Gettysburg College had just merged the library and the computer center. As reported elsewhere in this book, in July 1997 the two units separated at Gettysburg.
7. Arnold Hirshon, *Integrating Computing and Library Services: An Administrative Planning and Implementation Guide for Information Resources*, CAUSE Professional Paper Series 18 (Boulder, Colo.: CAUSE, 1998), 35-37. This publication contains a list of ninety institutions with integrated library and computer operations. The compiler (Arnold Hirshon) noted, "Institutional decisions to integrate or reverse integration, and the names of the CIOs, change frequently."
8. Raymond K. Neff, "Merging Libraries and Computer Centers: Manifest Destiny or Manifestly Deranged?" *Educom Bulletin* 20 (winter 1985): 8-16.
9. Everett M. Rogers, *Communication of Innovation* (New York: Free Press, 1971), 22-23.
10. Clifford N. Lynch, "Foreword," in Hirshon, *Integrating Computing and Library Services*, v.
11. Both the lists of integrated organizations and those who have moved away from an integration of the computer center and the library are dynamic. Some institutions who once had a more closely integrated operation and now have moved away from it include: Gettysburg College, St. John's College (Minn.), Schreiner College, Rice University, and California State University, Northridge.

CHAPTER NINE

Merged and Unmerged Services
Libraries and Computing in the University of Wisconsin System

EDWARD MEACHEN

As many universities and colleges have experimented with reorganizations of their information support services over the past ten years, a small amount of literature discussing this phenomenon has been produced. Until recently, however, the creation of merged library and computing services has gone unanalyzed. Opinion pieces and recounting of individual experiences appeared in the literature, but scarcely any research. University provosts and other administrators seemed willing to launch reorganization efforts without a base of analytical materials about the success or failure of other such efforts. There was a sense in the early 1990s that this was the right thing to do, but there were no data to back that up beyond a few scattered experiential pieces.[1]

As merged services became more commonplace, and as the administrative position of chief information officer (CIO) with responsibilities for libraries, computing, networking and media services became more commonplace, a few researchers finally began to examine the early experiments with this new organizational structure. Only in the past year have librarians and chief information officers been surveyed to determine how the new organizational structures really worked in practice. We now have a little data to inform decision making.

In particular, two studies based on survey information seem very useful to administrators faced with decisions about combining information support organizations. Larry Hardesty's "Computer Center-Library Relations at Smaller Institutions: A Look from Both Sides," in *Cause/Effect* 21, no. 1 (1998): 35-41, is based on interviews with computer center administrators and library directors at small colleges. Hardesty interviewed about ninety administrators from 1994 to 1996 and focused on the differences in cultures between libraries and computing operations. His findings, based on the experiences and insights of those in the trenches of support services, indicate that administrators ought to be very cautious about reorganizing and merging libraries and computing services.

In 1997, Arnold Hirshon undertook an e-mail survey of seventy institutions identified as having merged services under a CIO. He received forty-seven responses. Based upon his findings, he published a CAUSE professional paper that ought to be required reading for university and college administrators seeking to improve information support services by merging their libraries with their computing services operations. Hirshon's findings are quite cautionary. Clearly, the motives for reorganization and the particular cultures and personalities of different institutions have much to do with the perceived success or failure of merger experiments.[2]

Hirshon and Hardesty appear to be surveying first generation CIOs, many of whom have been promoted from within the organization. Their surveys provide valuable insights about how these newly merged organizations have been working or failing to work. But now we need to assess these organizations more formally as they come to maturation and as they seek second generation CIOs from outside the organization. Therefore, this study takes a slightly different perspective than those of Hirshon and Hardesty. It seeks to understand merged services from three perspectives: those of the chief academic officer to whom the CIO usually reports, the CIO who is responsible for the services, and library and computing staff who work on or close to the front lines of service delivery in the merged organization. Therefore, I developed three separate surveys, one for each of these three groups. From the results of these surveys, I sought to understand attitudes toward merged operations from a vertical perspective upward through the information services organization to the top levels of university administration. An equally interesting study might be to conduct a horizontal survey of faculty, staff, and students who use these merged services across the university. In fact, I have done something like that, without the personal interviews, in a general faculty and student satisfaction survey conducted in the spring term of 1998 for all the University of Wisconsin (UW) institutions. Some of that data is also used in this study.[3]

The eleven comprehensive universities in the University of Wisconsin System comprise the test bed for this study. These eleven universities, offering bachelor's and master's level degrees, have enrollments ranging from 2,500 to 10,000 full-time equivalent students. Nine of the eleven have had or now have merged library and computing services. These institutions provide an interesting environment for analyzing merged services because the institutions are administratively independent of one another, but collaborate in many support services. Overall, the University of Wisconsin System administration has general administrative responsibility for the eleven comprehensive institutions, as well as two doctoral institutions, thirteen two-year colleges, and an independent extension service.

For this study, I conducted phone interviews with twenty-eight individuals at nine institutions. These included all nine current CIOs, six of whom have responsibility for merged library and computing services. I interviewed eight of the nine chief academic officers of the universities who have responsibility for merged services or for the library operation. I also interviewed eleven staff members who have various hands-on responsibilities in the library or in computing services operations. I sent the surveys out in advance of the interviews and used them as a starting point for conversations aimed at analyzing attitudes about the information/library support services organization, and at exploring employees' understanding of how well support services are aligned with the overall campus mission, goals, and culture. I also guaranteed anonymity to all those surveyed. Thirty-six surveys were sent out, but several staff members declined to be interviewed. One administrator resigned about the time of the survey, and vacations made reaching several staff members impossible in the time allotted. I conducted all interviews in July and August 1998.

THE RISE OF THE NETWORK AND THE ADVENT OF MERGED SERVICES

Before I review the findings of the survey, I must put merged services in a broader context with the revolutionary developments taking place in higher education over the past decade. In that time there has been a good deal of experimentation in the organizational structure of the support services, particularly in small- to medium-sized colleges and universities. Libraries and computing operations have been merged and broken apart as administrators struggle with the revolution in digital technologies, particularly the convergence of electronic information resources and the search engines and tools used to access and manipulate them. The recognition of higher education administrators that information support services (libraries, media centers, and instructional design centers) might be usefully merged with technology support operations (academic and sometimes administrative computing, and networking) is exactly contemporaneous with the advent of campus networks and the rise of the Internet.

Without the campus network, there was no compelling reason for administrators to experiment with merged services. The mainframe-driven computing center provided rudimentary and highly specialized networked services to administrators who ran the business end of higher education. Generally, administrative computing enjoyed the lion's share of computing budgets and was more often than not under the responsibility of the university or college business officer. Academic computing, a far poorer cousin, experimented with Ethernet and Unix, and focused on programming and data manipulation for research or specialized teaching. Libraries tended to be isolated in their own dominions in the library building, sometimes running their own shop, sometimes contracting out to the computer center. These were three islands of academic support, as often as not isolated organizationally from one another and intensely competitive for institutional support.

Libraries, of course, in the 1980s moved vigorously to online public access catalogs (OPACs) and began to integrate electronic indexing and abstracting services into their academic support array. Their close working relationship with faculty and students (patrons), their public service philosophy built on teaching and research rather than on "customer" support, and their increasing use of desktop computing technology and electronic resources positioned libraries and their administrators to take on a leadership role in overall university support services when the campus network was born in the early 1990s. The question of why university administrators perceived advantages in merging library and computing services can be answered by examining the advent and development of the campus network.

At many higher education institutions the coming of the network took mainframe-computing establishments completely by surprise. They focused, not unnaturally, on limited access for a few administrative "customers" in a highly secure environment. Though they may not have been users of IBM hardware and software, the Token Ring and closed-ended environments with control as the operative concept shaped their perspectives. They protected data; they did not expose it. Librarians, on the other hand, believed strongly in the concept of open systems and universal access to information. They shied away from security except for protection of individual user's rights, and advertised the unrestricted use of information resources wherever possible. The network, driven by the Internet, which took off with astonishing speed after 1990 at almost all levels of higher education, drove computing into the hands of faculty and academic administrators. The network became the engine of change, driving desktop computing in completely different directions than a mainframe environment with connected CRT terminals. Librarians quickly grasped the power of networked resources in an open environment because their philosophical direction was exactly in compatibility with the open Ethernet and Unix architectures. Unix, the operating system that underpinned the Internet and largely dominated campus networks, invited access and discouraged security. To those who needed security as well as flexibility, it offered both a blessing and a curse. But it exactly suited librarians and their wide-open public service philosophy.

As the campus network began to dominate the business processes of the university, the tension between the secure, closed-ended world of administrative computing and the open, information-rich world of the faculty and academic support services grew intolerable at many institutions. The tension was played out in all sorts of venues. Struggles developed about who controlled the network and who would have access. Disagreements occurred over e-mail and its uses. Conflicts erupted between user support services supplied by the library in their own access labs and computing support services with competing labs. Some institutions worked out perfectly viable collaborations, and, depending upon the culture of the institution, moved quickly to partition the service array in rational and workable ways. But many institutions failed to grasp the dramatic changes wrought by the network and the personal computer and failed to develop technology plans. The personalities of those who headed up the support services drove most of this tension; rarely did universities launch information technology planning efforts that created alliances and collaboration rather than conflict. At many of these institutions administrators viewed the issue in terms of public service philosophy. They perceived computer center directors and their staffs as often as not at odds with the academic goals of the university. This perception remained an artifact of the history of campus computing before the network. The faculty's involvement in technology, made possible by the network, precipitated the chief academic officer's involvement in computing for the first time in many cases. Chief academic officers, almost always faculty members, made common cause with librarians in the struggle over vision and goals for the university.

Of course numerous exceptions existed. Chief information officers did not all grow up in the culture of the library. Institutions sometimes appointed computing professionals to responsibility over the library as well as network and computing services. But rarely have the older generation computer center directors been appointed CIOs. It turns out that knowledge of technology plays a lesser role in the success of a CIO than direct experience with teaching and learning. By and large, administrators do not have as their primary motive for creating merged services the saving of money or the supposed efficiencies of a single support organization. Instead, they seek the creation of a single vision for support services in harmony with the teaching and learning mission of the institution. This is primarily a faculty perspective rather than a business perspective, illustrative of the primacy of the network as an academic support tool. Even though business services will always play a critical role in the support of the university, they no longer dominate campus technology. Technology-enabled learning, driven by network and desktop technology advances (of which information and library resources play a major role), will transform and drive the business of universities.

Are merged services preferable or is collaboration just as viable at small- to medium-sized universities? Is organizational structure a particularly important factor in supplying information support services at the university, or is personality at least as important? Are university administrators on the right track in promoting the merger of libraries and computing operations, or will we see a reversal of this trend as the difficulties of blending diverse cultures become all too apparent? The answer to these questions at individual institutions is often found in the particular culture and business practices of the college or university. However, it is not likely that the relative growth in importance of technology for academic affairs as opposed to business affairs will change anytime soon. If the drivers of information technology in higher education are now clearly its teaching and learning applications, the library will continue to play a critical role in the management and planning of technology implementation. Merged services, therefore, will continue to be a viable option for university administrators. Personality, of course, will continue to be important in administration. There is no substitute for excellent management and leadership, but a viable organizational structure will grow increasingly important for information services. Organization will provide the glue to hold support services together in those times when less than brilliant leadership skills are available. Merged services and carefully thought out organizational structures are better guarantors of strategic alignment between support and academic mission within an educational bureaucracy than collaboration between organizations based on competent leadership. Nonetheless, there are no absolute guarantees in the dynamic environment of modern higher education, and many administrative models might work, as this study of the University of Wisconsin merged services will demonstrate.

MERGED AND UNMERGED SERVICES IN THE UNIVERSITY OF WISCONSIN SYSTEM

A wide variety of organizational structures and cultural differences are clearly apparent in the University of Wisconsin System. The two doctoral institutions, UW-Madison and UW-Milwaukee, have never merged library and computing services. Typical of larger institutions, support services tend to be more decentralized and functionally aligned with individual schools and departments. Two institutions, UW-Stout and UW-River Falls, never combined libraries with computing but experimented with various mergers of academic and administrative computing, networking, and telecommunications. The UW-Colleges, the thirteen two-year institutions spread around the state but administered centrally from Madison, have recently moved to a merged information services structure with the hiring of their first CIO responsible for libraries as well as computing. Three institutions, UW-La Crosse, UW-Superior, and UW-Stevens Point, had merged library and computing services, but for reasons we will explore later in more detail, split them apart and are currently operating in a collaborative, team-based environment. UW-Eau Claire has merged library and computing services under a CIO who did not have a library background, and that institution now has a "second generation" CIO without a library background. UW-Eau Claire now has the longest continuous history of merged services in the UW System, dating back to 1991. UW-Parkside in Kenosha merged library and computing services in 1992 under the library director, followed by UW-Whitewater, UW-Oshkosh, UW-Green Bay, and UW-Platteville, all following the same pattern: internal promotion of the library director to CIO responsible for computing, networking, media services, and the library.

Three Models

For the comprehensive institutions, then, we have three models. One is the collaborative model, in which independent technology support service directors plan and operate in a team environment. In three of the five institutions operating using this model, all members of the technology support departments report to the chief academic officer. In the other two cases, the administrative computing director reports to the institution's business officer. The second model operates as a merged organization with a non-librarian as CIO, but, unlike the other merged organizations, the CIO reports directly to the chancellor rather than to the chief academic officer. At the five institutions that created a merged services structure with the library director as CIO, that person reports directly to the chief academic officer. At four of these institutions, the library director's position was not refilled; rather, the librarian promoted to CIO continued to manage the library directly, though in an attenuated way.

Top-Down Mergers

The interviews elicited a variety of attitudes and insights leading to identification of issues pertinent to almost all the institutions. The most important of these is the manner in which the mergers occurred and the acceptance or resistance to the mergers by affected staff. In almost all instances, the merger occurred as a top-down process. The vice chancellors at three institutions stated that they had been responsible for merging services because, as one put it, "we needed the institutional philosophy to penetrate into computing services." Another said more bluntly that computing service simply was not working effectively anymore. At one institution a struggle over network priorities between library and computing services led the vice chancellor to direct the merger of the two services with the library director assuming the chief information officer position. At another institution, the computing center's failure to understand the network's crucial place in the academic mission led to a merger with the librarian taking on the role of CIO. At six other institutions the chancellor made the decision to merge services. In at least two of these instances, a faculty-led campus planning effort resulted in a recommendation to the chancellor that the library and computing services be brought under the same organizational umbrella with the rationale that they would work more effectively together. In several cases this reorganization involved moving computing from business services to academic services. At one institution the chancellor hired consultants who recommended merger of the services.

With the possible exception of the two universities where the planning process originated within the faculty governance structure, the merger of library and computing services was undertaken from the top down. Four of the CIOs interviewed believed one of the strongest motives for merger was budgetary. As one of the CIOs said, "It was made clear to me that we had to do more with less."

The vice chancellors at four institutions chose not to replace the library director or the computer center director, a prima facie argument, as far as these CIOs were concerned, that budget must be a motive for merger. Yet only two of the vice chancellors openly expressed budgetary motives, and both thought budget was, at best, not a particularly important reason for the reorganization. Perhaps the CIOs came closer to the vice chancellors' motives when later in the interviews all four expressed the opinion that computing services at their institutions had not been functioning effectively, and this ineffectualness played a primary role in the merger of information services.

Perceptions Are Critical

Repeatedly, the vice chancellors expressed perceptions of their library directors as technologically savvy and effective managers. In addition, they believed that since library directors worked closely with faculty and with the deans, they had a much higher credibility with faculty then did computing professionals. At least five vice chancellors clearly expressed these attitudes in the interviews. The fact that librarians had been working for many years with online systems and with electronic resources, and had pushed faculty to convert from paper to electronic subscriptions, seemed to give library directors credibility. In two instances, however, while vice chancellors expressed admiration for the library directors' management skills and had promoted them to chief information officers with responsibilities for merged services, they now expressed doubts about the ability of these CIOs to lead the campus's overall technology planning effort. In both cases vice chancellors and the chief information officer told anecdotal stories about faculty who had inadvertently or openly questioned the former library directors' grasp of new technologies. In both cases these faculty perceptions may not have been based upon empirical evidence (almost all the librarians-turned-CIOs possessed the same skills and faced the same difficult learning curve), but faculty opinions weighed heavily not only on the vice chancellors, but clearly on the CIOs. Both chose to step down from their positions within the first two years.

All the CIOs expressed some level of anxiety about "keeping up" with so many different areas of responsibility in technology. They had a strong sense that they would be seen as a "fool" in networking, or easily "deceived" in mainframe computing, or "unaware" of the next important advance in desktop video. All the CIOs interviewed expressed this sense in some way or another. Some admitted they simply could not keep up with the technical or trade literature in all areas for which they had responsibility. Others suspected they might not be able to analyze adequately the technical arguments of computing or networking staff for a particular solution. This occupational hazard seemed balanced against the excitement of grappling with new technologies every day. Most CIOs, with only a couple of exceptions, had no interest in returning to library responsibilities exclusively.

MERGER IS "SKIN DEEP"

Most of the staff interviewed, whether supportive of or opposed to the merger, agreed that it had not resulted in thoroughgoing organizational restructuring. Almost everyone reported increased communication, and while some thought this resulted in greater understanding between support areas and translated into improved services, others believed the meetings had become too frequent and wasted too much time. When asked about areas in which computer and library professionals worked together, almost all staff interviewed cited instruction and training. Some found that closer working relationships improved automation, network, and desktop computer solutions. One institution had combined librarians and computing professionals in a help desk function, but after several years of practice, the CIO reported many problems growing out of personnel differences between computing and library staff. Yet the majority of faculty and students, in a survey of service satisfaction, rated the help desk as good to very good (60 percent faculty, 63 percent students). Other universities with merged services reported collaboration between librarians and computing professionals in targeted projects such as faculty curricular support and multimedia applications.

Computing staff, in particular, doubted that substantive improvements had been created in service provisions as a result of a merger. At one institution where a merger had occurred, then been rescinded, the computer staff member interviewed claimed that from his perspective there had been almost no change in work patterns. At another institution, the computing staff member interviewed contended that real service improvements had occurred over the past three years since the merger, but that they would have occurred anyway—the merger had nothing to do with it. At a third institution, a computing staff member agreed that the merger was a good thing, that communication had improved with the library, but that no real perceptible improvements had been made in services that he could see. A fourth computing services employee believed that, while services had not changed much or improved perceptibly, the merger at her institution had improved management of the entire computing operation.

Frontline librarians shared some of the computing staffs' judgments about mergers. At least two librarians interviewed, both in public services, could see little change in their work since the merger. One pointed out that the old battles between computing application workshops and library information searching workshops seemed to have ended and that some joint workshops had improved service. Another public services librarian doubted that the merger had really improved anything, and may even have reduced the quality of service by refocusing the attention of the former library director more on technology. In fact, she stated, "library affairs have seemed to drift" since the director assumed the responsibility for computing. Two technical services librarians interviewed believed services had improved, particularly computing services to the library and to faculty. When pressed to elaborate, one mentioned that computing support personnel now seemed to understand better the significance and goals of library-provided technology services. At best, though, neither library nor computing frontline staff considered a merger an unalloyed good, and both believed the organization had a long way to go to achieve significant service improvements as a result.

A DIFFERENT PERSPECTIVE FROM THE TOP

Vice chancellors had a somewhat different perspective. One vice chancellor strongly argued that at his institution a merger simply was not needed: "a flat organizational structure," he asserted, "is more efficient." Another expressed the opinion that the library had been almost completely ignored during the merger era, hence the necessity to sever the joined organization. However, all the other vice chancellors believed the merger had improved the organization. One said that "turf issues have been reduced," and a definite cooperative spirit could be detected where none existed before. Another said that the new IT team was "more effective in integrating with faculty." One vice chancellor perceived real "efficiencies" around the new focus, which sees the university as "an information/learning environment. The service ethic and technical skills are a good marriage." Still another vice chancellor spoke about the lack of satisfactory leadership skills on the computer side to "meet university academic objectives." Yet another vice chancellor believed that "services have improved and are more seamless then before." And finally, another vice chancellor pointed out that at his institution he perceived efficiencies in human resources and "clear improvements in communication" within the information services merged organization.

THE VIEW FROM THE PILOT'S SEAT

Is the frontline staff more in touch with reality than the vice chancellors? Are the newly created chief information officers filtering the true state of affairs and selling the vice chancellors a vision of what they want to see, or are the vice chancellors pretty much on the mark? The chief information officers are probably in the best position to answer these questions, since their task is to both manage and lead the staff and translate support realities to their administrative superiors. While staff, administrators, and CIOs all have valid perceptions, the CIOs are most likely to be the group that sees the entire picture. Their perceptions are the best barometer of how well merged services are working.

Seeking to understand the relationship between university administration and the technology service organization, I asked the CIOs if they believed the administration's intentions were clear in creating a merged organization. I wanted to determine if the leader of this new hybrid organization clearly understood what was expected of them. I wanted to understand the rationale at each university for what was clearly a momentous decision. Five CIOs said unequivocally that they knew what administration expected. Three phrases typify their "marching" orders: "Do more with less," "Sort out personnel and technical issues," "Integrate support services." Four other CIOs were unclear from the start about the purpose of a merger. One said he didn't know if administration had any clear idea about what it expected (though, interestingly enough, the vice chancellor at this institution seemed to be very sure about what he wanted!). Another felt very uncertain because of the arrival of a new chancellor and the relative inexperience of the vice chancellor. Yet another complained that the chancellor and vice chancellor were completely divorced from technology and expected the CIO to make all technology decisions.

This latter point is a very good one, and other CIOs voiced it in other contexts. Several CIOs told me that one of the most important factors in making their position successful was the fairly in-depth involvement of both the vice chancellor and chancellor. One expressed the belief that to provide good services successfully, the vice chancellor had to understand technology and its limitations. Micromanagement might not be desirable, but ignorance of technology proved even more damaging.

In the top-down decision process typical of most UW information service organizations, the CIOs expressed a certain sense of disconnect and isolation. Although we did not discuss this subject directly, we did discuss attitudes that could lead to ambiguity. From the CIOs' perspective, their vice chancellors were not always clear about the goals of a merger. On the other side of the hierarchy, their staffs were not always convinced that the merger achieved service improvements. Despite this CIO anxiety and misgivings about inadequacy for the task, faculty and student satisfaction levels with IT and library services across the university system are very high.[4] At most institutions with merged services, the vice chancellor, the CIO, and the staff I interviewed generally agreed, despite misgivings, that organizational integration had improved communication and the merger was beneficial to the organization.

Much of the success of technology support services may be the result of the communication skills of the CIOs. They stressed that much of their job consisted of knitting together disparate service philosophies and goals within computing and libraries, and between faculty and computing services. As one CIO expressed it, his biggest challenges had been "managing the expectations of the faculty, overcoming the perceptions of IT people that they know what's best for the university, and convincing librarians that they have a role to play in IT." Another said convincing staff to confront change provided her biggest challenge. Several CIOs believed they had good management and leadership skills, but worried that they needed to get up to speed in understanding technology and where it was headed. Several said their biggest challenges involved personnel. This was particularly true of librarians who now had to deal with civil service unions, restrictive hiring practices, and personnel conflicts associated with information technology workers. All of these come down to leadership and management, exactly what the vice chancellors sought to resolve through the merger. They essentially took two diverse organizations with dramatically different service philosophies and amalgamated them under the manager who best exemplified their academic vision of the university's future. In every case involving internal promotion in the University of Wisconsin System, the manager chosen was the librarian, not the computing services director. This would suggest that vice chancellors and faculty were more comfortable with the philosophy and management style of their library directors than their technology counterparts.

THE EMERGENCE OF A NEW SERVICE MODEL

This shift of technology in higher education from business services to support for the business of higher education (i.e., the support of teaching, learning, and research) is further borne out when CIOs answered the question concerning what they believed would be lost if the merged organization were broken apart again. Several expressed their sense that the vision they had helped create through various joint planning efforts would be lost if the two organizations went their separate ways. Some talked about the potential of lost integration, which had been hard won even if incomplete. Others discussed budget leverage gained by combining both personnel and supply budgets. Four CIOs talked about the ability to move funding around within the much larger library-computing complex to fund critical projects. Several believed student budgeting and staffing were more flexible than under two umbrellas. One said the university would lose the "ability to create division-wide teams and to retain an integrative approach to projects."

From this analysis by the CIOs of their own gains and losses, a common set of opportunities to move support services in a unified direction can be identified. They are a unified budget, at least in some areas; joint planning and enhanced communication; and personnel flexibility. The common skills seen by both the vice chancellors and the CIOs are good management and leadership. For them leadership translates into an ability to bring support service goals into alignment with academic affairs' goals. The staff working on the frontlines providing service to faculty, staff, and students might be too focused to see this shift and make anything meaningful out of it. In fact, as we shall see later, for a variety of reasons such changes might seem threatening.

LESSONS LEARNED

As has been noted, most of the CIOs interviewed were promoted from within the organization, were new to the job, and had been library directors. Because the mergers created entirely new organizations, the CIOs often had to create their jobs from scratch. Only one of the nine CIOs interviewed had been hired from outside the university for a position already created. Because they were new to the work, and because they were feeling their way, I wondered what they had learned from the experience. A more veteran group surely would have answered differently, but the answers provided by these new CIOs are certainly valuable for anyone thinking of taking on this responsibility and for institutions thinking of creating such a merged structure and promoting from within. Although the CIOs mentioned many lessons learned, three stand out as nearly universal.

Many of the CIOs said they had dramatically altered their perspectives. When they were responsible for one department, generally the library, they focused narrowly on teaching, learning, and research issues. Technology created challenges of integration and management for their core business, but they did not see the overall support issues and tradeoffs confronted by technology managers every day. Like faculty, librarians tended to see only the user side of the technology equation. When they became CIOs and assumed responsibility for academic and administrative computing, networking, and computer labs, their perspective changed dramatically. One of the most valuable aspects of a merger, scarcely mentioned in the literature, is the librarian-turned-CIO's translation of this complexity into language faculty and academic administrators can understand. This understanding, this broadened perspective, may be the principal reason that vice chancellors see a merger as a success while some computing and library staffs see it in a different light.

The lack of technological expertise worried CIOs. They found themselves transformed from confident expertise in a single specialty to novices thrust among a vast array of technology initiatives. Many reported taking crash courses in telecommunications, networking, or mainframe operating systems, and yet still feeling that they had failed to master these arcane subjects with any degree of depth. The librarians-turned-CIOs reported spending all their spare time and much of their attention on the technology related parts of their organizations. The technology experts now responsible for the library found themselves spending much more time immersed in library culture. No CIO reported having finally reached a comfort level in this exercise, though some did take comfort in the knowledge that their management skills seemed good enough to float them through the troubled waters of technology decision making.

The CIOs in the University of Wisconsin System have learned that a merger, in the sense of true integration, is going to take a very long time. As one CIO said, "The verdict on the success of our merger will not be in for two years, or perhaps even for five years." "Integration takes time," said another, "and strategic planning is essential." There seemed to be a consensus among this "first generation" of CIOs that we should not rush to judgment about success or failure, but we should revisit the studies of these organizational efforts five or ten years out, and test them from a broader perspective.

MERGERS GONE AWRY

Three institutions in the University of Wisconsin System have stepped back from a merger. For a time they experimented with reorganizing the library and computing support services, but for one reason or another they decided that separating these services worked better for them. It is worthwhile to consider what happened at those institutions as an antidote to the optimism about mergers at some of the other institutions.

At one of the institutions, a campus-wide committee with broad faculty representation suggested that library and computing services be merged. It is not clear from the interviews that the librarians, who possess faculty status at the institution, fully bought into the merger idea. In any event, the campus chose a nonlibrarian from outside the campus as the CIO, and almost from the outset of his tenure, he ran afoul of the library faculty. His academic computing background turned out to be a poor fit with library service culture, and, not surprisingly, he quickly alienated faculty as well. His successor, on an interim basis, was the library director, who proved to be an excellent manager and leader. But library faculty, who saw a technology culture rather then a public service culture triumphant in the merged organization, convinced administration that the merged model was not productive. Some of the interviewees regretted the dissolution of the merger, arguing that the library would no longer be a "player at the technology table" if they were not a part of a merged organization. This person went on to argue that it was not the merger that failed, but the CIO chosen by the campus. Another interviewee saw the library faculty as the ultimate cause of the merger's failure because "they are unwilling to change the way they do business."

In the context of the CIO's own analysis of merged services, the two years of the merger were probably too short to provide a fair test for success. It is likely, too, that the skill set sought by the university—sophisticated knowledge of academic technology—was not as important as proven leadership and management skills and a dedication to the faculty/student service philosophy typified by the library profession. It is unlikely that the library faculty alone were to blame for the failure of the merger. Conversations with the vice chancellor and the CIO indicate that the more likely reason is the lack of clarity about university goals and the general direction of technology growth in higher education.

In this case, strong faculty input into the process instead of the more common "top-down" direction of most of the decision making at the universities in the Wisconsin System probably resulted in the university's pursuit of the wrong qualities in a CIO. It is easy to understand how a group of faculty members might believe intimate knowledge of technology trends might be more preferable than leadership skills for a CIO. This view held more legitimacy back in the early to mid-1990s before networked technologies permeated very far into teaching and learning.

Something very similar happened at one other university that experimented with merged services. Like the first institution, the second one chose a technologist rather then a librarian as the first CIO. Unlike the first institution, however, the chancellor drove the decision process. Interviewees here did not assign blame, but several told me that the library faculty led the charge for breaking the merger apart when the first CIO retired after about six years at the job. One of the explanations offered for the library's opposition, which I found very persuasive, was that the organization of the merged services severed the library from the vice chancellor and the dean's cabinet. Thus, the library's needs were always translated through a technology intermediary—the CIO who reported directly to the chancellor. I found this persuasive because another library director at an UW institution with merged library and computing services complained to me that he did not have a seat on the dean's council. Instead he had to report to a CIO who was a computing professional, who in turn reported directly to the chancellor. A disconnect developed, this director explained, because the library had a difficult time ascertaining the scope and level of support to provide to faculty without weekly, ongoing dialogue with the deans.

As at the first university, the interviewees at the second seemed satisfied with the new decentralized support services. The flatter organizational structure with shorter reporting lines between front line service providers and university administrators seemed to serve them well. Heads of departments seemed very collegial, and a council of four independent service providers (academic computing and networking, libraries, administrative computing, and media services) mapped budget and technology plans collaboratively. As one administrator explained, "merged services is simply not an issue here any longer. The current model seems to be working well." My own observation is that collegiality is remarkably well developed at this institution compared to most, and any organizational structure would probably work pretty well there.

CONCLUSIONS

The merger of library and computing services is now a well-established organizational structure within the University of Wisconsin System. Despite some misgivings on the part of line staff, CIOs, and even vice chancellors, the structure serves the academic mission of the university well. Merged services provide opportunities for leveraging both technology resources and vision in ways not readily available in nonmerged organizations. We are early into the merger experiment. But the discussions with CIOs and vice chancellors give evidence of its value as an organizational option in this transition from administrative support as technology driver to teaching and learning support as technology driver. Moreover, as libraries continue to play a pivotal role in teaching and learning support services, and as they transform themselves into complex centers for virtual, asynchronous learning, their administrators will provide a source of leadership for the more comprehensive information services.

The technology infrastructure of the university may become so ubiquitous and transparent that an organizational structure will emerge that separates infrastructure from application. Libraries may become exclusively involved on the applications side and no longer concerned about infrastructure, thereby making current forms of mergers irrelevant. But such a scenario is unlikely to happen very soon.

Investments are being made in CIOs who see the bigger picture of the university's mission and goals. This perspective is larger than the library and transcends the technology. It demands a service philosophy very much like that nurtured in library schools and imbued with library service philosophy. From this broader perspective, merged services fit well into the long-term trends of higher education where technology has been overwhelmingly adopted by faculty and students as standard tools of the enterprise. Even in those instances where a merger failed in the UW System, the issue of leadership in the use of the technology for teaching and learning brought library and computing services closer together. The discussions with CIOs, vice chancellors, and staff point to growth and maturation of merged support services rather than dissolution.

NOTES

1. Richard Dougherty began exploring the issue of mergers of collaborations in the late 1980s. His 1987 article, "Libraries and Computing Centers: A Blueprint for Collaboration," *College & Research Libraries* 48 (July 1987), 289-296, is emblematic of the type of "op ed" piece produced early on in this process. *Cause/Effect* has taken an interest in this subject from about the mid-1990s. The fall 1994 issue (volume 17, number 3) is devoted to the interrelationship between libraries and computing operations on campuses.

2. Arnold Hirshon, *Integrating Computing and Library Services: An Administrative Planning and Implementation Guide for Information Resources,* CAUSE Professional Paper Series 18, published in cooperation with the Coalition for Networked Information (Boulder, Colo.: CAUSE, 1998). More in-depth individual institutional studies of mergers can be found in Eugene A. Engeldinger and Edward Meachen, "Merging Libraries and Computing Centers at Smaller Academic Institutions," *Library Issues: Briefings for Faculty and Administrators* 16 (January 1996) (Ann Arbor, Mich.: Mountainside Publishing). See also Edward Meachen, "Positioning the Library for the Future," *College & Undergraduate Libraries* vol. 4, no. 1 (1997): 1-13.

3. "UW System Survey of Computing Services," Madison, Wis.: Wisconsin Survey Research Laboratory, University of Wisconsin-Extension, 1998.

4. "UW System Survey of Computing Services."

CHAPTER TEN

Conceptual Foundations for Library/Computing Center Relations

STEPHEN PETERSON
BERNARD HECKER

In October 1997 the Trustees of Trinity College voted to proceed with plans to design and build an addition to the college library that would include space for the computing center.[1] The decision to renovate and enlarge the college library responded to several long-standing deficiencies in the library facility. However, the original building proposal did not include space for the computing center.[2] The idea to physically integrate the library and the computing center arose rather late in the process of program definition, in discussions between the two department heads. Although these administrators quickly recognized several practical benefits of this inclusion, their sense of the concept as a prudent forward-looking proposal that would serve the college well over the planning time frame for the building chiefly propelled the proposal. The idea received swift and strong endorsement, first from college officers, and then faculty (both from formal committees and from individuals), as well as from both library and computing center staff. Following initial discussions of this proposal, the college undertook an extensive campus master-planning project. These planning discussions have produced even more widespread institutional confidence in the decision to build this facility. Indeed, the resulting master plan identified the proposed library and computing center as its first academic priority. Architectural design work for the facility began in the spring of 1998.

Yet, through nearly two years of planning, discussion about organizationally integrating the computing center and the college library at Trinity College[3] remains curiously absent—akin to Sherlock Holmes' curious incident of the dog in the night.[4] Although Trinity College officers were well aware of this type of organizational change taking place on other campuses, they simply did not seriously or even casually propose administratively integrating the library and computing center. Initially this discussion did not occur because thinking about the relationship between the library and the computing center at Trinity College has been driven by fundamental considerations of service. Many faculty members responded enthusiastically to the idea of placing the library and the computing center in a single centrally located facility because they saw the move as the foundation for a new quality of service—to themselves and to their students. They spoke about changes already under way in the patterns of their scholarship and in their expectations of students, and how these changes pointed to a redefinition of the relationship between computing and library services.

As Trinity College takes the library/computing center project to the architectural drawing board, it is clear to the authors, who shouldered most of the program development, that clearly this planning involved deeper conceptual issues. In this chapter we present the analytical framework from which we have come to understand the essential warrants for our library and computing center in the life of the college. This conceptual framework is informing and, in some ways, rationalizing our efforts to design new services and reinvent old ones. Additionally, the effort has helped us to understand more completely the unique developmental path we have found ourselves charting at Trinity College. Our analytic model is explicitly rooted in the core values of a liberal education, and although institutions articulate these values differently, we think there is sufficient common ground to indicate the experience at Trinity College will have applicability to other institutions.

STARTING WITH MISSION

The roles of the library and computing center must be illuminated, not by a sense of the day-to-day activities of each organization, but by a clear understanding of the aims of the college itself. Thus, only through a review of the mission statement of the institution can a conceptual framework emerge. Such a review anchors the reevaluation from the perspective of the needs of the entire institution—not just two departments. Liberal arts colleges are, by definition, open and self-directed communities. Faculty, students, and administrators expect a process that engages and involves them.[5] Therefore change must explicitly connect with first principles to move an academic community.

Trinity College is guided by the following mission statement, and recent planning efforts found it to be timely and appropriate, very much embodying the most essential of our community's beliefs:

> Trinity College is a community united in a quest for excellence in liberal arts education. Our paramount purpose is to foster critical thinking, free the mind of parochialism and prejudice, and prepare students to lead examined lives that are personally satisfying, civically responsible, and socially useful. (Trinity College Mission Statement, 1998)

Although this text is the result of an idiosyncratic evolution at Trinity, we think it resonates in the mission statements of many similar institutions. The power of these words comes in part from the grandness of their sweep, but indeed this abstraction makes it the more difficult to relate to the services of libraries and computing centers. How is the pursuit and appropriation of knowledge sustained by a mission statement? Through what instruments does an educational mission take root in individual students? And, of these instruments or mechanisms, which are most deeply engaged by libraries and computing organizations?

A SERVICE PARADIGM

Activating a mission statement—using a statement of goals to inform a specific plan of action—to plan a facility that would house both a library and a computing center necessitates a very methodical approach. For us, this approach required a critical first step in which we worked to flesh out the pedagogical structure that seemed embedded in the precepts of the mission statement. It is from this structure that the warrant for academic services—including information resources in the library and computing center—emerges. Our goal in this paper is to provide fresh insights into our changing departmental missions, how our two departments relate to other departments within the college, and how our departments fit within the college as a whole.

Trinity College's mission statement contains the structural presupposition that students mature in four developmental arenas. Weakness in any of these arenas will necessarily undermine the ability to deliver upon the goals of Trinity's stated mission. These arenas or components of liberal learning are:

1. academic skills
2. content competence
3. habits of mind and
4. personal values.

These components form the conceptual bridgework between the lyrical but abstract text of our mission statement and the service programs of the library and the computing center. This conceptual bridge is illustrated in figure 1.[6] Although these components may be listed separately and will be discussed here serially, they are in fact deeply interconnected. They interact with each other, separately and together, in complex ways. Moreover, the four components of liberal learning appear to cluster around two more general educational goals. One goal concerns personal development and the other concerns critical thinking. Both are indicated by flat ovals at the bottom of the diagram. Although personal development and critical thinking are equally important in our mission, it is with the latter that the services of libraries and computing centers are most directly relevant.

The First Goal: Critical Thinking

Critical thinking is a manner or discipline of organizing and applying other skills for the sake of generating the substantial intellectual outcome that is the core of the academic enterprise. Although it may be theoretically possible to teach critical thinking without attending to the cognitive skills on which it is based, the range and scope of these skills provide analytical depth and intellectual power to the exercise. A blacksmith's furnace may be used naively and will provide as much heat as a campfire. But replacing good coal for dry wood and learning the bellows yields a product that transcends the first. The cognitive skills are techniques of the mind as the smith's skills are techniques of the forge. Like the smith, our students must both master these techniques and apply them with purpose.

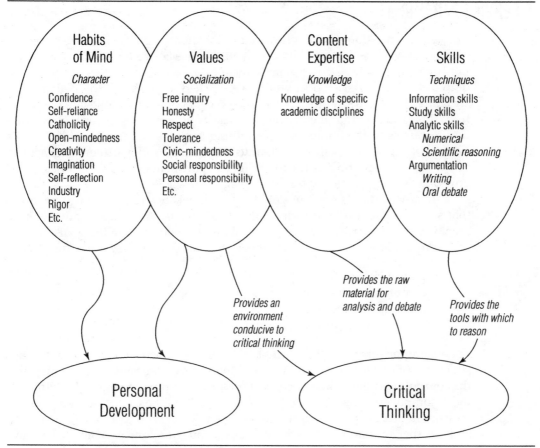

Figure 1   Components of Liberal Learning

Skills of Learning

Academic libraries and computing centers historically have recognized the importance of providing information skills training, but the programs are quixotic and the results are often disappointing. Yet developing certain skill sets is now a virtual prerequisite for effective learning in a technologically enriched teaching environment. To understand how intimate collaboration between the library and the computing center can improve this circumstance, we must take a much larger view of the problem. Figure 2 presents four basic skill groupings, along with some constituent skills.

Although the skills mentioned in figure 2 have a direct impact on the quality of a student's academic performance, they have not received equal attention within a traditional liberal arts education. Liberal arts colleges often want to dissociate themselves from skills, yet critics of higher education often point to inadequacies in basic skills like writing and numeracy among other deficiencies in contemporary college graduates.[7] The fact is that most college students need some help in these foundational skills to realize our most basic goal—students learning to be critical thinkers.

In our review, the skills upon which critical thinking depends settled into the four groups indicated in figure 2. Information skills concern the acquisition,

Information skills	Skills to acquire, organize, and evaluate information Technology skills
Analytic skills	Numerical skills Scientific reasoning—hypothesis testing
Argumentation skills	Writing Oral debate
Study skills	Reading Note-taking Time management Metacognitive skills (self-awareness of cognitive processes)

Figure 2   Types of Basic Learning Skills

organization, and evaluation of information. Considerable discussion is now taking place in higher education concerning the enhanced importance of information skills in the Information Age, with traditional research skills and the newer information technology skills often joined under the rubric of information literacy. For example, the American Library Association has developed a well-cited "Position Statement on Information Literacy" (http://www.ala.org/aasl/positions/PS_infolit.html). These skills are generic and universal, and apply to all disciplines as well as to learning beyond the academy. Faculty members and librarians agree about the importance of these skills, but the number of the constituent skills, their complexity, and the variety of contexts in which the skills can be applied make it difficult to agree about ways to cultivate these skills. Two things, however, seem clear. First, computers, and hence computing skills, are widely used in teaching these skills. Second, information or bibliographic literacy often is the goal or desired outcome of such skill training.

Study skills are the foundation of other learning skills, and the most essential study skill is reading, or more precisely, careful, critical reading. Teaching reading per se may always be rare, but critical reading is certainly promoted through the choice of reading assignments and faculty expectations of a student's comprehension. Also overlooked in most academic support systems are skills like time management, the challenges of which have unnecessarily undermined many a college career.

Analytic skills are well respected in higher education, and have traditionally been well represented in the curriculum. The numerical skills are formally covered and assessed in courses like mathematics, calculus, geometry, and statistics. The scientific method is discussed and demonstrated in science courses, so that virtually every graduate is exposed to hypothesis testing. A basic competence in these skills often is a degree requirement.

Argumentation skills include both writing and oral debate. Writing is near the center of liberal arts education, or at least near the center of most liberal arts colleges' rhetoric. In practice the teaching of writing often has to fight for respect. But the growing prevalence of writing centers and initiatives like writing across the curriculum are indications that this skill is not being ignored on campuses.

Oral skills are another matter. While discussion is the modus operandi of much liberal education, oral argumentation is not often taught, formally rehearsed, or even discussed—except perhaps within the confines of the debating team and the career counseling office. Without faculty guidance or extracurricular training, the casual and informal discussions of the classroom are unlikely to truly hone student skills.

This analysis holds several implications for the training programs conducted by libraries and computing centers. The first is efficiency—the removal of redundancy in class offerings, reduction in administrative overhead for scheduling and advertising workshops, and the streamlining of operations from the students' point of view. While these gains are not inconsequential, the greatest benefits will probably not arise from improved efficiency, but rather from the synergy that arises out of substantial collaborations between individuals with differing perspectives and experience. Training programs are built upon varied skills including course design, the design and execution of print and electronic materials, podium skills, one-on-one training skills, and faculty outreach. These skills are unlikely to be equally shared by the two separate departments. Further, the departments typically differ in their use of instructors (staff, student instructors, outside instructors), formats (free-standing workshops, in-class training sessions, help sessions, etc.), and modularity (one-shot, short course, intensive, etc.) Jointly developed training would benefit from a richer palette of options, as well as from the greater range of professional training, experience, and personal talents of its creators.

These considerations indicate that we should take even more seriously the training services that our organizations already provide and encourage us to think expansively about what training services should be offered in the future. Collaboration with other academic support organizations on campus that provide skill training beyond the library and the computing center would help to enhance the visibility of such training as a worthy cocurricular initiative. As we have seen, although training in academic skills is something of a poor stepchild on many liberal arts campuses, it shares fully the distinction of being a major part of our expectations for liberal arts graduates. A substantial collaboration between the library, computing center, math center, and writing center (and perhaps others) would help underscore the legitimacy of skills training while creating a more varied and flexible training program. It is tantalizing to imagine a truly integrated skill center around which tremendous vitality, professionalism, and visibility could be established. The interplay of skills training and content development could be cultivated creatively. To frame the services of such an organization as something more than ancillary is necessary. In an ideal scenario, a unified learning skills assessment would be administered to all entering students, and any skill deficiencies would be addressed in a customized curriculum.

The broader, unified skills training curriculum that derives from our analysis promises substantial pedagogical dividends. Realizing such a curriculum is a major undertaking in any campus context, with real academic implications. The idea should be implemented in phases. Bringing library and the computing center training programs together is a first step in moving from imagination to reality.

Content Competence

Liberally educated students are expected to know something, several somethings. As they mature educationally, their knowledge is expected to progress from general knowledge about something to specific knowledge, i.e., knowledge from within some field or discipline. They are, for example, expected to move from simply taking history courses to thinking and writing as historians think and write. Thus, content competence is a matter both of knowing something and knowing how to find out what one does not know. It is both mastery and method.

Traditionally, collegiate libraries have played an instrumental role in helping students with subject mastery and subject method. As recently as fifteen years ago a reasonably well-funded collegiate library would hold the texts, secondary literature, and instrumenta studiorum of the disciplines taught within a given institution's curriculum. Indeed, to some degree, a collegiate library would provide the basic informational framework for disciplines not actively taught in a curriculum but which had correlative importance for those fields. Collection development programs had the goal of assuring students the availability of essential works for subject mastery within the limitations of an undergraduate curriculum. That is, a well-selected collegiate library was the bibliographic equivalent of the collegiate curriculum, not comprehensive, but centered, focused, and possessing assured essential quality. In most cases, these collections included the tools that aided students in historical research and in tracking recent developments. The paradigm was reliable, often the results were commendatory, and the lack of financial support was the chief obstacle to ever-higher effectiveness.

This paradigm has disintegrated chiefly on the method axis, but in part also on the mastery axis. The disintegration is not because it was a defective paradigm, but because information technology has rendered it unsustainable. At least by the early 1960s librarians began to realize that computer technology—data processing, as it was called in those days—could and undoubtedly would have a profound and beneficial impact on library operations and library service. Reliance on, and optimism about, information technology now has swept unabated through every aspect of library service. Automation started with business and operations, moved quickly to bibliographic control, and now has, quite literally, revolutionized access. By the time the Web became a major source of documentation and information, all sophisticated academic libraries had become heavily dependent on technology for providing bibliographic access.[8] The traditional methods of access to the documents and information sources of most academic disciplines had moved from print sources to either a mixed environment—print and electronic—or largely to the electronic environment.

The paradigm has deteriorated on the mastery axis through the introduction of a much wider universe of documents and resources. The Web, as a means of publication, as well as the virtual repository of documentation with scholarly value, opened resources to colleges that they otherwise could not hope to provide to their students and faculty. Yet the chief difference between these Web resources and traditional college library resources is not their range and diversity, format, or even ready accessibility. Rather, most Web resources are presented to students without the traditional hallmarks of quality preassessment. Whereas most library collections represent a double quality control scrutiny—one provided by the publisher and the other offered by the library selection criteria—Web resources are presented in an open, unreviewed, unfettered democracy of expression.

The combination of these factors produces several unintended consequences for the undergraduate educational environment. First, the range or scope of content resources now presented to undergraduate students is both much larger and less well substantiated than was the case previously. Many Web resources represent bodies of content with which faculty members are unfamiliar and about whose quality faculty may hold suspicions. Although the Web does provide access to many classical texts, much of its secondary documentation is contemporary, leaving significant historical gaps in a student's awareness of a field.

The consequences for methodical inquiry also are complex. Many disciplines have distinctive bibliographic tools that are structured around the particular needs and characteristics of a given discipline. Thus, it was reasonable to expect students to gain proficiency in using these tools as part of their mastery of content. Now, with these tools and a certain measure of documentation both being presented electronically, students must master the distinctive and productive ways of searching for information and content electronically. Yet, with the gain in the use of a general method of inquiry, there is the risk of a distinct loss in the competence with discipline-specific inquiry.

Nevertheless, the erosion of one paradigm makes way for the development of a new paradigm for gaining subject knowledge. This new paradigm will integrate the discipline-based analytical tools with resource discovery and retrieval skills. Mastery and method will be ever more closely related. Although it is only now beginning to emerge and its contours are yet fluid, we believe it is clear that computing and libraries are inseparably linked in this paradigm. They now are directly engaged in teaching—not merely providing—subject content, and their pedagogical methods will sustain years of independent, self-reliant learning.

The Second Goal: Personal Development

Personal development ranks with development of critical thinking as a primary goal of liberal education. Trinity College's mission statement speaks of preparing students who will lead examined, satisfying, responsible, and useful lives. Formal classwork alone will not succeed on these matters. These more subtle lessons must be taught by example, through rituals, and through the fact and example of the life of the community itself. Thus they also are relevant, albeit perhaps indirectly, for the service programs of libraries and computing centers.

Values (Socialization to Academic Virtues)

The goals of critical thinking and personal development are deeply linked. We value rigor, honesty, respect, tolerance, and industry precisely because these are the qualities a community needs if it is to support free inquiry. Likewise, we value civic-mindedness and social responsibility, for without them academic enterprises are sterile, ungrounded, and ultimately amoral. Inculcating these values, what we might call socialization to academic virtues, is an indispensable part of our mission.

Libraries and computing centers certainly play a role in transmitting these values, not only those that concern the free flow of information, but also those that nurture a sense of community. With our first campus Internet connections came issues concerning access to information. For example, certain campus constituencies took offense with the content of some Usenet newsgroups. Many of us weathered political fallout in order to allow our clients to make their own choices from the broadest range of information alternatives, even though we found some of those alternatives to be personally offensive. In doing so we made a powerful statement about the importance of information access, and a belief in the judgment of the individuals who make up our community. This statement, of course, reinforces the long-standing resistance of libraries and librarians to censorship. As with all values, the importance of unimpeded access to information is communicated to students through our actions. In fact, there is no greater diversity on a college campus than the intellectual diversity represented by library collections and the Internet resources to which computing centers support access.

Similarly, we should take seriously our role in shaping the new virtual communities emerging on our campuses. Ideally, these communities will extend the vitality of our traditional campus communities and embody the same values we cherish, albeit in new and as yet unfamiliar forms. Both libraries and computing centers will be central agents in creating resources, establishing and perhaps monitoring membership, and setting the tone of these new learning communities.

Habits of Mind (Character)

The final component of liberal learning concerns personal character, the habits of mind that define a life that is constructive, purposeful, and expansive. First and perhaps foremost among these is the habit of self-reflection, echoing the ancient exhortation that an unexamined life is not worth living. Also included under this heading is catholicity—marking a mind with a broad range of interests and ambitions, which serves as a guard against arrogance and tunnel vision. Self-reliance and imagination encourage original contributions and creation. And responsibility embodies the moral imperative to acknowledge the connections between thought and action, action and consequence.

Taken together, these habits help create a life that is adaptive, productive, and useful. Academic libraries and computing centers have a propaedeutic role here as well, both while students are in residence and for their life of learning after graduation. Networked access to life on campus can help our alumni remain close to the best of our traditions, especially the rigors of self-examination and tolerance for diversity of opinions and draw from the creative energy that bristles within our walls.

SUMMARY AND CONCLUSION

In the paradigm that has emerged in our discussion, the library and the computing center have moved together in service, and together they have moved from being framed as support agencies to being direct educational partners with the subject classroom, the laboratory, and the performance stage. Their relationship to each other is not finally determined by convenience, efficiency, or, in Trinity's case, opportunity. Rather they are linked through the most essential goals of liberal education and in pedagogy—and, in an analogous fashion, with the institution as a whole. The pedagogical paradigm that has emerged in this discussion recapitulates the fundamental educational mission of the institution.

We have outlined in this paper a conceptual framework for productively relating libraries and computing centers to institutional goals. We are confident that there are strong and convincing conceptual reasons these departments can, and indeed will be, closely linked. This framework does not, however, compel a specific organizational solution. Rather, it provides benchmarks and signposts to guide our service design and to relate productively with the rest of campus. For many institutions, this may not be the time to link these organizations in administrative ways—indeed a precipitous rush to administrative vagaries may deprive institutions of the occasion to closely examine the conceptual and functional synergies in their libraries and computing centers. By keeping structural and administrative issues at the edge of the discussion while encouraging a close relationship between the departments, Trinity College has secured a valuable degree of flexibility to explore and test multiple options. Clarifying the conceptual and pedagogical linkages that are emerging between these organizations may forge even stronger future bonds and foster even more dynamic organizations.

NOTES

1. Both the Trinity College Computing Center and Trinity College Library are unitary organizations. The college never has encouraged the development of branch or departmental libraries. The Computing Center is organized into three groups, Academic Computing, Administrative Data Systems, and Technical Services, each reporting to the Director of Information Technology.

2. The Computing Center has been housed in a superb academic facility designed by Caesar Pelli and completed in the spring of 1991.

3. "Integration" in this paper is used in the sense defined by Arnold Hirshon, i.e., an organization in which both library and computing operations report to the same chief information officer (Arnold Hirshon, *Integrating Computing and Library Services: An Administrative Planning and Implementation Guide for Information Resources*, CAUSE Professional Paper Series 18 (Boulder, Colo.: CAUSE, 1998), vii.

4. "'Is there any point to which you would wish to call my attention?' 'To the curious incident of the dog in the night-time.' 'The dog did nothing in the night-time.' 'That was the curious incident,' remarked Sherlock Holmes." Doyle, *Silver Blaze*.

5. See John P. Kotter and James L. Heskett, *Corporate Culture and Performance* (New York: Free Press, 1992) and Patrick E. Connor and Linda K. Lake, *Managing Organizational Change* (New York: Praeger, 1988).

6. The authors wish to thank Susan Gilroy, Reference and Instruction Librarian in Trinity College, for her help in the early development of this model and for reviewing this manuscript.

7. For recent discussions see Ernest L. Boyer, *College: The Undergraduate Experience in America* (New York: Harper, 1987), Stanley M. Davis and James W. Botkin, *The Monster under the Bed: How Business Is Mastering the Opportunity of Knowledge for Profit* (New York: Simon & Schuster, 1994), and Lewis J. Perelman, *School's Out: Hyperlearning, the New Technology, and the End of Education* (New York: Morrow, 1992).

8. Although the term *information*, linked to technology, is in wide use, we find this term too narrow to define resources available on the Web. Documentation, itself a rather narrow term, may better describe resources that are constructive works of scholarship and research.

CHAPTER ELEVEN

The Service Imperative

A Case Study for Merging Libraries and Computing Centers at Smaller Academic Institutions

EUGENE A. ENGELDINGER

A strong, stable, service-oriented infrastructure is the most important contribution to a campus that academic information technology units can provide. Our academic constituents expect direct and indirect services from up-to-date, accessible, and dependable hardware and software and information resources. Additionally, they want service that will help them to learn personally how to use these tools and resources. Since one of the goals of higher education is to develop information literate and computer savvy graduates, it is *imperative* that we who work in information and instructional technology units provide the means and support the programs that will develop those graduates.

At most academic institutions, there is a tradition and culture of separate libraries and computing centers.[1] Such a situation existed at Carthage College, a four-year, residential, liberal arts institution at full enrollment with about 1,700 full-time-equivalent students, and about ninety-five full-time faculty members. The college is fully networked with a fiber optic backbone, with campus-wide LAN and Internet access from the library, all offices, residence hall rooms, computer labs, and classrooms. Until March 1993, academic and administrative computing reported to the Vice President for Business and Finance, the library director reported to the Academic Dean, and a rudimentary media services unit reported to administrative computing.

Nearly six years ago the college began the process of merging its library and academic computing units. In the fall of 1994, the college added media services responsibilities to the merged units, thereby rounding out Academic Information Services (AIS) with five computer services staff, one and a half positions in media services, and seven and a half positions in the library. The college administration appointed the library director as the new Vice President for Academic Information Services, reporting directly to the President of the College, and serving on the President's Advisory Council (PAC).

REASONS FOR MERGER

A caution often given in regard to combining library and computing services into a single unit is that such restructuring should not be done "to solve a problem."[2] On the contrary, I argue that fixing a problem is precisely the reason that it should be done. If things truly are working smoothly and there is active collaboration, there is no reason to reorganize. "If it ain't broke, don't fix it" is good advice in an area as complex as information technology. However, if there is inadequate user support, characteristically spotty, unstructured, and informal cooperation, and little meaningful communication between the computer services and the library, combining and reorganizing the two information technology units under good administrative management might provide considerable benefit.

We also hear that merging these units is rarely a grass roots initiative, rather that it is usually imposed from above. The implication is that because a merger is imposed from above, it is a flawed policy that will work poorly and will likely fail. Some observers further suggest that at best such a merger might create a very difficult and contentious "marriage." However, in my experience such results are far from inevitable.

Probably the least sagacious reason for combining the information and technology units is the belief that it will reduce the number of staff needed. In reality, staff reduction is a highly unlikely result. But even if it does happen, these benefits are likely to go unnoticed. Responding to the demands for more help to service the increasingly complex responsibilities will probably obfuscate any staff savings. On the other hand, there may be enhanced opportunities for improved staff efficiencies, since closer working relationships may increase the receptiveness of computing and library units to converge their goals and objectives. The various units are less likely to proceed along nonsynchronous paths, a situation that is more probable when they report to different officers, or under the "silo model" of organization, i.e. self-contained units under a single head, than under the merged model.

The major motivation behind an academic institution's decision to merge the library and computing center should be the desire to provide better information technology service to the academic community. This desire certainly provided the motivating force behind the decision to restructure the information service units at Carthage College. In our case, once the decision was made, three major management strategies facilitated our progress toward overcoming the legacy of our separate operations. Our initial merger success resulted from creation of a common vision, maintenance of clear and continuous communication throughout AIS, and resource sharing for the common good of the merged units. Frequent discussions regarding the vision, the completion of goals, mutual assistance to accomplish objectives, and the sharing of financial and staff resources all contributed to our successful merging.[3]

As Carthage moved beyond the initial challenges of restructuring and the units continued to work more closely together (a process that took two or three years to become very comfortable), the true raison d'être for Academic Information Services became increasingly obvious—providing improved, pertinent service to the college community. As we worked together on many projects, we recognized that the results enhanced immensely the service we provided to users. We focused on student and faculty needs through the more holistic lens of the combined unit, rather than separately through library, media, or computing foci. We saw clearly that as the components of information technology (hardware, software, and information resources) converged, the structurally merged organization could provide the new, more proactive service paradigm. Indeed, the users seemed to perceive their needs through that prism. Though users required help from library, media, or computer staff, many did not compartmentalize their needs that way. Rather they knew only that they needed assistance from someone who worked in AIS. Few knew to which unit they should apply for assistance.

INFRASTRUCTURE NEEDS

Most academic institutions understand that if information technology units are to provide dependable service, the technology and information infrastructures must be strengthened and maintained. This is particularly true of campus-wide networks, those utilities most academic communities have come to see as resources essential to the efficient functioning of the institution. At Carthage, too, we saw the network as a "mission-critical" resource for nearly all campus technical activities.

To meet service expectations, we had to ensure that information technology infrastructures functioned as reliably as possible. Most people probably view the technology infrastructure as consisting almost entirely of hardware and software. Because of this perception, they frequently overlook another important element of the infrastructure—one that requires equally close cooperation, unified vision, and continual development—the service infrastructure.

SERVICE INITIATIVES

Early in the Carthage merger, we realized that to facilitate closer group identification, cooperation, and empathy regarding the challenges each unit faced would require cross training and sharing of expertise among the units. With the constant expansion of technology on campus, computer staff had to install workstations, wiring, data outlets, LAN and Internet connections, software applications and equipment everywhere including the library. Library staff quickly developed a confidence in, and respect for, the computing staff's expertise and the challenges they faced. At the same time, the computer staff developed a greater awareness and appreciation for the role of librarianship, information resources, and librarians' contributions to the educational enterprise. Mutual understanding and confidence are particularly important in developing a proactive and cooperative attitude between the computer center and library staffs in addressing overlapping issues and problems, such as the online catalog, full-text databases, dial-in from off campus, user authentication, free or fee services, and user education.

That the library's resources should be accessible throughout the campus over the network became a basic philosophical tenet guiding our actions. Increasingly AIS staff recognized that the library existed not just as a singular part of the network, but rather that the network and the library intertwined until each became to the user indistinguishable from the other. Through the network, users gained access to considerable information, both print and electronic, in addition to word processing, spreadsheet, and other information presentation packages. E-mail, the Internet, World Wide Web and other communication features of the new technology assumed greater importance with our students and faculty. AIS staff became increasingly aware that the responsibility for improving the infrastructure and for guiding the Carthage College community in the best use of these new resources should be a shared responsibility. That the approach be collaborative and not competitive or confrontational became equally important to us. Neither unit should vie for exclusive control. Equally important, we believed neither unit should leave any service responsibility unclaimed, drifting without leadership or ownership in a rudderless wake. Each member of the staff possesses unique and valuable expertise that, when combined with that of other staff members, enhances the effectiveness of the services provided through the merger.

Few faculty members and students have sufficient time or inclination to maintain currency with all the rapid technological changes. Many faculty and staff members will become proficient with a few applications, and some will develop comfort with many applications. However, virtually no one will become facile with all the possible uses of information technology. Therefore, this makes it imperative that academic support units accept their responsibility to help the campus users meet their information needs.

Like many academic institutions, Carthage provides numerous opportunities for users to learn how to use information and instruction technology. Many of these are "just in case" services, such as workshops, point-of-use aids, classes, help screens, and e-mail announcements to the whole community regarding new services, databases, or software. However useful and much appreciated these services are, the service imperative demands more than "just in time" assistance. We must provide the right type of instruction at the moment of learning readiness, i.e., when the user is most motivated to learn new skills.

At Carthage we addressed this "just in time" service challenge through the development of a three-part strategy: a student-centered Information Technology Assistants (ITA) program, a Faculty/Staff tutoring program, and a Merged HelpDesk program. Adding these services to our traditional offerings enabled us to support more proactively most of our users' service needs. Not only did each of these three programs fill a unique need, but each complemented, reinforced, and provided support to the other services.

INFORMATION TECHNOLOGY ASSISTANTS

In the past, each of the AIS units had its own corps of student assistants to aid faculty and students in the computer labs and the library. The computer center annually hired, trained, and supervised about twenty lab assistants to help with word processing, spread sheets, e-mail, Internet, and other applications, as well as to service and maintain the equipment and facilities. The student reference assistants performed similar duties in the library, but also assisted with basic directional questions and worked with print reference sources. Each year the library staff hired, trained, and supervised about fifteen reference students. Finding and training a sufficient number of information-literate student assistants for each unit and scheduling all the service hours had proved an ongoing challenge for the library and computing staff. In fact, occasional competition had developed between the library and computer center for the better assistants. Differences in pay scales, as well as the need for providing consistent training and supervision, provided further concern.

Working through these challenges, we sought a solution that best addressed our users' needs. Early on, AIS subscribed to the precept that any information resource that could be networked would be. We had agreed, too, that we would network all college computers, regardless of their location. In practice this meant that since we networked all computer labs, faculty offices, and student residence hall rooms, as well as the twenty-four workstations in the library information commons, we should be able to use the same AIS staff and students to assist in any of those locations. However, we considered the library an exception because it contained reference books and other print materials not present elsewhere. For a few years we cross-trained the students, but the hiring and supervising remained with the separate units. As time went on, our ideas about this evolved. We came to believe that if we could pool both groups of students, properly train them so they would be interchangeable, we could then schedule them more efficiently. Thus, two years ago we pooled our student resources and started calling these students Information Technology Assistants (ITAs). We created a staff supervisor, developed a training program, and put our ideas to the test.

Overall the program has worked well, but we soon realized all too well that real differences exist in the quality of service individual students are capable of providing. Lab helpers, for example, must have considerable knowledge to respond successfully to the myriad questions and problems presented daily; since our campus did not yet have a computer science major, our student experts had to be home-grown within AIS. Success requires a well-thought-out training program extending over many months, indeed, several years.

Success also requires teamwork and cooperation from all AIS staff. Indeed, how we put the ITA program together offers a prime example of the way the AIS staff members worked together for the benefit of the whole campus. The two pools of students have been combined. A librarian supervises them and is responsible for scheduling both the computer labs and the library. However, since the ITAs receive many computer-related questions, we decided that the computer center staff should provide much of the initial training during each new term. Library staff would follow up by mid-term with information resource training. Both units now provide ongoing, routine supervision, and each submits evaluations at the end of each term.

Members from each unit of AIS contribute to the program and all benefit as a result. We schedule the ITAs to work in the library for some of their hours and in the labs during others. When the ITAs work their library hours, we usually schedule them alongside a regular public services staff member. This librarian acts as a mentor and supervisor during that shift, providing guidance and modeling proper service attitudes and help strategies. The special attention the ITAs receive during these shifts greatly improves their technical and people skills, thereby better preparing them for times they are scheduled to work alone.

When assigned to the computer labs, the ITAs usually work by themselves, but we encourage them to call the reference desk or the HelpDesk for backup assistance or advice. The reference staff member on duty and the ITA program supervisor conduct routine visits and inspection trips to the labs. As these students improve their skills, we tap them for the HelpDesk and, on occasion, for the Faculty/Staff Tutoring program.

TUTORING FACULTY/STAFF IN THEIR OFFICES

Few members of the academy doubt the necessity for the faculty and teaching staff to develop a moderate-to-high level of sophistication in using instructional technology to incorporate technology successfully into their classes. If the faculty is unable to make the technology a "natural" part of their courses, students are not likely to learn to use technology as well as they should. Of course, not all students need faculty encouragement, and some students will gravitate toward anything that smacks of technology. Such use, however, often will neither be as academically oriented nor as well guided as use driven by course requirements.

Like many other campuses, Carthage provides its faculty and staff with a variety of opportunities to learn and practice using the new technologies. We schedule workshops and demonstrations galore, but unfortunately these sessions are not always as well attended as they could be. Seeing this as a problem, and knowing that some of our faculty members seek help only at the actual time of need, indeed, at that certain "learning readiness" moment, we decided to provide them with "just in time" assistance. We determined to tutor in their offices, scheduled when they had an actual project with which they needed just such assistance. This assistance took advantage of the increased motivation to learn the needed skills and the opportunity to use the same office equipment on which the projects would be created.

At Carthage many of our faculty members use different computer operating platforms. Some use Macintosh; some use PCs. While most use Windows, the versions they use also differ. This diversity of hardware and software increased the difficulty of conducting general workshops, since a few participants always come to the demonstration or hands-on activity unfamiliar with whatever is being used. Too often when the workshop attendees return to their offices, they cannot apply what they just learned because they have different equipment or differently configured equipment.

The Faculty/Staff Tutoring Program also provides us with an opportunity to verify whether the user's equipment can actually handle the job to be accomplished. In short order, we can know if the learner has the right hardware and software, and if everything is configured properly. Working in the offices also offers us insights into the general technical literacy of the faculty or staff members, and whether their equipment needs upgrading or replacement during the next round in our four-year replacement schedule. The personal attention, though labor intensive, has proven to be very successful in focusing training on specific needs, at the time of need, thereby maximizing faculty satisfaction and AIS staff resources.

We began this program two years ago with some trepidation. Everything in our previous experience suggested that this would be very popular, and we would soon be drowning in a sea of unfilled requests for help. We rolled out the program with many announcements, both explaining what we hoped to accomplish with the service and recommending that faculty and staff members with specific instructional objectives contact us for appointments. Once an individual contacts us for an appointment, we establish a mutually agreeable time. If the individual needs additional sessions, we make the necessary arrangements. We encourage the assignment of appropriate library, media, or computer staff, depending upon the skill instruction desired, to a particular tutoring session. As it turned out, our original fears proved unfounded. While it is a popular service, requests have never inundated us. In fact, the program has allowed us to better schedule our daily workflow and to provide better instructional service in an atmosphere more conducive to learning. The pace and content of the instruction session can be tailored to the learner's real needs. All in all, we believe it is more efficient use of our time.[4]

THE MERGED HelpDesk

A third major "just in time" service initiative is the merged HelpDesk. Like many academic institutions' help desks, the purpose of ours is to provide immediate response to telephone, e-mail, and walk-in requests for help with technology questions regarding information sources, computing, and media resources. Unlike HelpDesks at many other institutions, ours is staffed with full-time professional AIS staff, using our best student assistants only as supplemental staff. In practice, we schedule librarians and media services staff, not just computing staff, at our HelpDesk. However, we do not expect all staff members to serve at the HelpDesk; we schedule only selected staff with sufficient interest and expertise, and we do not schedule paraprofessionals at the HelpDesk. Professional and paraprofessional library staff, as well as ITAs, take turns at the reference desk in the library. Although we do schedule members of media services at the reference desk, at present, while the matter is under consideration, we do not schedule computer staff members at the reference desk.

Using staff from each of the units distributes the workload, increases AIS staff awareness of user difficulties, improves teamwork of the staff, and ensures that users will get expert help. We assign a trouble ticket to questions and problems that cannot be answered immediately and then we delegate them to the appropriate staff to deal with in timely fashion. For example, when computer persons are at the HelpDesk, they refer any library resource question they cannot answer to a librarian. The same is true if a librarian is at the HelpDesk and is asked a difficult question about computers or the network. Through time, practice, and experience, the number of questions that each person answers successfully increases, while those requiring referral diminishes. On the other hand, if a question requires extended time and assistance, it becomes a candidate for the Faculty/Staff Tutoring Service. In such cases, we assign the most logical AIS expert to the task, and that person follows up by scheduling a mutually satisfactory time for tutoring in the user's office.

Unfortunately, the library and the computer center at Carthage are located in different buildings. Thus, we have maintained the HelpDesk in the computer center and the reference desk in the library. Because of the persuasiveness of the network with its computing and library resources, considerable similarity exists between the questions asked and the duties the staff must perform at each service point. We are currently considering merging these two service desks. However, because of logistics and user habits regarding which unit they are used to contacting, we have not reached a decision. We are also currently planning a new facility that will house together in a single building the library, media, and computing units. At that time, we plan to merge the two desks and complete the joining together of reference and HelpDesk service. As with the rationale behind the creation of our ITAs, the merging of technology and the resources available through the campus-wide network drive this decision. We desire to use the expertise of all our staff in providing the best possible assistance to the users. For staff members who lack the knowledge needed to feel comfortable at the service desks, we provide training. Indeed, several of our staff participate in the same training activities we provide for our ITAs.

CONCLUSION AND OBSERVATIONS

As Carthage enters its sixth year under the restructuring, there appears little doubt that the reorganization continues to deliver the originally hoped for results. Our common vision has become clearer, and communication has continued to cement our common purpose. The units have become more budgetarily focused on strengthening the technical and service infrastructures. Staff resources have become increasingly directed at satisfying the service imperative.

At Carthage, progress has been steady and evolutionary. While all members of AIS view each other as colleagues and as members of AIS, the idea that we are one unit has not always been easy for everyone to accept fully. Residual tendencies for some of us to see ourselves as librarians or computer staff still continue. Of course, their existence should not come as a surprise. People often want to identify specifically with their immediate job responsibilities, those with which they are most familiar, particularly if they have worked under the older, more traditional organizational structure. On the other hand, those individuals who have joined the staff since the reorganization seem less inclined to identify as strongly with their immediate unit. Generally they seem more comfortable with the merged structure. This suggests that some individuals prefer or reject the merged model based more on a desire for the familiar than on a desire to find a better approach to providing service. I believe that as individuals acquire longer experience with the additional benefits derived from the merger, such as the sharing of information, of desk schedules, and of improved service to their equipment, they will accept even more greatly the merger.

Anecdotal evidence and unsolicited comments from students and faculty suggest that these initiatives have resulted in improved service at Carthage. A reduction of staff has not resulted, and indeed that should not be the expectation of those who advocate restructuring. However, redeployment of staff, expansion of staff responsibilities, and far greater staff efficiencies have resulted. Until the rate of technology change slows and becomes more manageable, we should expect demands for service from the several technology units to grow continuously. In the meantime, planners and decision makers in higher education must organize their academic support staff in ways that further benefit the faculty and students.

I also must note a general upgrading of Carthage paraprofessional staff responsibilities over the past five or six years. Changes in technology have caused our professional library staff to assume more technical, instructional, and managerial duties, thereby leaving many of their traditional responsibilities to our paraprofessionals. In turn, we increasingly delegate clerical duties to students.

While not necessarily done easily or without adjustment difficulties and staff stress, our experience suggests that these units can be merged successfully. And it does take time. I also will note that even within nonmerged organizations often stress exists among staff members who have difficulty working toward the same goals. Difficulties arising from professional or job culture differences can result in quite pronounced stress. Therefore, we should not be surprised when librarians and computer staff from quite different cultures need time to learn to work together. And, indeed, we should not dismiss as unimportant the very real "cultural" differences between computer staff and librarians. Furthermore, we should be ever mindful of the possibility of staff burnout resulting from too high service expectations and too meager support resources. Working in this kind of environment is more stressful than in situations where each unit continues to deal with issues that are traditionally theirs.

Nevertheless, I doubt that cultural differences pose irreconcilable barriers. Indeed, I suspect that those who are opposed to the merger concept sometimes overplay that "card." After all, within libraries, we have catalogers and reference librarians with very dissimilar cultures and with different ways of viewing and doing things. If these two groups can adopt the same vision, improve communication among themselves, and thereby overcome their cultural differences to work harmoniously toward the same goals, as they do in most libraries, the computer staff and the library staff also can. The real key to successful merging requires the setting aside of narrow agendas, adoption of the institutional mission, and mutual acceptance of the service imperative.

NOTES

1. Both Hardesty and Hirshon have conducted interviews with the principals in the merging controversy. Those desiring more detailed arguments for and against mergers should consult their works: Larry Hardesty, "Computer Center-Library Relations at Smaller Institutions: A Look from Both Sides," *Cause/Effect* 21, no. 1 (1998): 35-41; Arnold Hirshon, *Integrating Computing and Library Services: An Administrative Planning and Implementation Guide for Information Resources,* CAUSE Professional Paper Series 18 (Boulder, Colo.: CAUSE, 1998).
2. Hirshon, *Integrating Computing and Library Services.*
3. Eugene A. Engeldinger and Edward Meachen, "Merging Libraries and Computer Centers at Smaller Academic Institutions," *Library Issues* 16 (January 1996): 1-4.
4. Eugene A. Engeldinger and Michael G. Love, "Taking Instruction to Where It Will Be Used: Tutoring Faculty in Their Offices," *Cause/Effect* 21, no. 2 (1998): 54-58.

CHAPTER TWELVE

Connecticut College
Working outside the Dictates of the Traditional Organizational Chart

CONNIE V. DOWELL
ANDREW W. WHITE

As the world enters the Information Age, colleges and universities, along with most other organizations, are struggling to respond to this new environment. Faced with leapfrogging demands and costs for technology and user services of all kinds, some institutions are responding by simply increasing resources. Other institutions are responding from the intellectual heart of their campuses by creating user-centered organizations guided by core values and traditions and infused with the critical new skills of the Information Age. The unification of libraries and computing centers into new merged environments allows institutions to plan more effectively and more efficiently for their rapidly changing information future while remaining grounded in their intellectual history. Pairing the historic role of libraries in the academy with the growing importance of technology in our institutions' missions makes a powerful combination.

The new merged environment, however, is more than simply a marriage of machines and content. Real organizational change occurs on the front lines of user services, staff member by staff member. The task of restructuring multiple units into a single cohesive user-centered organization while working toward common goals is not an easy one. Both library and computing staff are asked to view their professional responsibilities differently, not as guardians of a particular job description, but as user service representatives—each with valued expertise. The power of the perception of the cultural divide between staff in libraries and computing centers is significant. Acknowledging, however, that each profession has at its heart the same goal, connecting people to information, reveals the falseness of this perception. Creating the framework for common goals is instrumental in dismantling this perception and is an essential first step toward creating an environment for success.

The library and the computer center bring complementary qualities to the merged environment. Among these qualities are customer service orientation, willingness to take risks, management of intellectual content, as well as project planning and implementation. Combining the qualities from the two professions affords an opportunity to create a new profession. As technology becomes interwoven with content and user services converge, the demand for the next generation of information professionals will only increase. Individuals who understand the complex relationship between users, technology, and content are already in demand. A symbiotic relationship between the new information profession and the merged information environment will become apparent, each being necessary for the other to succeed. As the process evolves and as cultural differences diffuse, it is clear that perceived differences between the professions will be accepted as common strengths.

TOWARD A TEAM ENVIRONMENT

Connecticut College was among the first institutions to recognize these common strengths and the contributions they make to the new information profession. The college took the pioneering step of creating an environment where these strengths are fostered and valued. In 1994, the Strategic Planning Team for Technology recommended ". . . that the management [of Information Services] should be centralized, and that its connections to faculty, administrative staff and students be guided more from the perspective of users, than by the dictates of traditional organization charts." The strategic planning team of faculty, students, administrators, and staff created a blueprint for the college's technology future that would provide optimal support for learning, teaching, and the institutional mission. Their call to service resulted in the merger of Libraries, Academic Computing, Administrative Computing, Telecommunications, Networking, the Language Laboratory, and Media Services into Information Services (IS) under the leadership of the Dean of Information Services/Librarian of the College. The team recommended a central management structure and common service mission to eliminate duplication of effort and to support the following goals:

> Develop a system of [networked] user services that allows for easy and immediate assistance for students, faculty, and staff
>
> Support [multiplatform] faculty/student teaching and research
>
> Establish a purchasing policy that ensures best price flexibility, compatibility, and support
>
> Improve communications and information transfer across administrative offices, and between administrative and academic departments

Two years before the merger, the library staff had decided in a planning retreat to conduct its own reorganization. The success of this reorganization laid the groundwork and provided a working model for the later reorganization of Information Services as a whole. The library staff elected to divide the library into three functional reporting areas (see figure 1). Group leaders, appointed by the College Librarian for a term of three years, assumed responsibility for supervision of staff, policy implementation, and daily operations, and comprised the Librarian's Advisory Council. The establishment of activity groups, such as Reference/Liaison and Preservation, enhanced communication between the three reporting areas. Members of these activity groups were drawn from each of the three areas. Conveners had responsibility for calling meetings and forwarding policy recommendations to the College Librarian through the Advisory Council. While the College Librarian assumed ultimate responsibility for

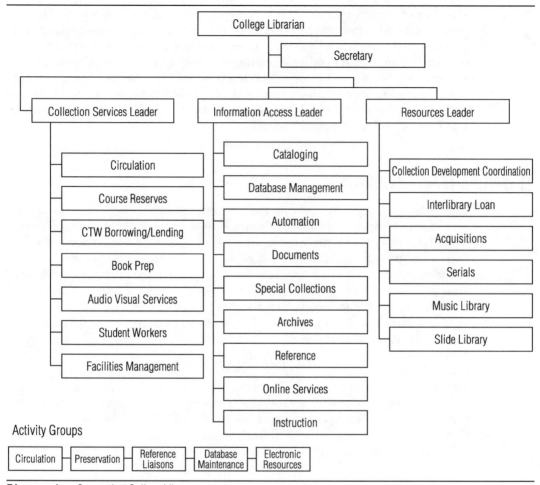

Figure 1   Connecticut College Library

approving new policies, new initiatives originated in the activity groups and were implemented through the functional reporting areas.

In June 1995, in response to the merger, the role of the Librarian's Advisory Council expanded to focus on all areas encompassed by Information Services. The name was changed to the Information Services Advisory Group and the Directors of Administrative and Academic Computing were added to the group (see figure 2). An important step toward unifying the organization and motivating staff to work on common projects and goals was the establishment of activity groups and task forces with staff from across Information Services. The activity groups were charged with fostering continuing communication and service coordination between staff; the task forces were charged with working on short-term projects, identifying problems and developing solutions. The task forces, including Space Planning, Communications, and Training, proved instrumental in breaking down barriers between areas and allowed many organization-wide projects to move forward more quickly, among them the IS Web site, the smooth relocation of offices, and the staff recommendation for coordination of instruction for research and technology applications.

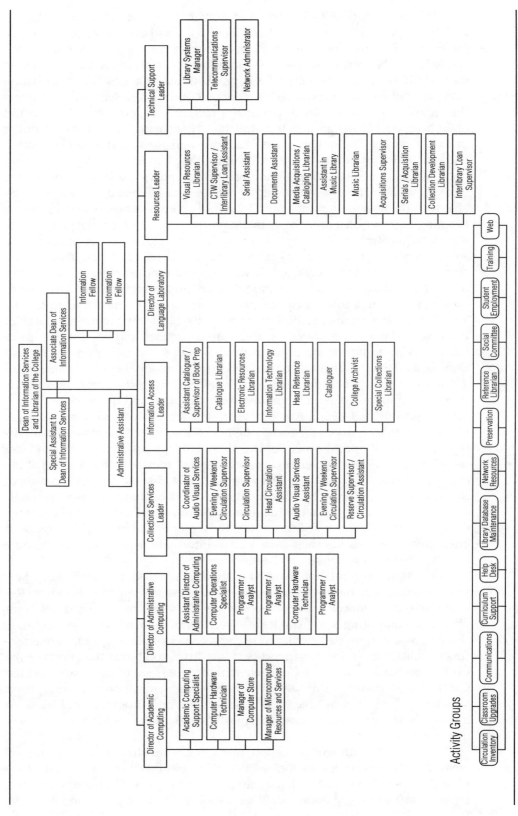

Figure 2 Connecticut College Information Services

Dean of Information Services and Librarian of the College

- Special Assistant to Dean of Information Services
- Associate Dean of Information Services
  - Information Fellow
  - Information Fellow
- Administrative Assistant

Director of Academic Computing
- Academic Computing Support Specialist
- Computer Hardware Technician
- Manager of Computer Store
- Manager of Microcomputer Resources and Services

Director of Administrative Computing
- Assistant Director of Administrative Computing
- Computer Operations Specialist
- Programmer / Analyst
- Programmer / Analyst
- Computer Hardware Technician
- Programmer / Analyst

Collections Services Leader
- Coordinator of Audio Visual Services
- Evening / Weekend Circulation Supervisor
- Circulation Supervisor
- Head Circulation Assistant
- Audio Visual Services Assistant
- Evening / Weekend Circulation Supervisor
- Reserve Supervisor / Circulation Assistant

Information Access Leader
- Assistant Cataloguer / Supervisor of Book Prep
- Catalogue Librarian
- Electronic Resources Librarian
- Information Technology Librarian
- Head Reference Librarian
- Cataloguer
- College Archivist
- Special Collections Librarian

Director of Language Laboratory

Resources Leader
- Visual Resources Librarian
- CTW Supervisor / Interlibrary Loan Assistant
- Serial Assistant
- Documents Assistant
- Media Acquisitions / Cataloging Librarian
- Assistant in Music Library
- Music Librarian
- Acquisitions Supervisor
- Serials / Acquisition Librarian
- Collection Development Librarian
- Interlibrary Loan Supervisor

Technical Support Leader
- Library Systems Manager
- Telecommunications Supervisor
- Network Administrator

Activity Groups

Circulation Inventory | Classroom Upgrades | Communications | Curriculum Support | Help Desk | Library Database Maintenance | Network Resources | Preservation | Reference Librarian | Social Committee | Student Employment | Training | Web

While the work of Task Forces and Activity Groups brought staff together and accomplished much, many traditional barriers between areas remained. Job titles and descriptions, as well as the preconceptions of users and staff, often created these barriers. In many ways, staff members felt uncertainty as to how they would be affected by impending organizational changes. Few Information Services staff had been consulted or apprised of the proposed changes during the Technology Teams strategic planning process. A smoother transition would have been possible if all affected staff had been made part of the planning process from the beginning. Since Academic and Administrative Computing had functioned as completely separate units, they had little history of cooperation that could be used to ease the transition or provide a familiar model for working with the library. Many steps were necessary to make the staff comfortable with the new environment and to identify common talents and strengths. Working together on a daily basis made this possible. To meet the goals established by the Strategic Planning Team for Technology, it was essential that the strengths of each area, including both technical expertise and customer service, be made available to the college as a whole. To accomplish this, the staff determined that Information Services should be an integrated user-centered organization rather than a collection of disparate units under a central management.

During the summer of 1997, two years after the formal merger, the staff of Information Services reviewed existing team structures and began to reformulate teams based not on job titles or old definitions, but rather on service and user needs. Their willingness to plan and implement another set of changes indicated just how much the staff had developed from the early days of the merger. The success of both the library reorganization and the work of various activity groups and task forces demonstrated the positive nature of change. During a holiday party at the end of the 1995 fall semester, library and computing staff stood at opposite sides of the room, talking only with their own team members, and appearing very ill at ease. One staff member later laughed at the experience, comparing it to the first visit with new in-laws. A recent opening of the school year party, on the other hand, could best be described as a neighborhood block party. Though a gradual process, staff recognized over the course of the merger that the more change occurs, the easier it is to predict, manage, and effect. By reformulating their own teams, Information Services staff became agents rather than recipients of change.

The staff reformulation resulted in five teams: Academic Technology Services, Institutional Information Management, Research Support Services, Resources, and Technical Support (see figure 3). No team consisted solely of library or computing staff. The teams were formed based on common tasks, shared goals, and unified service to users. As an example of appropriate cross-functionality, the Research Support Services Team combined the efforts of the College Webmaster with the College Archivist, the Head of Reference, and the Cataloging Librarian. As a direct result of the reorganization of existing team structures, the staff was able to look at services and programs and begin to imagine how their expectations of themselves and others could change to meet new goals.

Concurrent with reorganization of existing team structures, staff from all areas of Information Services formed the Help Line Task Force to design a telephone and e-mail help service for all campus technology needs. Initially, all interested IS staff, including library staff, hardware technicians, telecommunications

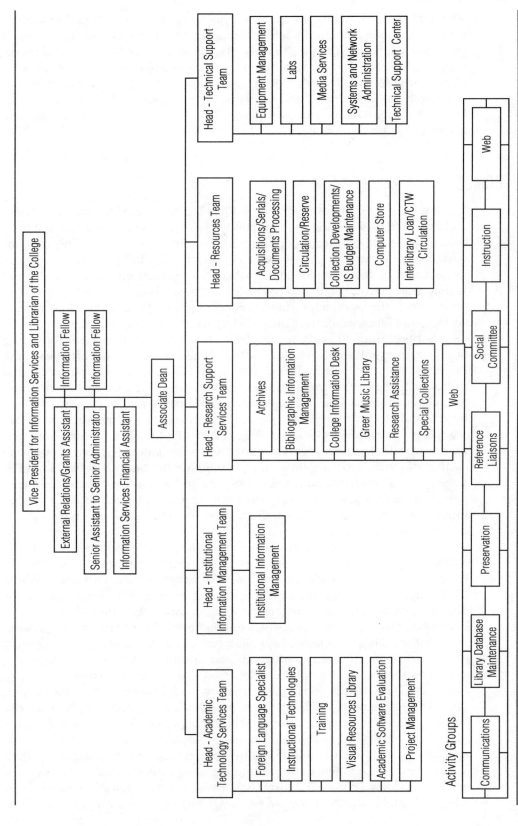

Figure 3 Connecticut College's Information Services Organization 1999

121

staff, and network managers answered phone calls and responded to e-mails from the campus community about computer, telephone, e-mail, and research questions. The willingness of all staff to plan, support, and staff a new and experimental user service was a powerful factor in the establishment of a formal Help Center facility. While today's Help Desk Service is staffed by hardware technicians, software consultants, and students, the initial response to user needs allowed the Information Services Advisory Group the time needed to reallocate resources for this important service.

OUTCOMES

Fulfillment of the goals of the Strategic Planning Team, the introduction of new and improved user services, and the ability to plan for the future would not have been possible without strong support from the college community. The most important local factors for success were the unwavering belief of the college administration in the rationale and goals of the merged environment and the willingness of faculty, staff, and students to embrace change and innovation. The promotion of the Dean of Information Services to Vice President for Information Services and Librarian of the College is testament to this commitment.

Support from all areas of campus manifested itself in successful funding of proposals over the entire history of the merger. Over the past three years, the Priorities, Planning, and Budget Committee (PPBC) awarded 88 percent of the college's strategic planning funds to Information Services and faculty-oriented technology projects. The decisions of the PPBC, composed of faculty, administrators, and students, reflect the belief that technology and research resources are integral components of the college's academic life. The funding has been used to update classrooms for technology and information delivery, to purchase additional multimedia resources, and to upgrade the campus network. At the same time, the Information Services baseline budget has been increased by 20 percent, and five new staff positions have been added. Both internal college funding and external foundation grants for new staff positions have added to the opportunities.

One reason proposals for outside funding have proved successful is that the college has given technology initiatives a high priority within the Development Office for external funding opportunities. Information Services staff has been able to plan and develop projects for outside funding because of the flexibility and cooperation ensured by the merger and reorganization. Funding agencies have been made aware of how a particular funding need fits into the larger strategic goals of the college. In a time of spiraling costs, external funding agencies have been increasingly attracted to situations and institutions where technology and associated services are thoughtfully delivered and supported across constituencies. This has resulted in seven major grants in the first three years of the merger.

An important example of the administration's support of goals of the strategic plan is the college's investment in PeopleSoft. The Technology Planning Team established as a goal the need to "improve communications and information transfer across administrative offices, and between administrative and academic departments, by encouraging more extensive use of the network and by developing coherent information management systems." PeopleSoft, an advanced, highly flexible software suite, was chosen not only as a replacement for an aging administrative computing system, but as a system that would transform the way the campus accessed, managed, and used information. The former systems librarian manages the project. Prior to the PeopleSoft implementation, he had been head of the Network Services Team, overseeing the campus technology infrastructure. The management of library information systems was formerly seen as a subset of the larger data management profession. In this new environment, professionals who understand the complex, mediated relationship between users and content are able to extend that understanding to campus-wide information solutions that are far beyond the scope of conventional library services. This ability, along with the strong technical skills, will be the hallmark of the new information profession.

As demonstration of its belief in the forging of a new profession, the Administration lent support to the creation of the Information Fellows Program. Committed to the thoughtful integration of technology into the curriculum, this unique post-graduate program is designed for recent graduates of master's programs in library/information science, computer science, or instructional technology. The president funded the pilot program and committed to pursuing grant support. Funded in 1996 by the Charles E. Culpeper Foundation, each Fellow is selected for a two-year term and reports to the Vice President for Information Services. The Fellow works closely with faculty, students, and Information Services staff incorporating technology into the curriculum and participates in campus-wide technology planning. Each Fellow is also given the opportunity to explore the possibilities of emerging technologies and their application to learning and research. This unique opportunity is designed to offer a set of experiences that prepares individuals to contribute to the new, merged profession.

A central goal of the Technology Planning Team was the introduction of new services "guided by the perspectives of users." These new services, identified by both Information Services staff and other campus constituencies, ranged from campus-wide technology instruction to digital media development. To plan, implement, and evaluate new services as varied as the computer lease program, Help Desk Services, and the Advanced Technology Lab, existing staff extended their understanding of their capabilities and responsibilities. During the opening day of the fall semester, the campus computer store was deluged with students picking up computers and requesting network connections. A number of staff from across IS pitched in to help set up, deliver, and provide instruction on new laptops and desktops. At one point, the Serials Librarian went with the Network Technician to help activate ethernet jacks in student dorms. Skills such as content management, instruction, customer service, technology troubleshooting, risk-taking, and community outreach are all integral parts of the daily professional lives of Information Services staff. Practicing these skills allows staff to envision, plan, and implement new services and facilities. The size, flexibility, and scope of responsibilities within the new organization have given current staff new opportunities for promotion and professional development, all within the context of the new profession. In the most recent six months, six staff members from nearly every team were promoted to positions of greater responsibility. The new merged environment has aided in recruitment of new staff at a time when many institutions are struggling to attract outstanding staff with technology skills. Whether seeking and hiring candidates with MLS, programming, or management credentials, an understanding of the convergence of data, delivery, support, and training is an essential characteristic.

The IS staff had exactly this characteristic in mind when they identified the need for comprehensive coordination of instruction across Information Services. In response to the recommendation of the Training and Technology Task Force, the new Technology Instruction Coordinator designs and implements an evolving, responsive technology and resource instruction program, utilizing staff across the five teams. Reflecting the merged environment of computing and libraries, training is offered in various areas such as bibliographic instruction, PeopleSoft training for campus-wide data management, a technology seminar series for faculty, and software instruction. This characteristic is also at the heart of the Academic Software Evaluator position, which provides expert advice, instruction, and technical support to faculty using academic software and other instructional materials for teaching and research. This three-year position is funded by a foundation grant. Through software workshops and a Web site, successful faculty use of software will be shared across the college and with peers at other institutions.

Just as staff responsibilities now reflect the merged environment, so do the public facilities managed by Information Services. All public campus workstations combine the full functionality of traditional computer labs with library research services. From a single desktop, faculty, students, and staff can access the broad range of tools necessary for scholarship and research, including general productivity software, discipline-specific software, media production tools, and all digital library resources. The bulk of these resources is also available from faculty offices and student dorm rooms. The primary public computing facility is located on the first floor of the library, adjacent to both research and technical assistance. Reference librarians are available to assist in research and resource instruction in concert with workstation consultants, who are stationed at the circulation desk and assist users with software instruction and workstation troubleshooting.

As the next step in the convergence of workstation tools and research materials, the IBM Digital Library and VideoCharger system provides desktop access to the full range of academic multimedia materials available on campus. Previously, digitized course materials were haphazardly stored on a variety of campus servers. From a Web interface, students and faculty select multimedia materials via keyword, author, and title searches, and stream materials directly to their desktops. Funded by the Keel Foundation, this system marries technological expertise and the management of intellectual content, allowing students and faculty the ability to integrate digitized academic course materials easily into their study and research.

The materials acquisitions and budgeting process also takes advantage of the merged environment by combining periodicals, books, CD-ROMs, videos, and software into a flexible pool of resources for individual departments. Treating all resources with equity regardless of format ensures budget flexibility and faculty choice. The faculty departments have a variety of options, and they are encouraged to look at the combined resources and new media options as opportunities to convey information in new ways and enhance the teaching and learning experience.

DEFINING GOALS FOR THE FUTURE

The Charles E. Shain Library, designed more than two decades ago when the information needs of the new century could not have been anticipated, is near capacity. At the same time, user services and demands and staff requirements are fast outstripping computing and network support facilities. In the fall of 1998, a team similar to the Strategic Planning Team for Technology began to plan a model facility for the twenty-first century, with the goal of creating a state-of-the-art information and technology center designed to meet campus needs well into the future. This new facility is a natural extension of the Information Services merger and will further underscore the common mission of all areas by uniting services and staff in one facility. The team's charge explicitly states that this important step toward the future

> be complemented by an equally strong regard for the history and character of Connecticut College and that it will enhance the central role of the library on the campus and in the life of the College. Therefore equal consideration is being given to recommendations for expanding special collections and archives space and plans for preserving the collections currently housed in Shain and Greer Music Library.

Part of the challenge of this project, as with the merger itself, is thinking anew about the ways people, services, and facilities remain at the core of student learning, as they always have in the liberal arts tradition. Those managing any merged environment and the new information profession face similar challenges. Recognition must be given to the importance of attending to the needs of users while planning for the institution's technology future with an eye to preserving the past.

While local factors made the successful merged environment at Connecticut College possible, there are also universal factors that enable success at any institution. Whether libraries and computing are merged under a single management structure or have a productive, collegial working relationship as separate units is not the determining factor for success. The convergence of content and technology inevitably will change user needs and expectations. Meeting these needs and expectations in a world where rapid change is the norm requires both institutional support and individual skills. The common goals of computing and libraries and the willingness of the staff both to embrace and lead change create an environment for success. While organizational structures must be agile enough to change according to user needs and expectations, information professionals must be prepared to work informally across units, reimagine their responsibilities, and provide leadership and expertise.

Almost four years ago when the technology planning team issued its call to service, uniting libraries and computing, the challenges presented seemed almost impossible to realize. With support from the campus community and the hard work of staff, Connecticut College transformed the traditional organizational chart and created a new merged environment where tradition, innovation, and service guide Information Services.

CHAPTER THIRTEEN

Toward a Model of Integrated Computer and Library Services

JOHN N. OLSGAARD
GEORGE D. TERRY

Economists have often described paper money as "a concept, backed by an idea." In other words, paper money is of value (or not of value) if everyone agrees that it is worth something; otherwise it is just so much paper printed with funny colored ink. Institutional change to instill unity of purpose and mission is much the same as paper money in the sense that everyone agrees that it is a concept of intrinsic value, but actually creating value requires more than changing "inks." It is often exceptionally difficult to bring the change to fruition.

In this paper the authors will examine the rationale for merging library and computer services in an academic environment (the "concept"); the common problems that many academic institutions have experienced in attempting this type of merger (the "idea"); and the mechanisms that will promote the successful merger (the "value").[1] In doing so, the authors will draw extensively on the experience of the merger of these services at the University of South Carolina.

THE CONCEPT

Over the past two decades there has been much discussion in the professional literature focusing on the convergence of technology and library services; one of the earliest and most well known being written by F. W. Lancaster in the early 1980s.[2] Most of the materials have dealt with specific issues, such as the innovative utilization of technology within the library setting. However, in recent years more attention has been placed on the trend within universities of placing computer services within the same organizational structure as the library and on how these two organizations can work together for the benefit of their institution. Since both operate in an increasingly digital environment, some observers believe it logical that a unity of purpose could be achieved through an organizational merger of the entities.[3]

What many academic institutions have discovered, however, is that while computer services and library services both function in a digital format, their respective organizational missions and philosophies tend to be radically different. Computer services units on most campuses had their beginnings in developing administrative processes and servicing high-end research projects. Since they worked in a relatively closed environment at the fringe of the academic enterprise and had a monopoly on the digital operations with a variety of users, many computer services units never developed a true broad-based customer relations model. For example, the staff at one computer services unit appeared rather proud of a poster in their building that read: "This isn't Burger King, you take it the way we give it to you, or you don't get any." A nice way of describing this environment within higher education's computer services during the 1970s and early 1980s would be "end-user hostile."

Academic library service units, on the other hand, have long had a strong tradition of user services. At better campuses, most faculty members and administrators considered libraries in the mainstream of the institution's academic mission. During the 1970s many campuses gave librarians faculty status. The beginning of the 1980s witnessed academic libraries that tended to be user friendly but often not technologically advanced.[4]

To write that the last half of the 1980s and the 1990s brought a wave of technological change is both a cliché and an understatement. The advent of microcomputers, LANs, WANs, the Internet, and universal high-speed networks on campuses brought those who serviced computer operations forcibly (some would say reluctantly) into the customer care business. In a similar fashion, the onslaught of electronic information resources such as online catalogs, circulation, online searching of databases, and CD-ROM towers brought librarians forcibly (and in some cases, reluctantly) into the world of technology. Given this environment as well as service philosophies that seemed to be at opposite ends of the continuum, the marriage of computer services and library services might appear doomed from the outset.

THE IDEA

Many academic institutions defined the merger of library and computer services as either hiring a chief information officer (CIO) and placing that person in charge of both organizations, or, alternatively, designating the director of one of the two organizational entities as the new CIO.[5] In a recent publication by Arnold Hirshon, the author states that despite the number of institutions that have united computing and library services within the same organizational structure, 71 percent "retained separate library and computing directors who now report to the CIO rather than the provost." More interestingly, he observed that 17 percent of the institutions responding to his survey stated that they had "a fully integrated organizational structure but that after close study, the previously existing subordinate organizations were essentially retained." His most telling conclusion, however, is that "most integrated operations today still reflect a strong library and computing lineage."[6] In other words, despite efforts to merge these two areas, both of which increasingly share common concerns over communication technologies, the unification does not go much deeper than the top management team.

Over the past several years, the validity of Hirshon's findings have become more apparent. As information professionals had the opportunity to observe organizational structures that relate to information technology, they have been struck by the tendency of central university administrators and CIOs throughout higher education to acknowledge only minimally the opportunity and potential that a fully integrated organization can provide to an institution.[7] Part of the reason for this approach to merge is that it follows a typical top-down approach to higher education administration. That is, the president or chief academic officer "fixes" the problem by moving the boxes around, or by creating a new box on the academic organizational chart, and then walks away from the process. This benign neglect exists partly because presidents and provosts have a great many other problems to address. They have little time for anything but minimal input into any long-term process. It is also because technology is not an area in which they usually have much expertise. In describing this process, some might use the negative cliché that central academic administrators are adept at "moving the deck chairs around on the Titanic." Probably a more appropriate description is that presidents and provosts take a "clockmaker" approach to their institution, meaning that they build an organizational clock, wind it up, and expect that it will start telling time. If the organizational creation they have forged does not function correctly, they simply build a new clock (i.e., they move the organizational boxes around into a different pattern). At the University of South Carolina, the organizational history of computer and library services, and the top-down decision to merge these entities, typified the above profile of the experience at many institutions.[8]

THE UNIVERSITY OF SOUTH CAROLINA EXPERIENCE

The University of South Carolina has eight campuses throughout the state serving approximately 37,000 students, with the flagship campus located in Columbia. The Columbia campus includes approximately 25,000 students (15,000 undergraduate and 10,000 graduate students), and 1,100 full-time faculty members. The Columbia campus is a comprehensive Carnegie Research II institution with a total annual revenue budget of approximately $400 million (including state appropriations, tuition, funded research, and gifts). Over sixty doctoral degree programs are offered on the Columbia campus and professional degrees are offered in law, medicine, and pharmacy.

Computer Services

In 1990, computer services at the University of South Carolina found itself isolated from much of the campus. This resulted from its historical development and perceived mission at that time. Computer services had assumed primarily an administrative role within the university, providing support for business, finance, and human resources networks and developing a comprehensive student information system. Because of the "homegrown" nature of many of the systems in use, computer services faced a large backlog of work in these areas. Reliance on a mainframe structure that had the unfortunate characteristics of combining outdated technology with an institutionally created system of software resulted in computer services finding itself almost strangled by the demands coming from administrative units across campus. The university also did not have a complete campus electronic network. Given the administrative vacuum, most of the individual colleges began to develop, with the help of a student technology fee, their own Local Area Networks (LANs) and technical support staff. Users rarely called upon computer services for assistance, nor did computer services usually offer any.

A compelling indication of the severity of the situation came from an unintended source. In the late 1980s, the university commissioned its first consultants' report to examine the state of technology on campus. The firm of Coopers & Lybrand studied, among other things, the utilization of technology for administrative purposes.[9] They graphically pointed out the deficiencies in administrative systems, describing some as "cumbersome" and "outdated." With the publication of this report in 1990, many found it obvious that computer services had become increasingly isolated from the university's educational mission. An institutional self-study completed in 1991 underscored this fact.[10] The authors of this report recommended strongly that computer services expand its activities to include more of the academic mission of the university. In the fall of 1993, after an extensive review of computer services' operations at the university, TASCOR, a second private consulting firm, recommended some dramatic changes to computing on campus. The initial report of the committee recommended that much of the central computing operations be performed by outside contractors. To begin with, they suggested that the initial networking of the campus be completed by outside contractors.[11]

The findings of other campus groups seemed to support this extreme position. In May, earlier that same year, the university had issued an internal planning report that looked at every academic and administrative unit on campus to determine how funds could be shifted away from administrative units to further enhance academic goals.[12] This report, which was presented to the president, was highly critical of computer services. In part, the report stated that the department "appears to be reluctant to take an aggressive role in completing the campus network or accelerating the inevitable decentralization of administrative and academic systems." The authors also recommended that the center's recurring budget be reduced by 12 percent and that these funds be reallocated to academic interests.[13] Obviously, there was a need to make a change in the way computer services operated.

Library Services

At the same time that computer services had been falling into such disrepute, the library system at USC had begun a significant expansion of its services. As with many academic libraries, technological innovations made possible many of these new services. The library, as a member of the Association of Research Libraries (ARL), contained extensive holdings built through traditional collection management procedures. However, with some rare exceptions, library services had not taken advantage of technological advances.[14] In the second half of the 1980s the environment began slowly to change. For example, the library readied itself for the eventual implementation of an online catalog system by having the entire collection prepared for conversion to AACR2 MARC format records. In 1988, the university mandated that the library complete the installation of an online system throughout the entire university system in just one year. This mandate necessitated the development of a close working relationship with computer services. The administrative leadership of computer services assigned a team of individuals from that unit specifically to the project, and together the library and computer services completed the online system in one year and sixteen days. This effort brought several individuals from the library and computer services into a close working relationship. In fact, the library hired from computer services a library automation administrator, whose job dealt specifically with issues relating to the online system and its functions on all of the campuses.[15]

The library took another significant step when it transformed a large and somewhat obsolete reserve reading room into the first of the university's public computing labs. The idea for the lab originated from conversations between the vice provost of computing and the vice provost and dean of libraries. They both shared a concern about the many students unable to gain access to one of the academic unit labs across campus. Students who had not declared a major, or who had classes in several academic disciplines and were unable, because of their lack of major, to use one or the other of the discipline-specific labs, particularly had this problem.

THE MERGER

Because of these early indications of successful collaboration, and with the specter of outsourcing looming as the price for failure, the provost decided to create a new university division by merging computer services and the library system. The provost also added the office of distance education and instructional support, a unit charged with using various digital technologies to support on-campus classroom instruction and with a long and successful history of telecommunication instruction off-campus, to this new organizational entity. Thus, in 1993 the Division of Library and Information Systems was born.[16] The vice provost and dean of libraries became the supervisor of this new division. The president and the provost granted his request that he be given a year to straighten out the problems that had been identified by the various studies.

The merger, however, proved to be not a universally accepted solution. In December of that year, several of his senior administrators advised the president that computing services at USC could not be salvaged and would best be served by outsourcing this service. If the university truly wanted a cohesive networked system, conducive to the growth and development of information technology, technological priorities would have to be set institutionally. The decentralization that had developed in the preceding years needed to be reexamined, since many local unit activities seemed counterproductive in broader institutional terms. Ultimately, the president decided that computer services would not be outsourced but would be given a last opportunity to succeed.

The completion of the campus electronic network system was established as the initial university-wide objective set forth for the division. This took approximately eighteen months. At the same time, the library began to work more closely with computer services on a number of other initiatives. Among the first of these initiatives included installing approximately forty workstations devoted to accessing CD-ROM databases and making online materials available across campus. The vice provost also charged computer services with changing both its image and philosophy of customer relations. The installation of a central "service station" strategically located in the lobby of the computer services building served as the first step in this process. The service station offered access to a broad range of assistance and information through a single telephone number, thereby eliminating the frustrations that developed when staff referred individuals from one office to another. Computer services intended this operation to remove the confusion caused when people who had problems called for advice the one employee they personally knew at computer services. It also served to enhance customer service communication and quality control.[17]

Another program objective involved department supervisors within computer services looking into changing the way they managed administrative computing services. Almost immediately after creation of the division, representatives from this unit, looking for ways to expedite the creation of data warehouses and a strategy that would enable them to move away from legacy technology, met with various consultants across the country. After a painstaking process of analysis and planning, the first modules of a new array of administrative software systems are currently being installed and should be in place during the calendar year 1999.

By 1994, less than a year after the creation of the Division of Libraries and Information Systems, the division had begun methodically to formulate its first strategic plan.[18] One of the most important goals of the planning process was to begin to integrate as well as capitalize on the value of each entity within the division. For example, the library quickly began to recognize the value of the campus-wide network and the network's ability to assist faculty research and student projects. The planning process also proved valuable in ways that had not been foreseen. Individuals from computer services, the library, and distance education and instructional support became colleagues for the first time. As they worked together in close collaboration, many things began to change. First and foremost came the realization that all of these entities truly had much in common and that they could provide needed support for each other. Since 1993, the division has formulated a number of intradivisional programs to combine the expertise of all its subunits. The four overall objectives of these intradivisional programs were to infuse technical expertise into the library services structure; to infuse customer service environment into the computer services structure; to save money through economy-of-scale consolidation of administrative services throughout the division; and to build a division-wide sense of unity of purpose. Several examples of programs designed to meet these objectives follow. A common personnel office within the division was created to serve the over 450 faculty and staff located in thirteen buildings across the campus. In a similar vein, a division business office intended to bring centrality to the organization was also created. These decisions resulted in savings of more than one hundred thousand dollars in duplicated services across the division.

The division learned the importance of simply bringing people and expertise together physically. Emulating a program initiated at the University of Tennessee, the division began to send not only faculty and staff from the library to visit other campuses in the Southeast but also included individuals from computing services and distance education. These visits had a twofold purpose. First, our employees could measure the accomplishments at other institutions against our current practice. We assigned each member of the trip a checklist of things to analyze on their return and then to report to the entire division the following week. These analyses identified deficiencies that we needed to consider. However, the fact that faculty and staff from computer services, the library, and distance education got to know each other on a personal as well as professional basis proved the biggest benefit. The benefits of these cross-divisional personal relationships formed during the visits cannot be overestimated. They quickly dispelled stereotypes among the personnel in the library, computer services, and distance education. In short, the division became a team. The realization at the individual level that these entities truly had much in common enhanced this sense of teamwork.

The vice provost appointed the new head of staff training at computer services, who also has a library degree, to a faculty position, and put her in charge of the liaison between computer services and the library. The vice provost also abolished the library's computer systems unit in favor of direct technical support from computer services. Members of the library still staffed the computer lab within the library, but computer services had a distinct presence within the facility. In addition, consultants working at computer services were moved to the library's public services area to allow them more visibility and people better access to these consultants. Division-wide standing committees, with members from all units, were formed to engender a spirit of loyalty for and identity with the division as a unit.

The creation of a division charged with meeting the information needs of the entire campus also necessitated the adoption of a new intradivisional organizational structure. Reorganizing the division to create eight unit managers instead of the former twenty simplified the reporting structure. In addition, four staff officers, including personnel and business supervisors, now report directly to the vice provost and dean of libraries to facilitate division-wide communication.[19] In addition to the change in organizational structure, we changed the process of work prioritization. All of the division managers were formally challenged to take stock of what they did in terms of service to the university, to reexamine their missions, and to identify obsolete or inefficient activities. The managers also looked for any enhancements they believed they should initiate into their current programs. This process, which took approximately three months to complete, resulted in the reconsideration and reassignment of many responsibilities.[20] Some of the decisions did not work as well as we had anticipated. Some, however, became true models of enhanced service to the university community.

The consolidation of administrative services across the division and the utilization of in-house technical expertise have realized a cost benefit for the division and for the university as a whole. However, these cost benefits are of the hardest variety to document because they are savings of money that did not have to be spent, rather than a reduction in workload. For example, rather than spending thirteen million dollars to outsource the networking of the campus, the university spent three million dollars (and pulled some fifteen miles of fiber optic cable) to complete the process. This savings of ten million dollars seemed only an expenditure of three million.

The library has embraced computer technology with greater frequency as one of the many tools to provide increased services to the faculty, staff, and students at the university. With the help of computer services, the library currently has well over 300 workstations providing more than 61,000 serial titles, some in full text and others in title only. Computer services has installed library multimedia classrooms that are utilized by our nationally recognized University 101 program to introduce students to information technology and the Internet. Computer services has also worked hard to provide remote access to library materials for faculty, staff, and students. Access to materials is available on every workstation throughout the campus, including each dormitory room.

At the University of South Carolina several of the overall objectives of the merger have been met, and tremendous strides are being made with others. The consolidation of the library and computer services benefited both entities. Librarians at the University of South Carolina have begun with new interest to look at the beneficial prospects of technological change. Computer technicians have begun to learn to communicate more effectively actions and activities that affect the entire technological infrastructure of the campus. Service has now become a more important aspect of the priorities and goals of computer services.

Getting the word out about these successes has been problematic. The library system over the past few years has been extremely successful in publicizing its various services and achievements. Computer services, however, lagged behind in terms of its efforts to provide the university with updates about new and enhanced services. Because of this, publication activity regarding new services and activities throughout the division have also been consolidated. In addition, new procedures have been developed to immediately notify the university community of events that might affect service.

One of the basic tenets of any strategic planning system is to constantly identify where the organization is and whether it is going in the correct direction. In November 1997, a group of consultants from Association of American Universities (AAU) institutions visited the university to facilitate this discussion.[21] Headed by Jay Lucker, former dean of libraries at MIT, the team included William Crowe, vice chancellor for information services and dean of libraries at the University of Kansas, and Naomi Schmidt, head of technology at MIT. Lucker observed that we had done an excellent job of integrating our technological services and functions and that it was probably one of the best in the country. But he also cautioned that the division had not completed the integration, and that this process needed to constantly renew itself in the face of changing technology. The division has taken this advice to heart and continues to look for additional ways to capitalize upon the collaboration between library services and computing. Information technology is changing every day and to ignore this change is to ignore reality.

THE VALUE

The model developed at the University of South Carolina is a good example of how a fully integrated system can create positive results. Over the past several years this integration has resulted in more productivity than would be the situation if either entity had worked with only partial support, let alone in full isolation, from the other. In other words, an organizational Hegalian synthesis can occur. A merger can work, but it requires more than a change in reporting line and a new name.

Much has been learned, and the learning process continues with the successful merger of computer services and library services. Outlined below are several characteristics that must be present for mergers to succeed.

A merger must have the strong support of the central university administration (top-down support). This support is essential particularly during the first eventful years of the merger when the changes may seem most threatening to individuals within the merged units and to other organizational units within the institution. People are remarkably adept at gauging the depth of support a president or a provost has for a program, and any indication of doubt on their part will have disastrous effects on the merger.

A process that encourages employee participation from within the division must begin soon after the consolidation (bottom-up support). A formal strategic planning process is a good place to start, but the key is to get members of each subunit working together on defining common goals. This will not only promote a divisional identity, but will also give employees the belief that they are at least partially in control of their future.

Similarly, common functions of the various subunits must merge into division-wide functions (side-to-side support). This will not only promote a divisional identity, but will provide financial savings to support other aspects of the merger.

The newly merged organization should also constantly seek advice from outside the institution and analyze the best practices of other universities for ideas and successful procedures.

This is a world in which a five-year technology plan can be considered an oxymoron. Emerging technology must be examined and reexamined in order to chart an organizational course in an ever-changing environment.

Likewise, the merged organizational unit and the individuals within it must be prepared to repeatedly realign the organizational structure in order to meet the technical and information services needs of the greater institution.

Finally, both campus computing and libraries must have a mutual system of administrative support as well as a clearly enunciated and understood mission.

Like paper money, the "concept" of the merger of computer and library services is reasonably well understood. The "idea" of the merger is progressing well in many different ways. The "value" is just now beginning to be recognized in realistic ways as the benefits of mergers start to bear fruit. What must always be remembered is that merging these services at any institution will always be a work in progress, a labor that may be understood but that will never be fully completed.

CONCLUSION

Our experience over the past five years has provided one important lesson. If units with complementary missions are to work together, there needs to be administrative support and a commitment from the individuals working in the units to make this integration successful. Some of the changes made in this merger have been unsuccessful, but for the most part the changes we have implemented to create this division have been most successful. We now have a division that has its own identity with an emphasis on service and the best utilization of information technology. Although there is much work left to do, the realization that we must continue to adapt our organizational structure to fit current trends is at the bedrock of our management philosophy. As technology changes, so do libraries and their willingness to embrace those changes. We are proud of what the division has accomplished over the past five years and optimistic in terms of our future.

NOTES Both authors wish to acknowledge the assistance of Don Kaplan in formatting the notes accompanying this essay.

1. The debate over consolidating libraries and computing has been a source of much discussion over the past fifteen years. The publication of *Libraries & Computing Centers: Issues of Mutual Concern,* published as an insert in the *Journal of Academic Librarianship,* for example, was established in March 1997 (and discontinued the next year) to allow librarians and members of the information technology world to debate this topic in an open forum.

2. F. Wildred Lancaster, *Libraries and Librarians in an Age of Electronics* (Arlington, Va.: Information Resources Pr., 1982).

3. For example, see Joan Betchel, "Libraries and Computing Centers Working Together: A Success Story" (*Libraries & Computing Centers: Issues of Mutual Concern* 7), an insert in *Journal of Academic Librarianship* 14 (March 1988): 34a-34b+; and William H. Sanders, "Libraries and Computing Centers: A Marriage in the Making?" in *Information Technology, It's for Everyone!: Proceedings of the LITA Third National Conference, Library and Information Technology Association, Denver, September 13-16, 1992,* ed. Thomas W. Leonhardt (Chicago: America Library Assn., 1992), 196-197.

4. We, of course, are not making blanket generalizations about either unit or profession in university environments.

5. See, for example, Carole Barone, "Planning and the Changing Role of the CIO in Higher Education," *Information Management* (summer 1989) 24; and Linda H. Fleit, "Chief Information Officers: New and Continuing Issues-Part 2," *Edutech Report* (July 1998), 4-5.

6. Arnold Hirshon, *Integrating Computing and Library Services: An Administrative Planning and Implementation Guide for Information Sources,* CAUSE Professional Paper Series 18 (Boulder, Colo.: CAUSE, 1998), passim.

7. An exception to this tendency is the work by Timothy J. Foley, "Combining Libraries, Computing, Telecommunications: A Work in Progress" (a paper presented at the ACM SIGUCCS Users Services Conference 24, Monterey, Calif., November 1997); also available from http://www.lehigh.edu/tjf0/public/www-data/acm97/acm97.htm. Accessed 12 November 1998.

8. There are many examples where colleges and universities have attempted to consolidate information technology and computing and libraries into one organization. Among the most notable are the University of Kentucky, University of California - Berkeley, and Vanderbilt University. See also "Relationships between Libraries and Computer Centers at Liberal Arts Colleges," *Research Brief Two* (Washington, D.C.: Council on Library and Information Resources, 1997). Available from http://www.clir.org/pubs/research/rb2.html. Accessed 15 November 1998.

9. Coopers & Lybrand, "A Study of the University of South Carolina Direct Charges for Services Study, Exposure Draft" (Columbia, S.C.: Coopers & Lybrand, 1990). This report included the interesting suggestion that computer services was underfunded to carry out administrative computing for the university.

10. "Institutional Self-Study for Reaffirmation of Accreditation by the Southern Association of Colleges and Schools" (Columbia, S.C.: Office of Institutional Planning, 1991).

11. "TASCOR Report" (Durham, N.C.: TASCOR, 1993).

12. "Investing in USC's Future: Report to the President" (Columbia, S.C.: Future Committee, University of South Carolina, 1993).
13. Ibid., 119-123.
14. A notable exception to this was the inauguration of the country's first online circulation system developed internally with our system's staff at the University of South Carolina-USC Circulation System, January 1974.
15. This individual, Patrick Calhoun, played a major role in the initial stages of integrating computing technology with library information resources at the university. He now holds the faculty position of Director of Academic Technologies.
16. University of South Carolina, Office of the Provost, "Proposal: Creation of a Vice Provost for Information Systems," internal memorandum, August 1993.
17. "Models of Service," Computer services internal document, 1995. In addition to this document, which looked at all aspects of services provided the university from computer services, there were a number of specialized services in 1994 and 1995 that dealt with the entire issue of a service operation.
18. George Terry, "Strategic Planning," internal memorandum, 20 September 1994. The division's first strategic plan accomplished several short-term and long-term goals. It also poised the division to have one of the most comprehensive planning documents on campus. The plan has been updated every year under the guidance of what is called a "monitoring committee." Every member of the division is informed as to the progress in achieving the action plans posed in the original document. We have embarked this year on a new strategic plan that commits us to integrate even more fully our goods and services.
19. Task Force on Personnel, Division of Libraries and Information Systems, "Report" (Columbia, S.C.: Division of Libraries and Information Systems, 1995); and Task Force on Business Practices, Division of Libraries and Information Systems, "Report" (Columbia, S.C.: Division of Libraries and Information Systems, 1995).
20. The models of service concept was developed during the process of our strategic planning in 1994-95. The concept was utilized throughout the division to look literally at every aspect of the services provided and to question the necessity of continuing various services as well the advisability of initiating new ones. The process stimulated debate and discussion about the purpose of the division.
21. Consultants to J. D. Odom, "Review of Division of Libraries and Information Systems," internal memorandum, January 6, 1998.

CHAPTER FOURTEEN

Wake Forest University

Pioneers and Partners

RHODA K. CHANNING
JAY L. DOMINICK

Both the organizational structure and the environment of Wake Forest University are highly unusual and, in some aspects, unique. In less than five years, the university has moved from a technologically challenged position to one of highly visible leadership in the provision and application of educational technology. This new commitment is among the factors that have propelled the university to the top of the national rankings and a role as a model for dozens of U.S. and foreign colleges and universities attempting to move in the same direction.[1] The university's strategic commitment to information technology, including its partnership with IBM, has radically changed perceptions of the institution. Many now see Wake Forest as a pioneer among liberal arts universities and have sent representatives to hear from those involved in the planning and implementation of this major change.[2]

The Reynolds Library and the Information Systems Department have moved from a customer-supplier relationship to a highly interactive partnership as part of Wake Forest's commitment to provide laptop computers to all undergraduates. The undergraduate technology plan, the recent technology initiative, includes creation of a steering committee for year-round technology planning. A faculty committee on information technology also offers input into decision making. Both the head of information systems, who is an assistant vice president and CIO, and the director of the library are members of these groups. In response to the new challenges, information systems (IS) recently has more than doubled its staff, from twenty-eight to fifty-eight, and has moved to a new building. The library, with an addition completed in 1992, has added five new slots, including three paraprofessional technical support positions related to the new initiative. Both IS and the library have undergone major organizational changes and continue to evolve with the needs of the university. The library is responsible for coordinating student training, development of training materials, and some staff and faculty training, and it plays an active role, in conjunction with IS, in the testing of software. Information systems is responsible for the support of Wake Forest community users and the design of the standard software suite to facilitate access to information resources, including those provided by the library. The two units also have the major responsibilities that characterize computing centers and libraries in all academic environments. In addition to the collaboration detailed above, which the technological initiative required, IS and the library have worked together on the selection of the next generation integrated library system. Although the cultures of the two units are very different and there is the inevitable tension from time to time, the present system has produced a high degree of collaboration and excitement about the future.

UNUSUAL REPORTING STRUCTURE

Wake Forest's claim to uniqueness is related to its reporting structure. The Director of the Library reports to the Vice President for Student Life and Instructional Resources, and the CIO reports to the Vice President for Finance and Administration. Neither reports to the chief academic officer, the Provost. In the traditional sense, there is no head of academic computing. In our decentralized computing environment, academic computing is not part of IS but consists of some seventeen academic computing specialists (ACS) who report to department chairs, and ultimately to the Dean of the College, who in turn reports to the Provost. The academic computing specialists are part of the technology partnership in that they "owe" 5 percent of their time to the library director to assist in computer orientation, and they serve on all the major technology committees. They also work with the library on digitizing initiatives and are often paired with librarians in subject-focused classroom instruction. The growth in IS, referred to earlier, does not include the creation of the seventeen ACS positions. These positions came about as a recommendation from the academic computing advisory committee, which included faculty and both directors.[3] Other partners in the technology initiative include the resident technology advisors, who are students who assist in training and support for other students in the residence halls, and STARS, or student technology advisors. STARS help faculty in courseware development on a one-to-one basis and also intern in the library multimedia lab, assisting students with their more sophisticated projects. These student experts report to IS but, as noted, contribute to the library's efforts as well.

INNOVATIVE TECHNOLOGY STRATEGY

The Wake Forest faculty voted overwhelmingly to support the plan that included entering into a long-term agreement with IBM to provide first-year students, beginning with the class of 2000, with ThinkPads fully loaded with powerful standardized software customized for the university.[4] Wake Forest has a strategy that involves supporting the standard hardware and software fully but providing no central support for other software. This customization allows a very tight integration of the technology with information resources at the university. For instance, the Windows start menu includes direct links to the library catalog, a very wide array of electronic resources, computer-based training courses, and the library CD-ROM network. The tight integration of the library resources with the standard computing environment helps assure the easiest possible access from constituents anywhere on the campus network and, through proxy servers, to our community off campus. Special software known as the Wake Forest template allows faculty and students in a class to interact in a secure environment with each other and with digitized materials. Other special software, such as SPSS and Maple, is available from a server and installed only if needed for academic work. The network is ubiquitous on campus with Ethernet in every classroom, in a combination of hardwired and wireless configurations, and simultaneous access available in every student room, as well as common spaces like the library and student center.

The technology is kept current for both students and faculty. The student laptops are turned in at the beginning of the junior year and replaced with the latest laptop and the new software load. When students graduate, they keep their by-then-two-year-old computers. Faculty and library trainers are on the same two-year cycle. ACS get new machines annually. Beginning in 1997, all students with ThinkPads also received color printers that are expected to last four years.

COLLABORATION ON CAMPUS

Although an explanation of the connection between the relationships among IS, the library, and the other participants in the technology picture at Wake Forest may seem a non sequitur after the description of the program, it is in fact very important. The scale and ramifications of the undergraduate technology plan require that all segments of the campus work closely together. Each year questions arise: what hardware configurations should we choose for our laptop and for our desktop machines; what changes are needed in the operating system or the software; what new links are needed? Wake Forest has refined a process using the committee on information technology for evaluating options and setting priorities with input from the faculty, IS, the library director, and others including our vendor partners. We determine what the load will include and what it will look like, and IS staff, library staff, and ACS work each spring to test everything from the modem card to the dialers, drivers, and links to assure that they operate smoothly. Only by testing thoroughly can we discover problems in time to find solutions before the freshmen arrive! Just as the library sends staff to assist in the testing, so IS sends staff to provide technical support during the training. We have developed a training and support loop in which the support staff from IS provide feedback on problems reported to the help desk, which then are translated into elements to be dealt with in training. Trainers (library staff) identify parts of the software or the processes that need refinement, and this information is fed back to IS. The training task force, which meets weekly all year, includes all the shareholders in training including library trainers, IS staff, ACS and student representatives.

Involvement in the technology initiative demands a lot of time from all players. We offer an option involving the early shipment of the ThinkPad to incoming students before they arrive on campus. Nevertheless, in the two days before classes start we are faced with the challenge of distributing over 500 machines and 1,000 printers to freshmen, collecting 1,000 two-year-old machines from juniors and replacing them with another 1,000 machines, plus offering computer orientation to an average of 1,040 first-year students and a handful of transfer students. We have no choice but to coordinate, plan, and work together!

MODEST BEGINNINGS

Our efforts at working together began less than a decade ago. Before the university had taken the first steps in its current direction, an ad hoc committee formed the academic computing advisory committee to determine a new hardware platform for the university. The committee consisted of computer-using faculty and the heads of both the computing center and the library. The committee collaborated so effectively that it became a regular faculty committee under the new name of Committee on Information Technology (CIT) and with a broader charge. Committee members played key roles in getting the faculty vote necessary for the plan, which we now call the undergraduate technology plan. The hiring of the ACS staff is one of the outcomes. Their reporting relationship to department chairs and the dean is another outcome of the CIT's recommendations to the faculty.

The library's relationship with IS and our history together developed further in 1992, when the university administration asked the library director to organize a computer camp for incoming freshmen. IS and the library forged interdepartmental personal and working relationships as they learned to share lab space, plan together, and work toward the success of that camp. The institution hosted the camp in the fall of 1993 and again in 1994, and it created demand from faculty and staff for similar exposure. The library staff relied heavily on faculty volunteers and IS personnel to deliver the program of instruction. IS and library staff continue to share objectives and enjoy actively experimenting with new initiatives, whether digital library projects, proxy servers, network PCs, or migrating data. There are two computer labs in the library and for a time the help desk was also located there until its space needs grew too great. As general-purpose labs are phased out on campus, one of the library labs will continue to operate in recognition of the library's role in training. The institution renovated the library's major electronic classroom with major assistance from IS. This renovation might not have been funded if the library had not been an integral part of the technology initiative.

Over the years, as we have worked together on the implementation of library automation and migration to another automated system, the library has tried to keep IS staff informed as much as possible concerning library operations and requirements. The CIO accompanied library staff on every field trip taken to see the systems under consideration and strongly supported the library's choice, both with his vote and with his budget! In fact, he was asked to be the project manager for the migration to and implementation of the new system.

CONTRASTS AND CONVERGENCES

The library and IS cultures are very different, although both directors hold MBA degrees. Until recently, the "culture clash" also reflected a white male culture in IS and a female, somewhat more diverse culture in the library. This is no longer the case. Although the library is not much changed, major positions in IS have gone to women and minorities, bringing the two organizations closer together. From a pattern of hiring recent graduates and "growing them" in IS, to the current practice of going outside to find experienced and expert staff, IS is moving towards the library model. The process of hiring new professionals clearly shows how far apart we still can be. The library uses a formal search committee structure with a faculty member or, if hiring for a position in the systems area, it asks someone from IS to join the committee. The library requires a presentation to the entire staff and, as with most academic searches, the process takes months. IS hires when the supervisor meets a qualified candidate without committees or outside participation.

The library staff recognizes and respects the skills of the IS staff and the ACS. The methods library staff use in training, which include team teaching, have given the ACS staff new appreciation for library staff skills in communication with students and in organizing a complex scenario from training scripts to logistics. The library staff regards IS staff and the ACS as resources that make many things possible as librarians work at designing interfaces and making information more accessible. Any veteran computer user at Wake Forest knows that customer service has become a much higher value for IS. Now, like the library, IS staffs its help desk with full-time employees and follows through to assure satisfaction.

From the perspective of the library director, some wonderful opportunities and strengths come about because of the relationship between the two units. When technical training is made available to IS staff, IS accommodates library staff whenever possible. The personal relationships that have been formed result in better communication, and better and earlier information. Several years ago, IS chose to switch its network software to a package that one of the library's primary information vendors did not support. This decision caused a major problem and cost the library considerable expense when it had to switch vendors. Such a gaffe is inconceivable now; library staff are in the loop. Often, indeed, library staff push the envelope, getting IS to help them find a way to effect a change.

During the past year, IS hired two library staff members. Perhaps the library director should be concerned, as they are very skilled and productive employees and are certainly missed. However, the library director is not dismayed for several reasons. First, talented people with technological skills can easily find jobs off campus, and it is wonderful that opportunities exist that keep skilled employees challenged, rewarded, and still available by telephone. Second, these people understand the library and know the staff. They are very responsive to library needs and help educate others in IS. Also, as the library director has worked to increase the salaries and job classes of her staff, the disparities in salaries between the library and IS have been noted and partially addressed.

Competition for resources is always a reality. Even at Wake Forest University, resources are not unlimited! By partnering with IS in the training role, library staff have earlier access to new equipment and software than other administrative units. Because the library's initiative in providing online resources is a major part of the undergraduate technology plan, more of the library's needs are met than in earlier years. IS, in its administrative computing aspect, is introducing new business methods and applications, many of which are Web-based and require a new level of staff skill. Library staff are working with the administrative computing staff on debugging, documenting, preparing training, and assuring that staff can make effective use of these applications. It is a new direction for the university, designed to move Wake Forest into the forefront of academic business applications, and it would be impossible without the cooperation and close collaboration of IS and the library.

Although unorthodox, our institutional arrangements work well for Wake Forest University. We are codependents, as the library looks to IS to maintain servers, networks, account control, and the rest of the technical structure. In turn, for the mission of IS to succeed, training is essential. Every person who is not trained adds to the workload of the support center. The partnership between the library and IS also gives the two units leverage in campus-wide, even university-wide projects. Our interests are very similar on many issues.

In the early 1990s, several divisions of the university, including IS and the library, embraced Total Quality Management, in the Crosby mode.[5] One of the basic tenets of that approach is that one should focus on the process, not the people involved in the process. Our experience at Wake Forest does not support that tenet. Compatible, flexible, and collegial staff can make any organizational pattern work. At Wake Forest, we enjoy working together on committees and projects, presenting together at EDUCOM and at the regular "fly-in" events for other academic institutions, and even collaborating on articles and chapters that tell the Wake Forest story.

NOTES

1. *U.S. News and World Report* moved Wake Forest University into the "national university" category from the "comprehensive regional university" category, and Wake Forest has been ranked from 25 to 31 in its new classification in recent years.
2. As of this writing representatives of three hundred universities, including thirty foreign universities, have visited Wake Forest University to learn about the technology initiative.
3. A standing committee of the faculty, the Committee on Information Technology replaced that ad hoc advisory committee.
4. The Plan for the Class of 2000 also featured adding forty faculty positions, mandatory first-year seminars and other benefits, supported by tuition increases.
5. In 1993, several administrative staff, including the library director and assistant directors and the head of the computing center, were exposed to the Philip J. Crosby approach to TQM as taught at Quality College in Winter Park, Florida. All library staff and all of the computing staff at the time had follow-up training on campus in the methods and purposes of TQM.

CHAPTER FIFTEEN

Beneficial Collaboration
Meeting Information Delivery Needs

JENNIFER CARGILL
RONALD D. HAY

During the information decade of the 1990s, the Louisiana State University Libraries and the Office of Computing Services collaborated in a number of efforts to facilitate meeting the information delivery needs of the university and the state. Four specific projects will be described in this essay. These projects underscore how essential it is to work cooperatively and collaboratively, identify effective partner(s), build trust among participants in projects, think creatively, and take risks. Another purpose of this chapter is to encourage other entities to seek partnerships that will further common goals and to pursue alternative approaches in reaching these goals.

BACKGROUND

The LSU Libraries and Office of Computing Services both are committed to supporting the missions of Louisiana State University and A & M College, the flagship institution of higher education in Louisiana. These two entities have worked cooperatively for many years in supporting the instructional efforts at LSU and within higher education within the state in general.

Louisiana State University and A & M College (hereafter referred to as LSU) is the largest and oldest campus within the LSU system and the premier public institution.[1] LSU is the state's comprehensive university, one of fifty-nine Research I institutions and one of only twenty-five universities in the nation designated both land grant and sea grant. It has more than forty research units as well as the traditional academic departments. LSU is in a position to be an important resource for the other educational institutions in Louisiana and the region.

The LSU system includes eight institutions on ten campuses located in five cities. The LSU system is headquartered in Baton Rouge, the location of three of the ten campuses within the system; the other LSU system institutions are located throughout the state. There are three other state-supported higher education systems. The four-institution Southern University system has its main campus and law school in Baton Rouge; its other two institutions are in New Orleans and Shreveport/Bossier City. The University of Louisiana system includes thirteen institutions scattered throughout the state. The LSU, Southern, and University of Louisiana systems include two-year through doctoral level institutions; the institutions range from a few hundred students to more than thirty thousand. A fourth system and board will come into being in 1999 to oversee the community colleges. The four higher education systems are under the oversight of the Board of Regents.[2]

The library is one of two Association of Research Libraries members in Louisiana. The collections are broad and deep in scope; services are diverse to serve both instructional and research needs. The LSU library system serves many people throughout the region; at any given time often 20 percent of library patrons in the LSU libraries come from outside the LSU academic community. The LSU computing services organization employs state-of-the-art computing technologies and a professional staff with considerable experience with library applications, operation of large systems, implementation of technology programs, and digitization.

The 1993 master plan for higher education designated the LSU library as the primary research library in the state. However, many years of financial constraints within Louisiana higher education portended continued inadequate support for the LSU libraries as well as for the other academic libraries in Louisiana. In the past fifteen years both LSU and other academic libraries in the state have cancelled many serial subscriptions. Document delivery is being used in several libraries as a substitute for canceled subscriptions as is interlibrary loan, and many of the libraries are purchasing relatively few monographs.

The state has been moving away from an almost total dependence on agriculture and the oil and gas industry. The dependence the state budget has on those economies has meant financial constraints during downturns in those industries. When financial constraints have hit the state budget, higher education has been among the first to be cut. While the academic institutions could be viewed as furthering the future of the state and its citizens, the state has not always put emphasis on the value of education. The rate of college graduation remains low in the state. The projects highlighted in this essay emerged from the background described, with LSU playing a leading role. These examples of cooperation underscore the importance of collaboration within the world of education and what can be accomplished with cooperation.

CREATION OF A STATEWIDE NETWORK

In contemplating the state of higher education in Louisiana in the late 1980s, the then Commissioner of Higher Education created a library task force chaired by the then LSU Provost. The LSU Provost had long tenure in her post, a high level of interest in libraries, and familiarity with the other universities and their administrators. She understood how critical libraries are to education and the state's economy and was determined that the academic libraries not be ignored in future planning. Before the task force accomplished everything it was charged to do, she stepped down from the provostship, returning to the classroom and freeing her time to focus on teaching, library projects, and writing grants. Since she knew higher education administration in the state and knew

how to facilitate ideas and projects, her increased availability provided a valuable asset to the libraries for any projects on which the libraries embarked.

For several months the library task force, composed primarily of academic
library directors, talked, assessed, and consulted. Under the chair's leadership,
the directors agreed that the academic libraries within the state had a number of
challenges but also had opportunities for collaboration and cooperation.[3] A
high priority emerged from the discussions: the desire and urgent need to automate the state-supported academic libraries. After further discussions and
meetings, the task force members' and the other library directors' goal of cooperation focused on automation of these academic libraries within the framework of an academic network. The interest in a statewide network with the
catalogs of the libraries online heightened after a consultant was brought in
from another academic library network and described the success of the network in his project and the benefits of collaboration. Some of the universities
had little or no Internet access, so the creation of a statewide telecommunications network presented a critical first step toward development of an academic
library network. The consultant's description of a statewide library network
and the sharing of databases excited the library directors; they decided to do all
they could to achieve their automation and network goals.

By 1990, only five of the public academic institutions had been automated;
not all of those libraries were using all capabilities of their chosen automation
system. The general funding situation in Louisiana, and more specifically in
higher education, led the library directors to be skeptical that they would obtain
institutional funding to automate in the foreseeable future. In assessing their
prospects for automation, the academic library directors determined that

> the software already most prevalent in the state would be the most direct
> route toward automation and the creation of a network; and

> any network would be best coordinated centrally, probably based at
> Louisiana State University with its experience and computer resources.

Once the directors and the task force decided to proceed with the network
concept, the libraries had to identify and seek funding. State funding for such a
project seemed unlikely, given the financial woes of the state budget. Therefore,
the library group decided to seek grant funding to create a small academic network and then use the initial pilot project as justification for obtaining some
state funding. This began a cycle of grant proposals to federal and state grant
awarding programs. The members of the Louisiana Board of Regents became
excited about the library network concept and provided $1.5 million from the
grant program it administered. Individual universities provided contributions
of equipment and staff time. Not until the 1995 legislative session did the legislature provide funds for ongoing support of the network. This funding continues in 1999 with 70 percent coming from the legislature and the remaining
amount being paid by the network participants.

As the academic network began, the concept expanded to include access
by public libraries and a pilot group of K-12 libraries. The enlarged network is
important in providing information access in a state that is largely rural. In
1998, the Gates Foundation provided further funding for expanding Internet access for public libraries throughout the state. Once the library network had been
created and become operational online, the interest in access to databases and
full text also began to emerge. A number of databases are now online.

Today we are looking at a successful project. How was this gem of an idea—a statewide academic library project—achieved? How did the concept become reality? There were some critical elements to the creation and development of the initial academic network:[4]

agreement on project goals;

faith in LSU's management of their bibliographic records;

trust in the state telecommunications office to create, fund, and maintain a statewide area network to support the library network; and

confidence that funding sources for the network would be identified.

Staffs in the Louisiana academic libraries are accustomed to a reasonable level of cooperation. For many years they have worked on a variety of projects of a more traditional nature. However, they found venturing into electronic cooperation a new and sometimes frightening step. Not all the academic libraries even belonged to OCLC. As the network project got started, the term of service for the Board of Regents' library task force expired. With the project in its infancy, a new organization had to be created—LALINC[5]—to continue working on various cooperative projects among the academic libraries of all sizes and to continue to explore the network concept. All academic libraries in Louisiana, public and private, are members of LALINC, although not all are part of the online academic library network. LALINC has several projects and interest areas: a borrowing card for faculty and graduate students to use at academic libraries in the state other than their home institution; a review of possible cooperative collection development; discussions of shared electronic journals; and cooperative distance education protocols.

While the library task force regrouped under the LALINC acronym, the participating libraries dubbed the emerging academic library network LOUIS.[6] LOUIS developed from the interests of the original library task force and its successor organization, LALINC, but reports to the Board of Regents. From the original group of academic libraries who wanted to be part of LOUIS, the network has grown to include almost all the public academic libraries; it will soon include a few of the private academic libraries. Communication among the LOUIS participants has increased, and this heightened interaction has spilled over to the entire LALINC community.

Just as the libraries had a history of collaboration, the LSU libraries and the LSU office of computing services also had a track record of collaboration. This history of collaboration proved essential. The successful creation of the network depended heavily upon the LSU libraries and their experience with the automated system that would be used by the entire network. The library system at LSU had been automated in the 1980s through the hard work of the office of computing services; ongoing cooperation had continued between the libraries and computing.

The planners realized that for the library network project to succeed, there had to be a commitment from the participating libraries. An element of risk also existed: efforts to make the library network concept a reality had to proceed without a guaranteed commitment or an absolute mandate from funding bodies. Monies had to be pooled from a patchwork of grants and institutional contributions, and an end product that worked had to be created by LSU computing services in a reasonable time frame. A network staff that had been assembled quickly automated the academic libraries and brought them into the network in phases. Libraries took turns, letting sister libraries "go first," based on the readiness of the individual libraries to come online. The libraries and LSU's computing services found themselves in a learning curve with many unknowns, dealing with many diverse institutions and patrons throughout the state. Flexibility and a tolerance for ambiguity proved essential. Library staffs focused on the larger goal and cooperated even more than they had in the past.

In the end, through the efforts of the LSU office of computing services, LSU libraries, the state's office of telecommunications, and the academic libraries that chose to join LOUIS, the project came to fruition. As the network moves into the millennium, it encompasses twenty academic libraries with six more to be automated in the near future, sixty-six public libraries, and a small number of school libraries that were part of the original pilot project. In 1998, a community college initiative in the state began with the creation of more institutions; it will undoubtedly lead to an increase in the number of network members. This larger network that expanded beyond the original academic-only network (LOUIS) began to be known as LLN.[7] As each academic library came online, a dedication "splash" took place to officially "cut the ribbon" on the new online service in each library. Libraries held contests to name the newly online academic catalogs, leading to opportunities for local publicity for the growing network. Newspapers around the state provided coverage of these online catalog opening ceremonies; legislators and other officials eagerly appeared and spoke at the celebrations. As the public and school libraries gained access to the network, additional publicity appeared in the media. The publicity led to increased interest in access to library collections and databases and heightened legislators' awareness of the importance of the network.

Success of the Louisiana Library Network (LLN) can be measured in many ways. Currently it is not unusual for library patrons to initiate more than 400,000 online transactions per day. Over the history of the project, annual transactions have grown from fifteen million to approximately sixty-two million.

The project resulted in a new level of cooperation among Louisiana librarians. Librarians now know their colleagues and institutional characteristics better. Librarians have expanded more communication concerning issues and problems, with extensive sharing of solutions. A critical mass of technological expertise, not formerly existing, is now in place, and librarians and institutions have a growing list of future projects that they want to explore. The library network has become an infrastructure on which to build other enhancements and projects.[8] The experience has positively influenced both the library and education communities. Students and faculty at the networked universities can more easily access and share information. Public library patrons have access to information never available to them before.

ELECTRONIC RESERVES

The success of the library network and the relationships and connections that evolved from that project led to brainstorming about other ways cooperative ventures might benefit individual libraries and higher education overall. The library network members became interested in areas or projects that might lend themselves to possible collaboration and product or service development. Having achieved one of the first statewide library networks, the librarians eagerly sought another success, preferably one with an element of innovation.

Course reserves is one service for which an enhanced product would be advantageous. Specifically, moving from print reserves to electronic reserves would provide a critical resource for instructional support. A Board of Regents priority is moving higher education into electronic distance education. The electronic reserve project would provide support at remote sites for students who did not have ready access to large library collections, and it seemed a natural adjunct as a support service for distance education classes.

During spring 1997, LSU libraries and the LSU computing services staff began developing an electronic reserves system; LSU libraries' staff and selected LSU classroom faculty did much of the testing. Developers sought to provide Internet access to course reserve materials for students, faculty, and staff at LSU. Librarians, computer analysts, and professors defined system requirements and brainstormed about interfaces. Computing services staff developed a prototype using the IBM/Lotus Notes[9] development environment.

In terms of security, copyright regulations required that access to individual reserve items be limited to registered LSU students with Lotus Notes IDs. After the initial development phase, students, staff, and faculty tested the prototype, using course reserves for a political science class. Staff evaluated professors' and students' comments and made refinements to the system. During the 1997-1998 fall and spring semesters, LSU piloted the system campus-wide. As a result of this pilot, and before launching the service to a wider audience, staff refined scanning procedures, determined copyright compliance criteria, and established implementation and use guidelines. A generic design template, derived from the pilot system, allowed creation and management of identical replicas of the system.

By summer 1998, the staff streamlined the electronic reserve system and put it into full production at LSU and five other network libraries. Students responded positively. During the fall 1998-1999 semester, four additional institutions chose to deliver the electronic reserve system. A U.S. Department of Education grant funded development and delivery of this system to these ten network participants. Additional institutions may elect to offer the reserve system, with the only associated costs those related to acquiring a scanning station. Maintenance is minimized through the use of the design template that replicates any changes to all systems.

Students, staff, and faculty are delighted with the advantages of electronic reserve: the ability to have reserves electronically available with authentication means no missing pages; electronic reserves are always available rather than being checked out; and they are available on a 24-hour basis. Copyright law, of course, prohibits all course reserves from being electronically available.

Having reserves available for distribution electronically also meant enhanced support for the embryonic distance education programs being advocated by the Board of Regents and the various universities. Forty of the sixty-four parishes (governmental entities comparable to counties in the other forty-nine states) are rural. The teaching of some courses from the LSU campus, for example, meant receiving the transmission in locations without collections to support adequately the courses. Being able to make course reserves available electronically provided critical augmentation to instructional support and is a vehicle for further development of course offerings. The electronic reserve system is yet another example of a successful collaboration among libraries within several institutions, and of the importance of the collaborative support of computing services. The availability of the reserve system for multi-institutional replication would not have been possible without the earlier successful network project.

COMPUTER LABORATORIES AND ELECTRONIC CLASSROOMS

With the experience of the network project on a statewide basis, the LSU libraries and LSU office of computing services looked to a campus-only need as a new collaborative project. With raised admission requirements, LSU has been experiencing dramatic enrollment growth as the best students clamor for admittance. A legislative-supported tuition program also meant more academically eligible students would be coming to LSU with tuition paid by the state for eight semesters. While LSU had sophisticated computer operations, the campus itself does not have adequate computer facilities for students working on course assignments. The university had few electronic classrooms. Schools and colleges within LSU do not require that students bring their own computers when enrolling; such a universal requirement is unlikely in the near future. Some of the existing computer laboratory facilities on campus have been limited to use by majors in specific fields.

More electronic classrooms equipped with instructor and student workstations seemed extremely desirable. With the increased use of software and databases in course work, having electronic classrooms available has become a necessity in today's education environment. The library skills course, for example, taught by faculty from LSU libraries had become more dependent on electronic resources as the university library system provided access to an increasing number of online databases and electronic journals. Library, computing, and university administration foresaw the desirability of electronic classrooms within the main library. Such facilities would enhance both the one-shot and "for credit" library instruction. The LSU libraries collaborated with the college of education and applied to the Board of Regents' grant program with a proposal for electronic classrooms. The proposal succeeded, and the funding level received supported development of two electronic classrooms.

The need for computer facilities and electronic classrooms escalated, and others learned of the success of the library grant proposal. Therefore, the library and computing services administrations explored how the two units could combine their efforts with the larger university community to provide a partial solution for computer needs on campus, using the recently funded grant as a springboard to a larger project. After reviewing campus sites and discussing student needs, the library and computing services administrators approached the university administrators with a proposal to create three public-access computer laboratories within the main library. This resulted in a new grant that funded the construction of an additional three electronic classrooms in the main library, one for university-wide use funded by the university and the other two for library instruction. The successful implementation of these labs and classrooms provides valuable experience in making the concept scalable to other sites on campus.

One of the first nonlibrary instructional uses of the electronic classrooms will be for nighttime astronomy laboratory exercises loaded onto the microcomputer clusters in one of the electronic teaching facilities. The astronomy instructors will train students to directly control the telescope from the facilities in the main library by the end of the semester. Students will be able to instruct the telescope to point to any specific object in the sky. They will be able to take a picture of an object using the telescope "camera" from a Web-based interface and transfer that picture back to the lab remotely.[10]

During the 1997-1998 academic year the LSU student body voted a technology fee assessment on themselves.[11] Because the university administration wanted the students to be closely involved with the decision-making process involving use of the monies, the university administration created a technology committee dominated by students and chaired by the Provost. While this meant some up-front preparation to educate the students of the technology opportunities in the LSU environment, it also meant the student leadership had an investment in the success of the fee assessment and the supported projects. The first group of approved technology fee projects includes some that will build on the examples of the labs and classrooms previously constructed in the library with university funds. Other projects will venture into wireless technology for computer access. Library space outside the main library will be used for additional computer laboratories and electronic classrooms. One branch library closed as a traditional library facility and will be converted to electronic classrooms and laboratory use.

Just as library patrons in recent years moved from taking notes to extensive photocopying, today's patrons rely increasingly upon electronic workspaces. Converting some patron areas into electronic learning space satisfies many objectives. Patrons respond well to the increased availability of electronic resources. The laboratories function at nearly 100 percent capacity most hours of operation.

DIGITAL LIBRARY

LSU libraries entered the electronic imaging arena in the early 1990s with a grant-funded project that resulted in a CD-ROM distributed by the LSU Press. As digitizing became more prevalent, the LSU office of computing services began exploring venturing into a digital library project. After many discussions involving computing services personnel, library staff, and faculty, LSU libraries and computing services embarked on another joint project.

The original LSU digital library pilot provided an electronic repository for the storage and dissemination of research collections provided by faculty at the university. The LSU Digital Library[12] has grown significantly in two years. A cataloger, manuscripts processor, and an applications analyst together defined system requirements and developed infrastructure. The data model derived could have been implemented in any environment; however, customized Lotus Notes databases provide the foundation for this system. As with electronic reserves, this software allows for collaborative and distributed work that is scalable, replicable, and designed to emphasize discovery and intellectual access.

Using a combination of Dublin Core metadata and a locally designed cataloging template, the digital library permits resource discovery through commercial search engines as well as locally written search routines. The LSU Digital Library is based upon a descriptive scheme designed for "generic resource description," meaning that objects from most knowledge domains and physical formats can be captured and described. Current collections in the digital library include

> several thousand scanned and cataloged items from a geography and anthropology distinguished professor's research career;
>
> five hundred aerial photographs from the 1940s and 1950s of the Mississippi River Delta region;
>
> nineteenth century correspondence related to the 1863 siege of Port Hudson, Louisiana;
>
> letters from the 1800-1860 period from members of a prominent plantation family, builders and owners of the largest surviving plantation house; and
>
> two hundred scanned and cataloged images of the original architectural drawings for LSU, organized by building.

While this is a "work in progress," with refinements regularly being added, it provides a successful pilot project that may lead to similar enterprises.

FUTURE DIRECTIONS

The experience of the LSU libraries and the office of computing services in collaborating on a number of projects has been positive and rewarding. Possibilities of further cooperative ventures building on earlier successes are being explored. The successful creation of a statewide network led to "thinking outside the box" and contemplation of use of the network and the lessons learned for other projects.

The lessons learned at LSU in working on cooperative projects are indisputable:

> identify partner(s) and explore each other's strengths and weaknesses;
>
> develop relationship(s) based on trust;
>
> exploit the relationship(s) for the benefit of the parent institution and the larger community;
>
> think beyond the traditional; and
>
> be willing to leap and take risks.

And—engage in the collaboration, the partnership, with your audience in mind and the benefits that can result remaining foremost in your plans and thoughts.

NOTES
1. Founded 1859 and designated Louisiana State University and Agricultural and Mechanical College in 1977.
2. For further information on higher education in Louisiana and access to the various institutional Web sites, access http://webserv.regents.state.la.us
3. Sammie W. Cosper, "Setting the Stage for a Library Network," *Library Hi Tech* 13, consecutive issue 49-50 (special issue 1995): 88-89.
4. Ronald D. Hay, "Technology as a Strategic Investment," *Library Hi Tech* 13, consecutive issue 49-50 (special issue 1995): 100.
5. LALINC means the Louisiana Academic Library Information Network Consortium.
6. LOUIS means Louisiana Online University Information System.

7. LLN means Louisiana Library Network.
8. For further information, see http://www.lsu.edu/OCS/LOUIS/catdat.htm
   See also the following articles:
   Jennifer Cargill, "A Target of Opportunity: Creation of the LOUIS Network," *Library Hi Tech* 13, consecutive issue 49-50 (special issue 1995): 87-107.
   Jennifer Cargill and Ronald D. Hay, "Achieving a Vision of a Statewide Academic Library Network," *Journal of Academic Librarianship* 19 (January 1994): 386-387.
   Nancy N. Colyar, Charles F. Thomas, and Kelly Boudreaux, "Interinstitutional Use of the Louisiana Online University Information System by Academic Libraries," *Information Technology and Libraries* 16 (September 1997): 132-134.
   Jill Fatzer, "Budget Stringency as a Stimulus to Innovation: The Cases of Louisiana and Ohio," *Journal of Library Administration* 22, no. 2/3 (1996): 57-77.
   William Gray Potter, "Recent Trends in Statewide Academic Library Consortia," *Library Trends* 45 (winter 1997): 416-434.
9. Lotus Notes is an IBM product.
10. Astronomy lab project under Joel Tohline, Professor of Physics and Astronomy, Louisiana State University and A & M College.
11. $5.00 per credit hour per semester for a maximum per semester of $75.00.
12. http://diglib.lsu.edu/digitallibrary

CHAPTER SIXTEEN

Service and Instruction
A Strategic Focus

SUE SAMSON
KIM GRANATH
VICKI PENGELLY

TRANSITION OF PLACE AND TIME

The revolutionary aspect of the Information Age has led to new ways of thinking and to fundamental changes in how people work and interact throughout the world and in business and academia.[1] One example, electronic mail, has not only improved communication—its primary purpose—but has changed interactions within organizations, families, and culture, a secondary but significant consequence of this new technology. Within higher education, information technology has offered a new platform for curricular development and the expansion of the classroom to remote locations. It is in this arena that libraries and computer centers are providing leadership and creating new applications of information technology. Within this framework of new information technology, we describe the effective role of service and instruction as a focus for collaboration between computing centers and libraries. We also stress the importance of integrating this instruction into the curriculum by focusing on the faculty through teaching and collaboration.

Service and Source

A case in point: the University of Montana has a student population of approximately twelve thousand graduate and undergraduate students, four hundred and eight faculty, and nine hundred staff. Administratively, library services operates within academic governance with a dean and faculty structure. Computing and information services (CIS) operates within the administrative structure with an executive director of information technology who reports directly to the president. An Information Technology Resource Center operates separately within academic governance. In addition, the Montana Board of Regents recently reorganized the university system statewide so that the University of Montana now encompasses entities beyond its Missoula campus, including

Western Montana College in Dillon, Montana Tech in Butte, Helena College of Technology, and College of Technology in Missoula.

Evolving Expertise

The alliance between CIS and the Mansfield Library began with Internet instruction. As access to the Internet became widely available in the academic environment, so did the need for instruction. Both CIS and the library fielded numerous Internet-related questions and, in spring 1991, they began collaboration on a series of Internet classes. They also jointly offered Internet classes through curriculum-integrated instruction in all disciplines, through departmental workshops and seminars, through conference workshops, and in a formal Honors College three-credit course.

Since cooperative Internet classes began, collaboration has evolved in other areas. A campus-wide strategic planning process that included both the library and CIS developed the University of Montana Information Technology Plan. The library and CIS cosponsored two information technology conferences, an Internet teleconference, and jointly planned, designed, and maintained the university gopher with additional guidance from university communications. In addition, library faculty and CIS personnel have collaborated on several publications.

During the 1993-1994 academic year, the Mansfield Library's CD-ROM local area network and library catalog became accessible to remote users. Users dialed into the campus modem pool, accessed their university computer accounts, and used the university gopher to access library resources. The need for greater collaboration between the departments became immediately apparent to personnel in each department. CIS provided technical support for questions about dial-in access to the library catalog and network, along with instructions for access cowritten by CIS and library staff. Questions dealing with software and hardware were referred to CIS, while reference librarians supported questions dealing with information access.

Help Desks, Interfaces, and Personnel

In fall semester 1994, the CIS help desk and the library reference desk conducted a staff exchange with the goals of providing continuing education about services offered at each site, establishing a knowledgeable basis for referrals, and further expanding open communication between the two departments.[2] At about the same time, the library made available a public Internet station with multimedia access—the only one then available to all students and faculty members on the campus. In this case, CIS could not provide technical software support due to restrictions in the university's contract with its Internet provider.

As a result of a strategic planning process conducted in the early 1990s, a new position of executive director of information technology was created. When this position was filled in August 1994, more than the usual amount of change ensued. One change, the outsourcing of dial-up access, had a significant impact on services, particularly those of the library; students, faculty, and staff who wanted to access their e-mail accounts or "surf the Net" from off campus could either elect to purchase service at special rates from the commercial vendor that won the bid or could select any other vendor. The university chose outsourcing as the cost-effective method to improve the previously inadequate dial-up service, which provided only forty-eight modems at a maximum capacity of 14.4 baud.

This apparent step forward in general dial-up access resulted in two steps backward for the library. With the new Internet Service Provider (ISP) and the database climate changing from text-based to GUI (graphical user interface), we once again had to restrict databases to use only with the library. We also had to eliminate direct dial-in access to the catalog. During the academic year, library personnel had to become proficient at advising users on how to configure their Internet browser to access Telnet and link to our catalog through the library's Web site. For some users, the university's ISP added to the confusion by not supplying its subscribers with a Telnet client, a condition specifically written into the contract. Help instructions both in paper and on the library Web site underwent many a revision.

To handle the changes made by outsourcing Internet service, the library's automation specialist quickly arranged a meeting with CIS and initiated collaboration at yet another level. The library had to establish three levels of access to its licensed databases—in-library, on-campus, and off-campus. Each level of access had its own Web page menu. Initially, the library only provided access to the library's Web databases. To authenticate licensed users, the library provided database vendors with the university's Class-B Internet Protocol (IP) range for on-campus users and a range of IP addresses used by the university's ISP for off-campus users. CIS and the library considered this only a short-term solution for accessing library resources.

IP address authentication enabled both on-campus and off-campus users access to a limited number of databases. However, this method required off-campus users to use the university's ISP to obtain graphical access to the Web databases. Users with other ISPs could obtain access only by connecting to the Internet through their provider, logging into their university computer account, and accessing the databases with a non-graphical Web browser. Since most Web databases are designed for graphical access, this process proved to be difficult and awkward for many remote users. This solution particularly frustrated distance education students. The university's ISP made no provision (e.g., a toll-free phone number) for students outside of the local dialing area. These students could not establish an account with the university's ISP without making a long distance phone call to access the library's resources. As their only option, students had to use their local ISP (if one was available) and access the databases non-graphically.

During the next academic year, the librarians actively worked to increase the number of resources for remote access. By changing database formats from CD-ROM to their corresponding Web interfaces and by establishing a procedure for downloading the client software, on-campus users could access CD-ROM databases. While this increased remote access for on-campus users and university ISP users, it still did not address the larger remote-access problem for the outside ISP users. The preferred long-term solution, of course, would have been to create an overall campus authentication system that would be used by the library as well as other departments on campus. However, lack of resources precluded this solution. Without this authentication system in place and with rising user demands for remote access, the library's automation specialist decided that the library would have to solve its own authentication problems. By the end of the academic year, technicians at CIS and the library's automation specialist had collaborated to build a library authentication system.

Remote users must still establish a university computer account available only to valid students, faculty, and staff, but remote access is now independent of the ISP or physical location of the user. Another additional authentication measure that is being adopted by more of the library's database vendors is the use of URL referral. With this process, the user links to a database from a secure library Web menu using a site-specific URL, and the database vendor then verifies this URL before the user can access the database. This process is completely hidden to the user, but adds another level of security for the database vendor.

Meanwhile, back at CIS, client services experienced its own grand evolution. The introduction of the Internet to the campus resulted in explosive growth in the interest among faculty, staff, and students in e-mail and all sorts of Internet resources. The number of e-mail accounts went from a few hundred in 1991 to several thousand just a few years later. With no extra support staff, client services tried to serve a greatly expanded user base along with an increased number and variety of applications. Steve Gilbert refers to this situation as the "support service crisis" and identifies, among other symptoms, the rapidly widening gap between available resources and the expectations of faculty and students. He also explains how and why faculty and students need more help from librarians and faculty development professionals.[3]

At the same time that this interest in the Internet was growing, some departments and administrators initiated a move on campus to decentralize some aspects of computer support. This should have decreased the workload for computer center personnel, but it required service at a higher level of expertise. Currently we are seeing a trend toward recentralization as our campuses sort out which kinds of services can be reasonably shifted to departments and which can be best served by the staff of the computer center.[4]

ELECTRONIC LEARNING ENVIRONMENTS

Throughout this mosaic of intertwining activities of the library and the computer center, both together and separately, the concept of teaching and learning remained a constant component of our expanding programs (figure 1). Sheila Creth emphasizes the concept of the "teaching library" as a core issue in building partnerships in universities.[5] Traditionally, computing center staffs have also had a role in instructing computer users.[6] The computer help desk and reference and information desk exemplify the service missions of each unit. With the advent of electronic learning environments, the need for help reaches far beyond the desk to enhance the learning and teaching needs of students and faculty. Karen Diller describes the advent of one jointly organized and administered program designed to meet the instructional needs of an entire campus in an electronic learning environment.[7] Her description of the collaboration necessary to meet these needs also uncovers the basic differences of each unit. These differences provided conflict at the University of Montana as well.

Access versus Security

One of the first collaborative conflicts occurred when the Mansfield Library established the first workstation that provided Internet access to all students, faculty, and staff. Librarians considered this a significant accomplishment in providing access to new information resources at the library. Some CIS personnel, however, expressed concern about the effects of this access on our license with the university network provider that did not cover open access. Some CIS personnel

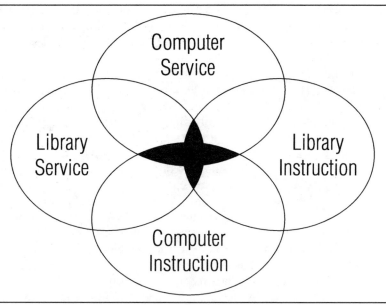

Figure 1   Service and instruction provide a core of collaboration between computer specialists and librarians in support of users.

also had considerable concern about security issues dealing with an unmonitored system. Librarians took some steps to address these concerns, including consultation with the university's legal counsel to prepare a disclaimer posted on the workstation. As discussion of the issues continued and the station became a component of the library's ready reference service, CIS's concern abated.

Subsequently, this same issue reappeared almost in reverse with regard to access to the library electronic databases. Licensing for these databases requires that remote access be available only to university students, faculty, and staff. However, as described earlier, once the university outsourced Internet access to a commercial vendor, the vendor placed little control on who was allowed to set up an account. In fact, more customers, whoever they were, made the vendor happier. CIS made software packets for establishing accounts with the university ISP freely available from several locations on campus, including the library. While the university's ISP provided a range of IP addresses to use for remote authentication, no one could guarantee that the persons using these addresses were valid university students, faculty, and staff. Negotiating licenses for remote access to the databases became more difficult. Eventually, the ISP removed most of its public software distribution points, and there is now more control over who can obtain the software package for establishing an account. Without verification of the status of new clients, this issue of uncertainty in the pool of remote users again underscored the need for the library to develop its own authentication system.

Content and Delivery Issues

Throughout our collaborative efforts, other differences between the perspectives of computer center and library personnel became apparent. Library users generally need information resources in support of specific subjects. They require access to specific types of databases or Web sites that support a particular kind of downloading capability or other access. Computer users, in contrast, tend to have more technical needs. They often need to identify files or resources that can be transferred in alternate ways. For example, CIS continued offering short courses on File Transfer Protocol (FTP) procedures long after some librarians deemed those courses of little or no value. The librarians reasoned that for their clientele the Web provided access to many FTP sites, so why subject users to the arcane procedures of the original FTP procedures? But the CIS classes served a broader group of users, some of whom did not have access to Web browsers or who needed to exchange files in the absence of an e-mail program that could handle binary attachments. The benefits of our collaborative instruction provide the necessary expertise to meet the needs of a variety of students.

Other examples of content and delivery issues include the establishment and management of electronic mailing lists and e-mail groups for classroom instruction, the design and implementation of Web pages for use with students, and access to and use of electronic databases. Computer center personnel and library personnel bring their separate perspectives to address the questions that arise as students and faculty members implement these new technologies. For example, CIS addresses access to the Web and appropriate software and hardware questions; librarians provide expertise in locating information resources and emphasize critical thinking and evaluation skills.

Technical Implementation versus User Impacts

The greatest collaborative challenge at the University of Montana has been ensuring that user impacts are adequately addressed before implementation of technical changes. We are fortunate in having a client services unit within CIS. Their technical expertise is focused on serving the user and provides an excellent cooperative venue with the library. The challenges arise mainly with those technical staff within CIS who focus on technical implementation. The most recent examples include the previously discussed outsourcing of Internet access and the delayed response in establishing a method to provide controlled access to the library databases. Both of these actions had a significant impact on the library user, while the library had only limited input in the decision-making process.

As described earlier, when Internet access was initially outsourced, remote access to the library's databases became a problem. To alleviate this, staff members from the library and the computer center designed an authentication process that provides remote access. In the meantime, librarians and CIS help desk personnel fielded numerous questions and concerns with regard to access. Clearly the need for and the development of an authentication process has been a long-standing issue and a significant challenge for both departments.

FOCUS ON FACULTY

Stephen Franklin describes the university's most valued asset as its faculty. He further suggests that universities should "leverage the value of this asset by recognizing and assisting well-established faculty and institutional strategies in these ways: foster autonomy and initiative, cultivate collaboration, promote intramural ties, facilitate discipline-based ties, and balance competing demands."[8] Creth discusses the importance of teaching as an essential element in the role of university libraries and emphasizes the need for librarians to "move beyond the limiting nature of bibliographic instruction to a more comprehensive concept of the 'teaching library.'"[9] This concept would move the library from its focus on users who come to the library to a focus on the needs of individual users wherever they are located. This parallels the teaching and mission needs of the computer center staff who also address the needs of remote users.

Form and Function

In the spring of 1997, the University of Montana CIS unit completed a user survey of faculty and students. In the results of this survey, the faculty expressed a clear desire to receive intensive training on the use of the Internet. This focus on faculty also complements the library's instructional strategy, which emphasizes partnership and collaboration with faculty to embed information literacy throughout the curriculum.[10] Another Library/CIS collaboration was born.

The survey resulted in a "Focus on Faculty Internet Workshop" series. CIS and the library scheduled the first of these series for four two-hour sessions on Friday afternoons during the 1997 fall semester. We limited attendance to twenty faculty members to match the number of computers available for hands-on instruction. Each session began with a demonstration by a faculty member already using the aspect of Internet that was to be that day's focus. The demonstration was then followed by instruction designed to teach faculty how to do what they had just seen.

With three instructors always present, individual questions and problems could be addressed with ease during the course of each instructional presentation. Sessions focused on e-mail and mailing lists; introduction to the World Wide Web; advanced searching on the Web and the use of electronic databases; and the design of Web pages using a basic Hypertext Markup Language (HTML) freeware editor. A class mailing list provided a hands-on implementation of one of the instructional aspects of the class plus expanded communication opportunities for the class members completing the assignments that accompanied each session.

Evaluation was twofold: faculty members completed one-minute evaluations at the end of each session and provided a comprehensive evaluation at the end of the last class session. In the one-minute evaluations, faculty members were asked to e-mail their comments on the one best thing they learned from the session and the one thing they wanted to learn but did not. Instructors responded immediately to these evaluations, answering questions on the mailing list and following up in the next session.

Inspired by positive evaluations, the instructors incorporated suggestions by the first participants in a second workshop series offered during the intersession between fall and spring semesters. This series was offered in two three-hour sessions on consecutive days. Even though they used a larger lab to expand enrollment to thirty, a waiting list developed. As before, a faculty demonstration began each session. The first session included e-mail and mailing lists, beginning and advanced Web searching, and access to electronic databases. Instructors devoted the second session to the design of Web pages and the use of HTML. They distributed a comprehensive evaluation at the end of the second session.

The CIS director of client services instructed the class in e-mail basics, subscribing and unsubscribing to online discussion groups, and using news groups.

The Mansfield Library electronic resources librarian introduced users to basic Web navigation and searching, and the library instruction coordinator covered advanced Web searching and access to and use of electronic databases. The university's Webmaster taught basic HTML using software that is freely available across campus.

With the exception of the Webmaster, the instructors met at the beginning of the semester to plan the first workshop. Discussions covered topics to include possible faculty presenters, available dates, number of participants, assignments to link the sessions, and administrative details including creation of the announcement and registration form. CIS assumed the administrative responsibilities of mailing the announcements, reserving lab space and equipment, creating a registration list, and preparing information packets for all participants.

Service and Students

The success of these "Focus on Faculty Internet Workshops" resulted in large part from the strong collaborative culture CIS and the library had developed over a period of years. Our shared experiences at help desks, our dialog with faculty and students, our systematic efforts at feedback from our primary users have made us more and more aware of the need to serve our students through our faculty (figure 2). For the most part, students use the computer center labs and library resources to complete assignments given to them by faculty. If these assignments are based on a lack of understanding of the services available, the impact becomes a major challenge for the student, for the computer center, and for the library.

A review of the literature reveals that the value of teaching the teachers is at the core of many current models of library reference service that have evolved as a result of the electronic information revolution. Jackie Mardikian and Martin Kesselman describe partnerships with teaching faculty at Rutgers in a program called LINCS, Library Instruction Cooperative Service, designed to promote information literacy.[11] They emphasize the importance of involving the teaching faculty to develop effective library assignments and serve students who are motivated to learn and complete their assignments.

Another effect of the technological revolution is the switch from services confined by a specific location. Chris Ferguson and Charles Bunge discuss alternatives to the traditional reference service as defined by place.[12] They emphasize the value of tiered reference service, roving librarians, and research consultations. Another alternative proposed by Suellen Cox is "going out to the user."[13] In this model, reference librarians work directly with users in their workplace. The link to computer services evolved with the advent of electronic workstations in the reference area. An early discussion in the literature proposes reference technology assistants to address the new wave of questions dealing with hardware, software, printers, and similar issues.[14] This evolution of traditional reference is strengthened by collaboration.

Computer center personnel have identified these trends as well.[15] At the University of Montana, CIS is proposing a program that would pair a qualified student with a faculty member who wants to incorporate technology into the curriculum. A committee whose members include reference librarians, computer center personnel, and representatives from other departments will direct

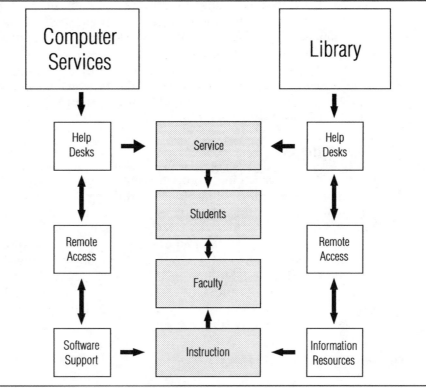

Figure 2   Service and instruction provide a base for new models of outreach in support of users.

the program. Again, instruction becomes a focal point that fosters collaboration. At the University of Montana, we believe that the role of instruction in the university library and computer center is a primary and critical service around which other services should function.

CONCLUSION

Close to a decade of collaboration between CIS and the Mansfield Library at the University of Montana provides an array of experiences for developing a working model that can be implemented in universities where separate computer centers and libraries exist.

What Works

The narrow model of service as place has been made passé by the access available through technology. Users now seek consultation from remote sites and are well served by those familiar with hardware and software as well as electronic information resources. Computer center and library personnel have gained a better understanding of frequently asked questions at each site and have established a goal of sharing information resources by forming information teams.

Instruction has become the focal point of all other services. Instruction serves as the major model of collaboration and builds on the strengths of each unit. Collaborative efforts to embed information literacy and computer literacy into the curriculum have gained significant momentum at a time when the demand for instruction in these areas is increasing. Effective electronic learning environments require the complementary expertise of computer specialists and librarians in instructional teams.

To best serve students, the primary users of both units, it is critical to form an information bridge to faculty. Well-informed faculty with knowledge and expertise relative to information and computer technology provide the best source possible to students for the proper utilization of resources available.

Areas of Challenge

Point of view is everything. Computer center specialists and librarians come to the same table for different meals. Their training and expertise are unique, yet they share the same clientele. Collaboration requires respect and compromise, time and commitment, and a search for common goals.

Decision making without all of the facts on the table is perhaps the most critical challenge to successful collaboration. Building partnerships at all levels remains essential to establishing effective electronic learning environments. It is essential to impress directors, deans, and administrators at all levels with the value of this collaboration for our users. Collaborative planning lays the groundwork for cohesive programs.

The Future Is Already Here

We find it difficult to imagine a more exciting profession than the one in which we operate. The magnitude of new hardware, new software releases, new and evolving information resources make each day a learning experience for computer and library professionals. New alliances and new experiences create opportunities for new models of service.

We have described the value of service and instruction as a focus for collaboration for computing centers and libraries operating within this new wave of information technology. We are limited only by imagination as we establish these new levels of collaboration. The alliance of computer center and library personnel to integrate computer literacy and information literacy into the curriculum is an important component of developing a comprehensive program of instruction and service to faculty that will result in improved services and informed and satisfied library and computer users.

NOTES

1. Lee Sproull and Sara Kiesler, *Connections: New Ways of Working in the Networked Organization* (Cambridge, Mass.: MIT, 1991).
2. Sue Samson, Vicki Pengelly, and Barry Brown, "The Collaborative Advantage: The Library and Computing Services at the University of Montana," *RQ* 36 (spring 1997): 370-374.
3. Steve Gilbert, *Symptoms of Support Service Crisis,* e-mail communication with Vicki Pengelly, 12 May 1997. Available e-mail <pengelly@selway.umt.edu from gilbert@clark.net>.
4. Don M. Wee, "Re-centralizing: The Pendulum Wobbles Back," *SIGUCCS Newsletter* (September/December 1997): 8-14.

5. Sheila D. Creth, "Creating a Virtual Information Organization: Collaborative Relationships between Libraries and Computing Centers," *Journal of Library Administration* 19 (1993): 111-132.

6. Anne G. Lipow and Sheila D. Creth, eds., *Building Partnerships: Computing and Library Professionals* (Berkeley, Calif.: Library Solutions Pr., 1995).

7. Karen R. Diller, "Helping Your Campus Navigate Electronic Environments: Collaboration Is a Necessity," *Research Strategies* 15 (1997): 187-192.

8. Stephen D. Franklin, "Libraries and Academic Computing Centers: Forging New Relationships in a Networked Information Environment," in *Building Partnerships: Computing and Library Professionals,* ed. Anne G. Lipow and Sheila D. Creth (Berkeley, Calif.: Library Solutions Press, 1995).

9. Creth, "Creating a Virtual Information Organization."

10. Sue Samson, *Mansfield Library Instructional Strategy* (The University of Montana Maureen and Mike Mansfield Library, 1996). Available at <http://www.lib.umt.edu/inst/strategy.htm>.

11. Jackie Mardikian and Martin Kesselman, "Beyond the Desk: Enhanced Reference Staffing for the Electronic Library," *Reference Services Review* 23 (spring 1995): 27-28.

12. Chris D. Ferguson and Charles A. Bunge, "The Shape of Services to Come: Values-Based Reference Service for the Largely Digital Library," *College & Research Libraries* 58 (May 1997): 252-265.

13. Suellen Cox, *Rethinking Reference Models* (University of Southern California Doheny Memorial Library, Doheny Reference Center, 1996). Available at <http://www-lib.usc.edu/Info/Ref/Cox/rethink_ref.html >.

14. Bruce Bonta and Sally Kalin, "CD-ROM Implementation: A Reference Staff Takes Charge," *Reference Services Review* 17 (summer 1989): 7-11.

15. Jennifer Fajman, "Collaborations within Higher Education," *SIGUCCS Newsletter* (Dec. 1995): 18-19.

CHAPTER SEVENTEEN

The Gettysburg Experience

ROBIN WAGNER

In February 1994, Gettysburg College launched an ambitious experiment that joined computing and the library into a new organization known as Information Resources.[1] Gettysburg College, one of the first liberal arts colleges to undertake such a merger, sought, along with only a handful of other institutions, a level of integration so complete that all vestiges of the traditional library disappeared. This is the story of that merger and why it failed despite the best efforts of many.

To ensure the successful merging of computing and the library the chemistry must be right. First of all, there must be compelling reasons to integrate. Those involved must plan the marriage carefully, enlist grassroots support, and then create a flexible new structure. Most importantly, those involved must be realistic about what can be accomplished and have the flexibility to change the recipe if things do not jell. Arnold Hirshon's 1998 CAUSE publication, *Integrating Computing and Library Services*, provides a textbook on how to do it right. In the chapter titled "Making the Decision," he outlines the readiness indicators for integrating and presents an equally impressive list of poor reasons for coming together.[2] Gettysburg College could claim just two of the essential readiness factors—an institutional mission and desire to expand service. However, Gettysburg College could claim nearly all of the negative factors.[3] Had Hirshon's guidebook been available in 1994, the results of the Gettysburg experience might have been different. Unfortunately, from the start Gettysburg College had the ingredients for an unhappy union resulting in misunderstandings, staffing departures, and ill will.

I joined the newly formed information resources unit seven months into the experiment, near the completion of the planning phase. I participated on three different teams during the three-and-a-half-year union and served as team leader from 1996 until the redivision of information resources in July of 1997. In trying to understand what happened at Gettysburg College, I examined the written record (what little remains), relied on my own notes from this period, and collected the stories of current and past employees who experienced the merger.[4]

My evidence suggests that there were many explanations for the failure of the merger. Some were linked directly to the leadership of information resources. In this essay I will concentrate on three areas: the planning process, the organizational structure itself, and the cultural differences between the library and the computing staff. From the beginning, a leadership that seemed to have little interest in libraries or books and did not understand the culture of libraries defined the culture of information resources. Leadership had minimal contact with the rank and file. A perpetual disconnect seemed to exist from the everyday needs of staff and from the responsibilities of managing an organizational change of this size and character. Based on my experiences, the leadership preferred to dream the big dreams rather than to deal with everyday realities.[5]

BACKGROUND

The Gettysburg College community learned of the merger via e-mail from the provost in January 1994. The provost presented the merger as an accomplished fact. The college had just been through a strategic planning process, and the college leadership explained the merger as a way to meet critical technology goals, specifically "to develop the best possible computer-based information resources and programs."[6] The need to consolidate resources and eliminate redundancy was also emphasized. The unofficial but commonly held explanation took a slightly different spin: the library had lagged technologically and had more money than it could spend well in a given year. The computer center positioned itself on the cutting edge—but lacked the budget or staff to do the innovative experimentation that would put Gettysburg College on the map.

Almost immediately following the official announcement three important events occurred. The college joined the library and computing administratively, and the new unit took on the name Information Resources. Nearly everyone from computing moved into the library, a building too small for the number of people it would now house. A reengineering process began, entailing advice from consultants and the establishment of a four-person core planning group. This group ultimately proposed a flat, process-based organizational structure. Overall, the changes effected in early 1994 were dramatic and far-reaching; they also proved to be unrealistic and in the end, unworkable.

With the marriage announcement, the partners took up residence together and began sharing the same checkbook. The new vice president for information resources, who had been the director of the computer center prior to the merger, held the checkbook. This individual had had a meteoric career at Gettysburg College. In his brief tenure as head of computing he had been credited with networking the campus, advancing technology, and working effectively to integrate computing into the curriculum. Some considered him a visionary and others hailed him as a miracle worker. He had hired an able staff and had revitalized computing on campus. His staff went to the merger with a positive attitude.

On the other hand, as many interviewees recalled, the library staff seemed uncooperative and resistant from the outset. According to one member of the library staff, reaction to the merger and the choice of leadership was "mixed, though heavily weighted to anxiety and dread of what was to come." She wrote,

> I, myself, was more hopeful, since I believed that the library could benefit greatly from moving to a position of more technical strength. I was naive

enough to think that [the VP] would be moderately reasonable once he'd settled himself into his new position, and second, that the workers in the library would see the advantages to upgrading the technical aspects of their jobs and finding ways to improve them. I felt [VP] should be given the benefit of a doubt, and be allowed to at least try a few changes.

As one can tell from the tone of these comments, the leadership failed in the end to ameliorate these concerns and to change attitudes. A hostile work environment set up for failure resulted.

PLANNING MISTAKES

In looking back, three major problem areas can be identified that collectively led to a breakdown of cooperation and the end of the merger. First, the planning process failed to include a majority of the staff in a meaningful way. The lack of cooperation appears to be an inevitable result of a process more exclusive than inclusive. A small and select group, meeting almost daily with consultants or with each other, designed the reengineered organization. The vice president and three close advisors comprised this team. No librarian served on the core team.

Librarians played a modest role at the next level, the extended team, in serving as intermediaries between the core designers and everyone else in the organization. The extended team had eight members, and, according to an interviewee (a librarian), many quickly labeled it the "rubber stamp team." This librarian had served on the extended team and described the role of intermediary as awkward and frustrating, observing:

> The consultants worked with the highest ranking work group [core team] to form the teams. I think it became clear after a while that [two individuals] were the masterminds behind the new structure. There were meetings of smaller groups, and of the whole of information resources to discuss the options, but nothing that was said in those meetings seemed to have been taken into account when the teams were formed. The few group meetings that did occur were called "all hands" meetings (as in "all hands on deck"). Some ridiculed these meetings as pointless. Others labeled them as "mass indoctrination sessions."

Commented a long time library staff member:

> Officially all of us were part of the planning process. Only it wasn't planning, it was more like reeducation. We would all march off to these silly meetings in Pennsylvania Hall, led by the consultant hired by [the VP] who was around twenty-four years old [the consultant], and didn't know anything about libraries. We pasted circles on priorities like "perform selection on a more efficient basis." All this stuff was obvious. Who isn't for efficiency and excellence?

Library staff members commented over and over that they felt estranged from the planning process and troubled by the fact that the consultants seemed not to understand the library environment.

Reengineering planning continued for eleven months, mostly behind closed doors. Library and computer staff, still not united on teams, occupied the same cramped space and saw each other every day. However, leadership made little effort to bring these groups together in any meaningful way. Everyone waited anxiously for the plan to be unveiled. Conditions created a perfect environment for suspicion and innuendo to flourish. This, therefore, was a critical time to encourage dialogue, cooperation, and joint planning, but no one did. The vice president and his advisors missed an important opportunity.

Staff remember this as an uneasy period. Each side viewed the other with suspicion. Computing staff felt like barely tolerated visitors in their new home. Library staff described themselves as having been "conquered" by an occupying force. Librarians and computing staff continued to identify with their original group in spite of working side by side for eleven months. The core team had placed the integration of staff further down on the "to do" list and did not acknowledge or even recognize that the time to start working on these issues was the very beginning of the marriage.

In this secretive climate, fears took precedence over hopes. Some people feared they might lose their jobs. Others feared they might lose their offices (some did). Others feared they might lose their status as manager (most did). Finger-pointing and blame became the operating principles. Rumors raged. Tempers flared. The core team continued meeting privately. By the late fall of 1994, when the core team unveiled the new plan, many staff on both sides of the house felt disenfranchised.

Leadership presented the new structure in two volumes entitled *Business Renewal Project, Final Report.*[7] They told people to go home and read it over Christmas vacation because they would become teammates in January. Staff expressed uniformly negative comments about the planning process and final report. They spoke specifically about the lack of meaningful participation, the negativity directed toward library staff, the use of incomprehensible language in the final report, the overt business orientation, their inability to understand the value of the new structure, and their difficulty relating to the organization's new goals. One member of the support staff later reflected:

> We were always being told we had to keep up with the future and that what we were doing was NOT the future. The planning sessions all dealt with corporate America like GE and Ford. Never higher education or libraries. I felt as if every week we heard jargon from the latest management book on the *New York Times* bestseller list. It was exhausting.

STRUCTURE PROBLEMS

The new structure, which seemed unwieldy and illogical to constituents, presented the second problem. Implementation began in January 1995. The new information resources had at its core six self-managed (leaderless) teams organized by process, not function. The philosophy behind self-managed teams was that natural leaders would "bubble up" and assume leadership roles. Instead of bubbling up, they boiled over. On some teams everyone wanted to be in charge. On other teams no one wanted to be in charge. Leaderless teams proved unworkable, and after a year team leaders were appointed.

The process-based structure proved equally problematic. Departments like acquisitions, circulation cataloging, reference, and interlibrary loan ceased to exist. Instead, teams arranged work around a process—for example, the process of delivering a book or a computer or an overhead projector or a piece of electronic mail to a user. The delivery process became the basis for the delivery team.

The leadership also viewed ordering as a singular enterprise, whether one ordered a journal, software, telephone service, pens, pencils, or the weekly supply of coffee. Ordering was ordering! Therefore everyone who did any ordering should sit together and be on the same team—in this case, the selection team. Expertise was not a factor.

Six teams served as the bedrock of the new information resources. The core team conceived these teams as planets orbiting around a central customer. The teams had names meant to clarify the process, but members of the community, faculty members in particular, never managed to unravel the team structure or to make sense of the language. The teams included: planning, response, delivery, selection, training, and new initiatives. People did not know which team to call for assistance. The confusion, real or imagined, translated into misunderstandings and a perceived decline in service.

The planning team had responsibility for allocating resources, creating an evaluation system, organizing communications, and staying on top of public relations. Other members of information resources quickly labeled this team as "a group of people operating in a vacuum." Not on the front lines and not dealing directly with constituents, they were seen as decision makers with little knowledge of the rest of the organization, much less of the essentials of providing user services. I served on the planning team for a time and feel comfortable in saying that this perception is fairly close to the truth. The planning team earned this wrath, deserved or not, by remaining separate from the other planets. Salary inequity became a sore point. The planning team had to deal with the disparities of income on supposedly egalitarian teams, which made this team the lightning rod for general discontent—a situation exacerbated by the limited increases available for salaries.

The response team acted as the chief customer service unit. It consisted of former help desk employees and reference librarians who staffed a new, joint information desk—part reference desk, part clinic, part complaint bureau, and part repair shop. "One stop shopping" became the buzz phrase. The rationale for this combination went something like this: The "process," in this case, consisted of answering short-duration questions. All the following fell in the "short-duration" category: What is the population of Botswana? The printer is jammed. What does "fatal disk error" mean? Where is the bathroom? In theory, difficult, complicated questions would be referred to other teams. Harder questions would be handed off to the training team, for instance, which was supposed to contact the faculty and invite them in for a training session with their class. (This presupposed that all class assignments generated all reference questions.)

Reference librarians scoffed at the notion that all they did was answer short, simple questions. They pointed out that reference service often involved time-consuming research, complex search procedures, and sometimes follow-up days later. Librarians despaired that their jobs had been reengineered and their service restricted to answering simple questions. Anyone who had ever worked as a reference librarian found this approach to reference service confounding.

In the original plan all "library people" would learn enough about computing to respond to basic questions and the computer staff would learn enough about the library to answer reference questions. This required a shared base of minimum knowledge, and everyone spent hours in training sessions trying to get to the lowest common rung. Librarians often felt inadequate when dealing with technical questions they believed either they could not answer or were not their responsibility. They wearied of dealing with problems related to student telephone bills or dorm hookups.

Likewise, response team members with a computing background felt out of their element when users came shopping for statistics, literary criticism, or the text of the latest congressional hearing. Try as they might (and they really did try), the library staff never felt comfortable, let alone competent, making "house calls" to offices and dormitory rooms to troubleshoot computer problems—any more than former computer help desk staff felt comfortable fielding reference questions. Users grew impatient.

The leadership's lack of understanding of the training and experience necessary to perform as a reference librarian proved even more problematic. The core team continually downplayed the importance of professional credentials. The core planners viewed all library people as the same. Paraprofessional library staff assigned to the response team included the former head of circulation, a serials check-in clerk, staff from reserve, support staff from media services, and other paraprofessionals from the library who had never worked at the reference desk. The core team planners expected these diverse members to act as seasoned reference professionals when, in fact, they had not answered any more than the most rudimentary of reference question in the past. Running the reserve book room does not qualify one as reference librarian, no matter how positive one's customer service attitude is.

Indeed, core team planners cited attitude and personality as the most important traits for response team members. The *Business Renewal Project Final Report (II)* included a "Knowledge, Skills and Abilities Matrix" that enumerated these personality traits: pleasant, outgoing disposition, patient, adaptable, personable, customer-service oriented. Authors of this report defined essential knowledge as "basic knowledge to be able to respond to the majority of user requests for information and service."[8] Unfortunately, many staff felt ill equipped to deal with the depth and breadth of questions, not to mention the variety. Staff remarked that they felt set up to fail.

Opinion also remained divided about who should sit at the response team desk. The computer center traditionally employed many students on its help desk and saw no reason to discontinue this practice. While technically able, these students lacked preparation to assume the role of reference librarian. Librarians chafed at the presence of students at the desk and felt it represented the ultimate denigration of their role.

The one clear process to come out of the response team was a method of logging, responding, and tracking information desk calls. Considerable energy and resources went into developing this process while the team put other business on hold. Reference statistics during this period suggest that many users stopped thinking of the information desk as a place to come for library help. With only two bona fide librarians on this team, a reference load once shared by many on a rotating basis fell on a few.

This process-based model also destroyed the reference-bibliographer model of library service. The structure no longer permitted reference librarians to engage in collection development or bibliographic instruction. The reference librarians' involvement in collection development enables them to respond to user needs with greater knowledge of the collection. Conversely, they become aware of patron requests and are able to recommend purchases that will improve service on the front lines. Knowing what materials have just come in and recommending new sources for a particular class make it possible to do a better job as a reference librarian. The inauguration of the narrowly defined, process-based response team broke the natural, logical circle of reference bibliographer. Selection became a matter for another team; teaching became a responsibility for yet another. Reference librarians could only recommend to colleagues in training the readiness of class x for an instruction session and then could only hope that someone in selection had enough information to purchase the sources required to perform well on the front lines. The situation became demoralizing.

Of all the teams, the training team probably worked best. Librarians and information technologists had already worked collaboratively before the merger, and the area had many intersections. Yet the rigidity of the model soon led to the resignation of the librarian on this team. This individual did not want a steady diet of bibliographic instruction and, as she said in parting, had not gone to library school "to teach umpteen classes in e-mail and Netscape." Without the opportunity for a more varied day's work, entailing selection and reference duties as well as instruction, this librarian soured on Gettysburg College and accepted a more traditional position at another college. At this juncture, the training team became a unit of two and library instruction took a back seat. The team limped along trying to keep up with the demand and had difficulty recruiting new members. Indeed, it had become reduced to a team of one by the time the organization collapsed.

The selection team served as the purchasing agents for information resources. This team became home base for many former library support staff workers, a telecommunications administrator and several catalogers. In addition to books, journals, videos, supplies, and phone and cable service, this team had responsibility for the purchase of all desktop computers, software, and hardware. During the first year of the reorganization no one on selection possessed a strong computing background. The team spent a lot of time trying to get up to speed, never had the expertise needed to perform well, and often floundered. Observed a long time support staff member and experienced cataloger:

> I was a member of the selection team. I truly feel that we were the people they planned to dispose of and replace with computing specialists. We were expected to be involved in the ordering of computer software and eventually hardware, as well as library items and telecommunications stuff. Can you imagine? Of course it didn't work out, we were set up to fail!

If the selection team lacked expertise, the delivery team had more than enough experts to go around. In what became popularly known as "IR-speak," core team planners created the delivery team to "add value to new and existing resources, maintain these resources and ensure resource availability for the college user community."[9] Delivery processes were delivery processes—no matter what system was involved! It included such endeavors as the delivery of cable television, the campus network, the online catalog, telephone service, electronic mail, circulation, reserves, a cart with a VCR, and an overhead projector. Many of these processes, of course, had no relation to each other. Moreover the delivery team had great disparity of education, expertise, and background within it. Network engineers and stack assistants made up the team. They had vastly different goals, expectations, interests, and salaries. Members of this team found they had little in common and as a result became frustrated with the philosophy of the organization that lumped them together as a unit.

The vice president and his close advisors never clearly defined the remaining team, new initiatives. Staffed by one—the former library director—it ceased to exist when he left Gettysburg.

In its operation the process model had many conceptual flaws. Cataloging provides a good example. The wisdom of the day considered copy cataloging a selection team process because one "selected" a record from the database to download. But the core team considered database maintenance, the act of correcting mistakes in the online catalog, withdrawing records, or practicing authority control a value-added service, hence a matter for the delivery team. Catalogers had to decide if they wanted to be selectors or deliverers. In addition, many catalogers believe they quickly lose their edge, if not their sanity, if forced to spend eight hours a day doing copy cataloging. However, in the new organization, trained catalogers who elected to stay on the selection team (some selection team members did some original cataloging) were no longer permitted to fix database problems. Catalog maintenance fell into the hands of people on the delivery team—with little catalog training.

The library's one professional cataloger resigned and left the college, as did a support staff cataloger assigned to the delivery team who found herself running the circulation desk (value-added service). A second paraprofessional cataloger resigned, and a new professional cataloger left after only nine months on the job. The former head of acquisitions, working as a member of the selection team, left after two years of trying to oversee purchasing with an ever-diminishing staff. An acquisitions assistant from the selection team and a delivery team assistant, both former library employees unable to meet job expectations, resigned. Because of the dearth of professional and paraprofessional expertise, information resources ended up outsourcing nearly all cataloging to a vendor at a price tag that far exceeded the cost of the employees who had resigned.[10]

A parallel situation in interlibrary loan further amplifies the flaws of a process-based model. As with cataloging, the reengineering document outlined an interlibrary loan split along selection and delivery team lines. The document defined the borrowing aspect of interlibrary loan as a selection duty since one had to find the record online and select the institution to which the request would go. Lending, on the other hand, it defined as a delivery task, because the item must be retrieved and mailed. An awkward division of service and imbalance in the workload resulted. The selection team member faced a crushing workload. Meanwhile, the delivery team person had so much spare time that the team had to struggle to find other tasks for her to perform within the range of her skills and capabilities. This particular example illustrates the folly of a process-based model that removes experienced staff from tasks they perform well and places them in situations where they are left feeling underutilized and incompetent or completely overwhelmed.

One individual who left the organization reflected on the awkwardness of the process-based model:

> The reasoning behind the idea that the library and computing services should be combined into one organizational unit seems to be as follows: (A) computing services is in charge of acquiring, installing and administering computer hardware and software and the network on which it runs, (B) the library uses a lot of computers, therefore (C) the library and computing "do the same thing" and, furthermore, should be merged to eliminate redundancy and

increase efficiency and effectiveness. This makes about as much sense as saying that because the admissions office uses phones and fax machines a lot, it should be merged with or run by the department which installs and maintains the campus telephone system. The fact that one department is a frequent user of the tools installed and maintained by the other does not mean that the two departments "do the same thing."

CULTURAL DIFFERENCE

The third problem relates to the cultural differences between the library and the computing staff. Not recognized initially as an important factor, these differences should have been addressed in order to build a healthy and harmonious new organization.

When the computer center and library merged they found themselves in close quarters. With space on campus at a premium, leadership made a decision to move computing into the library. Musselman Library, built in the early 1980s, had an open floor plan. Little space had been set aside for offices and barely accommodated the twenty-five members of the library staff. With the merger, an additional twenty members of computing and assorted student assistants required lodging.

Extensive and, in most cases, cheaply orchestrated renovations became necessary to make everyone fit. Some of these renovations impacted the heating and ventilation systems. Staff found themselves in cramped makeshift offices with no air conditioning in the summer and no heat in the winter. Stacks had to be consolidated, and all carefully measured collection growth space disappeared. "Go electronic" and "buy fewer books" became the message. Renovation plans turned student study areas and open stacks into newly fashioned labs and offices. The library became a perpetual construction site. The renovations cut technical processing space in half.

With the identification of teams, private offices all but disappeared and communal workspace became the arrangement of the day. Large shared offices were integral to the new organization's philosophy. The core team planners believed housing team members together in close quarters would facilitate innovation, foster creativity, and encourage the "bubbling up" of leaders. In reality, the large communal workspaces more closely resembled overcrowded bedrooms shared by squabbling siblings. Almost everyone got one or two roommates. One team office had nine inhabitants. People used to a quiet environment found it hard to concentrate.

From the library perspective, these new roommates brought "a lot of stuff" with them—messy stuff with wires, draping cords, and loose parts. They needed work space and storage space—both in short supply. In a house too small, housekeeping quickly became a flash point. No one had anticipated the differences in culture, much less had worked to channel those differences into positive energy. The new roommates did not know each other very well, but they soon learned that they had strikingly different habits, values, goals, and even reasons for coming to work.

I have talked to colleagues who contend that cultural difference is an overplayed issue. They argue that people in computing and those from a library background are really more alike than not—all have customer needs at heart. They maintain that the "difference in culture problem" is exaggerated. Based on my Gettysburg experience, I disagree. Based on conversations with staff on both sides of the house, I believe that many, though not all, viewed each other with suspicion, much of it based on circumstances. They entered the merger with many stereotypes about their new partners—stereotypes that had a large grain of truth. Instead of recognizing these differences as a potential problem and dealing with them to build a stronger organization, some used stereotypes in a destructive manner—to create an IN (cooperative) group and an OUT (uncooperative) group—which contributed to an overwhelmingly negative climate.

At the time of the union, while believing themselves understaffed, busy, and innovative, some in computing viewed the library as overstaffed, underworked, lacking innovation, and resistant to change. Said a colleague in computing, "[The library staff] didn't seem to work very hard. We were there at all hours running from office to office on campus. Helping everyone. There was never enough time, never enough people for all the demands. We never went home on time."

Indeed, arrivals and departures became a point of contention. Some library staff believed that computing staff hung around the building all the time, "playing with their gadgets." Said a library staff member, "They wore it like a badge, how they could never leave, had so much to do." On the other hand, many library staff members left each day at 4:30 sharp. Some computing staff viewed this as a lack of commitment. As one library staff member explained, "This is a job for us, not a career. It doesn't make us less dedicated."

Gender and status also became factors. The library staff consisted of predominantly older female workers. The library employed greater numbers of hourly workers than did computing. Both librarians and staff earned substantially lower salaries than their counterparts in computing. Despite the perception of being uncommitted, library staff consisted mostly of long-term employees of the college. By contrast, computing employed a higher percentage of younger males and had many more administrative staff than hourly employees. Compared to the library, they were high earners. Computing staff had more fluidity among its ranks. With more opportunities in the private sector, computing had a higher turnover than the library.

The library had been operated on a hierarchical basis prior to the merger, and many had a difficult adjustment to a flattened organization. Library staff had been comfortable with hierarchy and welcomed authority and direct supervision. Library employees also held affiliation as a primary value. People came to work partly to enjoy the friendships. They had close personal relationships with each other and had many "ceremonial" occasions as a group—recognizing birthdays, births, anniversaries, and so on. Breaks were a regular part of the workday and staff gathered like clockwork in the staff room at set times. By contrast, computing had a flatter, more egalitarian structure, with more employees at the same level. Some computer staff joked that everyone wanted to be the boss, which resulted in everyone being a director of something. Computing staff viewed themselves as more businesslike, and the regular breaks and celebrations of the library staff baffled them.

Both groups found they had habits that irritated their new partners and occasionally escalated beyond annoyance to open argument. The library had a long-standing food ban in public spaces. Computer staff ate and drank in the open, took soft drinks to the information desk, and ordered food for their student workers. Members of the library staff often brought a brown bag lunch and ate in the staff room. Computing staff felt unwelcome in the staff room and ate lunch at their desks. The smell and sight of open food created vocal complaints from librarians, concerned about the consequences of food in the library. Computing staff could not understand the librarians' perceived obsession with banning food.

Other differences ranged from security to spending habits. The library staff was security conscious, carefully locking outside doors and parceling out keys on a limited basis. The vice president issued master keys to everyone on the staff. Some computer student workers had access to the master key; and those who did not occasionally propped the back door open when the building was closed. While the computing staff tried to monitor their student employees, library staff perceived computing as lax.

The library never overspent its budget and seldom requested or got major enhancements. The library was technology poor, complained about it, but remained in this state for years. Librarians spread spending throughout the year in keeping with the publishing cycle. By contrast, computing, being more action-oriented, adopted the philosophy of spending everything whenever receiving a new allocation and then looking for additional funding later. They could not fathom the library staff sitting on a pile of money and measuring it out slowly. One former library employee wrote:

> I believe that the culture of computing, with its rapidly changing knowledge base and hardware options, resulted in the attitude of patch-it-together. It is good enough for today because everything will change tomorrow anyway. [This] is so diametrically opposed to the library culture of preservation, thoroughness and attention to detail, that it takes a great deal of effort and a lot of tolerance from both sides to bridge the gap.

What happens when you marry two groups with different habits, motivations, and perspectives? Without proper counseling and preparation, small matters are likely to grow into major incidents. Small misunderstandings turn into major grudges. Minor suspicions become major issues of mistrust. Instead of acknowledging difference and channeling it in a positive direction, difference becomes a wedge. Difference soon became not only an impediment to full integration but also the basis of much ill will. A highly respected library support staff member reflected:

> Originally we had a culture of benign neglect under a regime which offered little leadership but which encouraged civility and fellowship. Bad behavior was seldom rewarded; consequently there was little incentive for people to practice treachery, deception and those other refined arts we've come to know so well. There was little or no sense of careerism among the [library] staff. Emphasis was on collegiality, nurturing, and so forth. Long-term staff pretty much understood that they had traded any prospect of salary or promotion for a pleasant work atmosphere. When computing moved in it was like an occupation. Suddenly there were two groups of people, immediately labeled first class/valid/good people and second class/invalid/bad people. The library staff was second class. Indeed we were forbidden to even use the word "library."

With this shift, the reward system for behavior changed radically. People who wanted to be identified with the privileged first class, or who wanted to escape stigmatization as part of the second class, discovered that they would now be rewarded for behavior which would previously have been discouraged. The new environment encouraged and rewarded careerism; lack of compassion became a virtue. For many, the whole social values system seemed turned upside down.

SEPARATING INFORMATION RESOURCES

Eventually faculty and other employees noticed the change. Fewer and fewer of them visited. When they did, they often came with complaints. They had questions but could not always find the team with the answers. Indeed, the team concept confused them. They talked about us behind our backs and to each other. They said we were disorganized, dysfunctional, unhelpful, and chaotic. Many of the members of this dysfunctional, newly blended family left home. Teams soon had vacancies that they could not fill and more work fell on those who remained. A nearly complete organizational breakdown followed. In February 1997, the faculty began a barrage of public e-mails related to problems in information resources and publicly criticized the organization and its leadership.

Department chairs weighed in, urging a vote of no confidence at an upcoming faculty meeting. While this vote did not occur, the college administration altered reporting relationships shortly thereafter. Information resources came under the academic wing of the institution, reporting directly to the provost. Soon afterwards the vice president for information resources left Gettysburg. In July 1997, the college separated information resources. At the time of this restructuring the library professional cohort consisted of only three librarians and an archivist—an all-time low.

The most interesting story, perhaps, revolves around the events of the past two years, as the Musselman Library and our information resources colleagues (we kept the house, they kept the name) have struggled to build new, separate organizations and identities and win back the goodwill of our constituents. We still live together, awaiting availability of new quarters for information resources, but we address space and turf issues more openly. We also have begun to identify the natural intersections of our two units and move in the direction of collaboration when it makes sense. A joint effort to design an "electronic classroom" in the library for both sides of the house to use is the first example of the collaboration. We have been talking about joining forces for freshman orientation. Such efforts are still awkward at times, and many resentments linger, particularly on the part of library staff members, but we are doing better.

"No!" Each interviewee almost always responded when I asked, "Was there anything good in it from your perspective?" However, some staff members did acknowledge that the library moved forward technologically as a result of the experience. Said one former employee, "It was easier to get more state-of-the-art computer equipment for library staff and librarians. We were always at the end of the line for new equipment [before the merger] and we did move pretty quickly into purchasing electronic products." Everyone agrees that library users have benefited from the highly networked environment. They now have wide choices of electronic journals and indexes, document delivery, electronic reserves, online tables of contents, Web catalog and electronic ordering and claiming. Some of our outsourcing arrangements and our approval plan, made in desperation, have worked well for us and we have kept them with modifications. These are positive outgrowths of the merger. A library staff member offers this observation:

> I think, as an organization and as a college, we are stronger for having survived this. Also, we were forced in the library to rethink what we were doing in our jobs, which wasn't all bad. The cost was too great, though, and we'll be years getting over it.

The challenge for the current leadership is to help the staff put grievances aside and move on to build a strong new library for the next century.

CONCLUSIONS

What lessons can be learned from this episode in Gettysburg College's history? Many institutions have been curious about the Gettysburg experiment, and in the early days we hosted dozens of delegations from various colleges and universities who were considering merging their library and computer center. Few, however, adopted our model; few sought a level of integration so complete that most vestiges of library culture disappeared. Nevertheless, many colleges and universities have merged services and found a comfortable middle ground.

The Gettysburg experiment began with a great deal of optimism on the part of its planners, but they could never forge an effective partnership between library and computing personnel. The vice president for information resources and his close advisors became caught up in reengineering—the management rage in mainstream business at the time. They trusted outside consultants who lacked the necessary understanding of how libraries function. The organization of the project left key constituencies, from the college's administration to the faculty, out of the loop.

The team structure quickly became unwieldy as teams became too large and remained unorganized for more than a year while the vice president and his advisors continued to insist on self-management rather than team leaders. Teams spent too much time in definition—trying to figure out their role and defining their boundaries vis-à-vis other teams. The organization lost a critical moment to establish clear, unified service. Beyond the problem of leaderless teams, an organization arranged around process and the logical rhythms of work ground to a halt. An organization that could not function effectively resulted. Morale diminished, as did the quality of service. Once patrons began to expect the worst, it became a self-fulfilling prophecy.

Moreover, we saw that vocabulary does make a difference. Clear definitions of teams and work groups are essential considerations when serving an academic clientele and contemplating changes away from a traditional model. Gettysburg faculty wanted to know who to call with a specific problem and they did not want to think about whether it was a delivery team or a selection team matter. The business language became an impediment to academic users who felt uncomfortable with language such as "value-added services" and "goals measurement matrix."

Quite real, but not insurmountable, cultural differences existed between the library and the computer center staff. Recognizing the differences and working with them constructively would have made a world of difference. Had the vice president and his core team engaged from outside the college some skillful trainers, experienced in working with organizations and change, instead of trying to manage the transition completely in house, many flash points might have been avoided. Allowing people to work together for a time, collaborate on projects and get used to each other, before throwing everyone into the same house and imposing a new structure would have been a more measured and possibly more successful approach.

Gettysburg College tried to do three things at once—merge administratively, move into the same space, and throw away the old framework and reengineer a new one. The new structure was not sensible, and the rank and file staff on both sides did not feel invested in the pursuit. Overall, a dubious project was undertaken, with little consultation with those who would be responsible for providing patron services and making information resources operate effectively. These errors, and the error of trying to merge instantaneously proved fatal to any hope of a successful merger.

NOTES

1. Gettysburg is a four-year, non-sectarian liberal arts college founded in 1832. The college enrolls 2,200 students and has 160 full-time faculty. At the time of reorganization the combined organizations had fifty-two employees.
2. Arnold Hirshon, *Integrating Computing and Library Services: An Administrative Planning and Implementation Guide for Information Resources,* CAUSE Professional Paper Series 18 (Boulder, Colo.: CAUSE, 1998), 6-9.
3. Ibid., pp. 6-7. Hirshon's list of poor reasons for integrating include climbing on the academic bandwagon, improving a weak operation by marrying it to a stronger one, saving money, saving space, eliminating an ineffective administrator, eliminating faculty status for professional staff or reducing compensation, and reducing the number of direct reports to the provost or president.
4. In addition to oral interviews, staff were sent a questionnaire with eleven questions related to the merger. All names have been omitted in this essay.
5. An example of this disconnect— "dreaming the big dream"—was a public meeting in which the vice president for information resources suggested that we give our book budget to Cornell University, let them use it to buy books, and let Gettysburg College borrow anything we wanted, whenever we wanted, thereby increasing our collection size dramatically by having access to all the volumes available at Cornell. Faculty members present at the meeting did not endorse this idea.
6. Gettysburg College, Information Resources Division, *Business Renewal Project: Final Report, Part I: Executive Summary and Recommendations.* December 6, 1994, p. 3.
7. Gettysburg College, Information Resources Division, *Business Renewal Project: Final Report, Part I: Executive Summary and Recommendations* and *Part II: Deliverables.* December 6, 1994.
8. Gettysburg College, Information Resources Division, *Business Renewal Project: Final Report, Part II: Deliverables,* December 6, 1994, p. 81.
9. Ibid., 91.
10. By 1997, information resources had lost most of its cataloging and acquisitions staff. What few staff members remained spent most of their time checking the work of the vendors and supervising students. During the merger we initiated an approval plan with Yankee Book Peddler and established a contract with an excellent independent acquisitions jobber, Siena Library Company, and continue to use their services.

CHAPTER EIGHTEEN

The Computing Center and the Library at a Teaching University

Application of Management Theories in the Restructuring of Information Technology

THERESA C. TRAWICK
JEFFRY T. HART

INFORMATION MANAGEMENT IN CRISIS

Increased demands for electronic information, static budgets, and overworked, inadequately trained staff have created a crisis in information management on our campuses. Through observation and interviews, the authors have confirmed the existence of the crisis among librarians, computer staff, and top university management in teaching universities. We believe that the resolution to this crisis demands those management theories applied in the corporate environment also be applied to management of higher education's information technology. However, such purposefully incorporated quality management practice in this area is lacking.

The ninth annual "Campus Computing Survey" conducted in 1998 sheds light on this management crisis. Based on data provided by officials at 1,623 higher education institutions in the United States, this study revealed an exponential growth in demands for electronic information. Classes using e-mail grew from 32.8 percent in 1997 to 44.4 percent in 1998; class syllabi reflect that 33.3 percent of classes have Internet components, compared to 24.8 percent the previous year.[1]

Such growth in demands would tax even the most competent management. However, this 1998 study revealed that less than 40 percent of the participating campuses report a working financial plan for IT (information technology), up from 1996 (28.1 percent). In the study, information officers expressed a need for integration of information services into the universities' goals. The study found that information officers consider the following as the top challenges for campus computing:

> Integrating instruction and technology
>
> Supporting users[2]

To meet these two challenges, universities must develop the ability to manage technology as a single entity instead of technology-related units trying to work separately to obtain bigger budgets, technology, and additional staff.

BEGINNINGS: COLLABORATION AT TROY STATE UNIVERSITY

Before the late 1980s, minimal ongoing cooperation existed between the library and the computing center at Troy State University, mostly with the computing center providing limited support to the library through computer maintenance. The computing center and the library operated worlds apart with well-defined boundaries as part of a traditional structure. The small computing staff consisted mainly of males; the small library staff consisted mainly of females, with the exception of the library director. Library technical staff and computing center staff held in common the careful processing of information. In contrast, the library's public services department practiced "people skills"; the staff observed, inquired, reacted, and interacted as they assisted patrons.

Within this human culture, a technological culture grew. Troy State University's computing center, until recently, served mainly as administrative computing in a mainframe environment. Requests for new services or changes slowly channeled from the university administration to the director of computing and then to the staff. Somewhat stable environments in the computing center and the library did not require their managers to have a full appreciation of the interrelation between the two units.

During the 1980s, the library staff began experiencing increasingly longer lines of students waiting to use stand-alone workstations, which the staff took as evidence of a need to provide more access points for the electronic delivery of full-text information. As a result, the library director sought permission to use existing staff funds (from retirements) to form a new position in the library of information technology coordinator. The computing center staff, reacting positively to the newly created position, showed respect for the coordinator's technical skills and expressed relief that he would be the one to handle library projects. Once the coordinator was in place, the library began unrolling a technology plan in phases. An early project in the plan included building a local area network to deliver full-text articles and the catalog. The network developed while the acquisition of full-text journal resources and a public access catalog/circulation system on CD-ROM further developed.

Further "bottom-up" changes began in 1994. After much discussion among the library director, the coordinator of information technology in the library, the head of reference and collection management, and the other library staff, the director asked the university to create a new administrative position— electronic services librarian. This librarian would lead the planning, selection, installation, and continuing development of an integrated library system and related systems. After approval by the university, the librarian who served as head of reference and collection management laterally transferred to the position of electronic services.

Until this time, the library at Troy and its campuses had maintained a CD-ROM-based catalog and circulation system. The librarians began a push for an integrated library system. The library director appointed a committee from the library's public and technical services staff, who spent several years selecting and choosing a system. Once this group met its charge, the director then appointed a library system implementation committee. This committee consisted of the Troy campus's electronic services librarian (as chair), the library technology coordinator (in the library), the library technical services chair, and the Dothan campus's assistant library director. Only months after this committee began planning for installation, the university transferred the library's technology coordinator to the computing center. As a result, the library had to hire another library technical coordinator. The project to implement an integrated system needed collaborative input, including contributions from the computing center. Ironically, the person who moved from the library to computing now represented computing.

The committee spent months preparing configuration manuals, outlining and structuring the project with Gantt charts, and integrating the library system into broader information systems plans. This cross-functional committee remained in close contact with both the library and computing center administrative offices as various parties made decisions about information delivery systems. Several committee members expressed interest in management techniques applied in the corporate environment and wanted to apply that knowledge in the university committee work. Along with an interest in management, the members shared strong informal relationships that existed before appointment.

Through 1997, the original structure of this cross-functional group remained basically the same. Additions included the library's Webmaster and the technical-support student assigned by the computing center to the library. Informally, this group grew into a self-directed, cohesive team. Formally, the library and computing directors supported the group but did not label the group as a "team."

Once the committee put the integrated system in place, the committee functioned in a broader sense as a systems committee. Plans unfolded for the design and implementation of the library's Intranet for patrons. Time-consuming questions included how to select and integrate databases, how to handle user authentication, how to answer routine questions and general information, and how to design Web pages that presented information in an effective way.

OUTCOMES OF THE LIBRARY SYSTEMS COMMITTEE EFFORTS

The broad range of desirable outcomes that the library system committee helped bring to Troy State University includes:

> Gained recognition from the university's information technology coordinator for the planned management in selecting, installing, and developing the integrated library system.
>
> Created and had approved the first internal documents outlining the MIS department's and other departments' responsibilities dealing with networking costs.
>
> Created systemwide planning for library system development.
>
> Publicized the need to have computers and networking as part of the operating budget.

Established the precedent for handling library system upgrades.

Assisted the library's public service desk in computer/Internet training.

Was represented on the university's administrative user support group.

Was represented on the university's systemwide (all campuses) development committee.

Troy State University has also incorporated the following strategies to ensure a high level of cooperation between the library and the computing center:

1. The computing center has provided a full-time staff member to support information technology within the library. This staff member is responsible for PC hardware, desktop applications, online database access, OPAC software support, and administrative software support.

2. The host systems for Web servers, OPAC servers, etc., are housed in the Troy State University main computer room. Backup functions for these hosts are performed by computing staff. This staff is also responsible for the operating system software on these hosts. Backup schedules are coordinated with the library to ensure continuity of system services.

3. Software upgrades to operating system software and application software are the responsibility of the computing staff. Application software upgrades are coordinated with the library to ensure continuity of system services.

4. The computing center provides the library with network access and network support. All network hardware and software are the responsibility of the computing center. Network security and Internet access are also the responsibility of computing.

5. The library is responsible for all contract negotiations with regard to application software, online databases, and levels of access. TSU has multiple sites and libraries that require different levels of access to certain online services. Computing provides access to different sites or groups of users based on the library's request.

6. The library is responsible for determining the services that its patrons need. All evaluation of services and decisions as to which services to add, delete, or change is the responsibility of the library.

7. The library is responsible for providing a staff member to act as Webmaster for its Web site. This individual is responsible for the layout, development, testing, and changes to the library Web site.

Troy State University's assistant director of computing served as a key player responsible for the successful outcomes listed above. He had been the library technology coordinator and a member of the library system committee. With an interest in management theory and application (and some background in library services), he provided a broad knowledge base to draw upon as a leader in the computing center. His encouragement to restructure the computing center into academic and administrative computing with coordinators for each, and his efforts to reward these individuals, helped improve the organization.

From the mid-1990s through 1997, the relationship between the library system group and senior administrators became closer, and the senior administrators left more decision-making power with the group. Troy State University began strengthening the collaboration between libraries and computing by bringing workplace democracy to the organization. The relationship between the system committee and its additions of sub-groups to build Web pages and to develop the serials module displayed this democratic effort. The library systems group profited from both continuity of membership and flexibility in changing the membership.

The library and computing center also profited from observing how others handle restructuring issues. In the mid-1990s, the new acting director of the Troy State University libraries promoted the merger of the libraries with the newly formed information technology department, which included telecommunications, radio and television, computing and distance education. Not only was the acting library director new to the position, the head of information technology was new in a newly created position. The library systems committee did not support the merger at that particular time for several reasons:

1. Such a restructuring had not been a formal part of the university's strategic planning; therefore, a strategy to truly integrate the two departments had not been designed.

2. Leadership previously had been defined as only one person at the top.

3. Collaboration between the two entities had been sporadic and informal, except for the formal and planned collaborative effort with the library systems committee.

4. Staff of the two units had not been asked for input.

5. The two new directors had not been employed long enough to obtain the profound knowledge of the social/psychological/economic factors affecting the university and the two departments.

6. The two directors had not been employed long enough to obtain the process task knowledge of systems and subsystems within the two units.

Not surprisingly, the proposed merger did not occur. Fully successful collaboration between the library and computing center in other areas, such as user training, also did not succeed. The library and computing staff often struggled with how to handle the large demand for training. Coordinated training between the library and computing center still is not yet in place. The library does much staff and patron training in computers, databases, and the Internet. The computing center does provide a help desk to handle technical questions but struggles to staff it.

This lack of collaboration in training is not uncommon. A study by Nancy Schiller published in the summer 1994 issue of *Internet Research* found that only "half of the librarians (50.7 percent) and slightly more than a third of the computing services staff (37.1 percent)" indicated that the library and computing center worked together to provide Internet instruction. Those units that did work together divided instruction with the computing center covering how the Internet works and the librarians covering where to find the information. Many personnel from both units thought "the two service groups brought to Internet training and instruction different and complementary expertise and knowledge, and that they should work together to provide Internet instruction."[3] Schiller concludes that "experiences varied greatly from institution to institution and that local traditions and personal, organizational, and instructional politics and attitudes can greatly facilitate or impede cooperation between the two groups."[4] At Troy State University, the computing staff must overcome existing workloads in order to develop a training program in collaboration with the library.

BEYOND RUDIMENTARY COLLABORATION: ELEMENTS REQUIRED FOR SUCCESSFUL RESTRUCTURING

Many of the factors required for successful restructuring of an organization to support technology are intertwined. These complex factors can be readily deconstructed into simple terms. For example, teams cannot lead without plans. Leadership within the library and computing centers is directly dependent on the executive support for information technology. The support is directly related to how well the integration of technology into strategic development planning takes place. Libraries and computing centers cannot take leadership roles unless the senior university administrators willingly relinquish some decision making to them. Teams must be self-directing and prominent on campus.

The beginning of successful redesign of organizational plans for information technology is very dependent on librarians', computing staffs', and top administrators' insight into the complexity of applying management theories. In the following section we briefly analyze relevant management theory in three broad areas: planning, communication, and training. Mastering of these management areas undergirds the restructuring of information technology that is necessary for complete and effective collaboration (see figure 1).

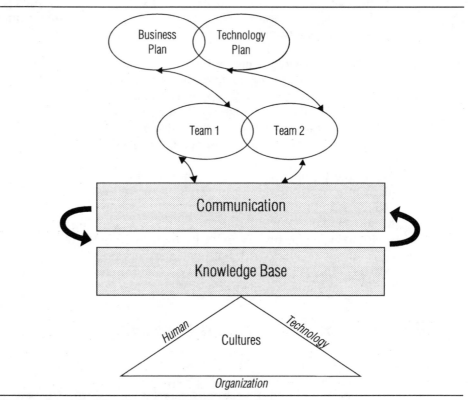

Figure 1   Information Management in the Twenty-first Century

Managed Restructuring Requires Planning

Knowledge Base Required for Planning   Understanding the interrelation of the concepts mentioned above requires a broad knowledge base. As a knowledge base becomes strengthened, staff are able to plan. Managers begin to see that technology plans should fold into the university's strategic plan. As said by the Global Institute for Interactive Multimedia:

> Strategic planning, on a continuous, rolling basis, is the only way an institution can hope to cope with the sea changes taking place in its environment caused by Internet/Web technology and the effects that the sea changes are having on other aspects of the institution's environment.[5]

Planned Change   Another factor related to planning for information technology is planning for change rather than being forced to change. Troy State University, as with many institutions, is forced into change. The open communication/information network made possible by the World Wide Web forced the library and computing departments to maximize resources. As library and computing staff began to informally discuss student and staff expectations and to react to technology changes, these staff members realized that the university could not provide the electronic services being demanded without a change in management. On a small scale, the library system committee became one answer to handling change at Troy State University. To have more integrated restructuring on a large scale will require full support of team management from top administrators. Implementing team management requires planning for change.

Planning Job Positions   Another important area of planning that demands attention is the restructuring of job positions for team management. Such restructuring is often not welcomed by all, especially when resources and salaries are of concern. The resistance to change is so strong that John Lubans Jr. believes that it will take another generation of library and computer center staff truly to collaborate for the good of the parent organization. At Duke University, Lubans found that staff at the top and bottom, when introduced to team structure, "did not know what to do with this new-found freedom. . . . A generation of librarians raised in a competitive and hierarchical model, with independence as a core value, was not ready for the implicit collaboration and consulting required by the new model."[6] Considering the difficulty of forming teams, Troy State University has been fortunate to have individuals from the library and the computing center who could work with one another and see very positive outcomes because of their work. One would wish that this success story would prove an incentive for similar team efforts.

Managed Restructuring Requires Communication

Establishing Communication   The need for effective communication parallels the importance of planning. Top management philosophically and functionally support effective communication. A direct relationship exists between effective communication and effective information delivery. Nevertheless, if a long-standing awareness of the importance of communication exists, why then the failure or poor utilization of communication?

Reinsch's survey of entering MBA students indicated that a combination teaching approach "that situates practical 'know-how' in a framework of theoretical 'know-why'" is needed in management/business communication courses.[7] A major but simple premise is that any one in the workforce needs to know how to communicate; however, communication is complex. Don Mankin in *Teams and Technology* points out those information technology professionals "often cannot communicate with users, tend to subordinate user desires to broader, corporate imperatives, and view corporate management, rather than end-user units, as their client."[8] A solution to "whom do I serve," according to Mankin, is in the hands of a select few who deliver technology.[9]

Communication Feedback   One way to avoid losing sight of the customer and becoming enmeshed in the politics of an organization is to practice communication feedback. Feedback is defined as a communication path as well as an integral part of communication structure: it is a cyclical evaluation of output to input. Effective feedback is characterized by

> Feedback coming from other team members, from team leaders, from customers, and from the organization.
>
> Feedback in the form of numbers and words.
>
> Feedback that is formal (scheduled and official) and feedback that is informal (spontaneous and open).
>
> Feedback of long-term, broad outcomes, as well as of short-term, small outcomes.[10]

Knowing how to communicate as individuals, in groups, and within the organization means acquiring understanding of the paths in which communication flows, with a cyclical path preferred. Simpler concepts, such as nonverbal communication, are also important to collaboration; face-to-face communication not only offers words to convey the message but also facial expressions, gestures, voice, personality, and immediate feedback. In summary, the element of communication and its importance to effective collaboration in technology efforts must be understood in order for team members to manage.

Managed Restructuring Requires Training

Training for Technology and Management   Staff training is also a key element in collaboration. Staff training in both technical and management areas is critical. Training is not only needed in the use of technology but in the management of technology. With the academic environment slowly adopting some of the management approaches of the corporate world, the authors hope that universities will become better at formally planning, financing, and rewarding staff training, especially for staff supporting information delivery and use. Training provides the strong knowledge base required for collaborative results.

The failure of institutions of higher education to educate staff in technology management is undesirable. Because of the lack of classes in technology management, some corporations have decided to expand their internal training efforts rather than depend on higher education. The information technology leader Andrew Weiss at Fannie Mae describes a case in point. He could not find universities with courses that taught information technologists how to manage teams and projects; therefore Fannie Mae began its own educational program. As the corporation moved to client/server technologies, the technology leader knew that a closer relationship with users and business managers would become more important. He found that these groups would not even talk to the information technology group. He soon realized that "so-called 'soft skills' of how to work in teams with end users" had to improve.[11] If corporations are taking steps to correct the lack of knowledge in regard to information management and communication, the university should take note.

Building a base for information management within library/computing units requires a continuous commitment to education. As previously mentioned, many corporations show strong commitment to research and training. "Motorola says every $1 it invests in training returns $30 in productivity gains within three years,"[12] Lubans from Duke University points out:

> Many academic libraries, strangely enough, provide little opportunity for training and development. Unlike industry, where sizable budgets and release time for training are common, the academic sector struggles with putting even the most modest percentage of an operating budget into training and development. I know of few change efforts in academe with a training commitment even approaching a tenth of what is needed.[13]

CONCLUSIONS AND RECOMMENDATIONS

Ideally, information services restructuring would permeate the organization as a result of strategic planning and as a result of teams formed to provide certain user services. The authors of a CAUSE document titled *Reinvesting in the Information Job Family* emphasized that job evaluation systems have not changed for decades on many campuses. They suggested the formation of cross-organizational teams to manage the system attentively and work with human resource managers and researchers to "develop new factors . . . in determining the worth of jobs."[14] Once universities realize that job descriptions and hiring processes must change, this awareness will facilitate collaboration between libraries and computing centers. Such restructuring will seem radical and threatening to many people. In a recent issue of *OCLC Systems and Services,* Neil Jones noted, "Taking into account the risk involved, it is unsurprising that even the more dynamic of library managers, with the support of well-converged computing departments, are reluctant to initiate the fundamental rebuilding that new technologies and new ways of using libraries are beginning to demand."[15]

In fact, many libraries that apparently restructured for better collaboration have made only superficial changes. Arnold Hirshon's study affirms that much of the traditional structure of separate departments remains as is (according to 71 percent of the respondents to his survey). Seventeen percent of the integrated organizations reported to him that they had placed the library and computing center under a chief information officer (CIO), but the directors of both units remained.[16]

During the Information Age, if the university does not completely redefine its organizational structure and fully integrate information technology into all phases of the organization, it will be considered less essential than in the past. The university's libraries and information systems staffs are essential change agents for this integration process. Restructuring with more team integration is crucial to meet today's demands for information technology (see figure 2). The structuring process must be done in a team environment and must be more than simply moving libraries and computing centers under the same manager.

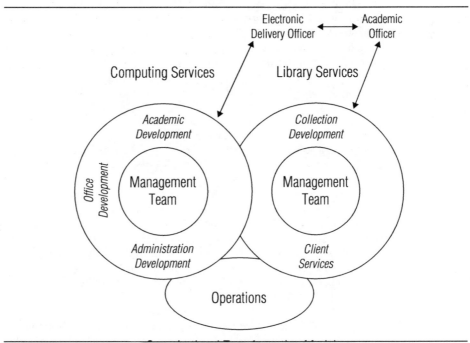

Figure 2   Organizational Transformation Model

Implementing cross-functional and self-managed teams, consisting of all levels of the present hierarchical structures, must be priority. Teams must be organized around tasks or customer needs, dependent on goals and environment. The university must strategically plan to integrate management applications into the restructuring of information technology. Over time, with the integration of organizational management, communication and collaboration, information technology will evolve into a truly reengineered area rather than one that has merely shifted around traditional responsibilities and lines of authority. As expressed by Kristin McDonough, "Clearly, among the daunting challenges that lie before campus information providers, the human issue of cooperation is as important—and as thorny—as the technological ones of connectivity and networking." [17]

NOTES

1. Kenneth C. Green, "The Campus Computing Project: The 1997 National Survey of Information Technology in Higher Education." <http://ericir.syr.edu/Projects/Campus_computing/1997/index.html>, October 1997.
2. Ibid.
3. Nancy Schiller, "Internet Training and Support: Academic Libraries and Computer Centers: Who's Doing What?" *Internet Research* 4 (summer 1994): 40-41.

4. Ibid.

5. The Global Institute for Interactive Multimedia, "Using Strategic Planning and Other Planning Processes to Facilitate Success in Responding to the Digital Revolution," <http://www.edgorg.com/management.htm>, October 1998.

6. John Lubans Jr., "How Can Something That Sounds So Good Make Me Feel So Bad? The Dilbertean Dilemma," *Library Administration & Management* 12 (winter 1998): 10.

7. N. Lamar Reinsch Jr. and Annette N. Shelby, "What Communication Abilities Do Practitioners Need? Evidence from MBA Students," *Business Communication Quarterly* 60 (December 1997): 25.

8. Donald Mankin and others, *Teams and Technology: Fulfilling the Promise of the New Organization* (Boston: Harvard Business School Pr., 1996), 83.

9. Ibid.

10. Harvey Robbins and Michael Finley, *Why Teams Don't Work: What Went Wrong and How to Make It Right* (Princeton, N.J.: Peterson's/Pacesetter Books, 1995), 126.

11. Jeff Moad, "Change of Course: IT Execs, Stymied by IAS Schools, Are Growing Their Staffs' Soft Skills," *PC Week* 12 (April 24, 1995): 1.

12. Stephen P. Robbins, *Organizational Behavior: Concepts, Controversies, Applications*, 7th ed. (Englewood Cliffs, N.J.: Prentice Hall, 1996), 114.

13. Lubans, 10.

14. Anne Woodsworth and Theresa Maylone, *Reinvesting in the Information Job Family: Context, Changes, New Jobs, and Models for Evaluation and Compensation*, CAUSE Professional Paper Series 11 (Association of College and Research Libraries; CAUSE; Apple Computer, Council on Library Resources, 1993), 11, ERIC, ED 365327, microfiche.

15. Neil Jones, "Network-Accessible Resources and the Redefinition of Technical Services," *OCLC Systems and Services* 14, no.1 (1998): 20.

16. Arnold Hirshon, *Integrating Computing and Library Services: An Administrative Planning and Implementation Guide for Information Resources*, CAUSE Professional Paper Series 18 (Boulder, Colo.: CAUSE, 1998), ix.

17. Kristin McDonough, "Prior Consent: Not-So-Strange Bedfellows Plan Library/Computing Partnerships"(April 12, 1992) EDRS, ED 364225, microfiche.

CHAPTER NINETEEN

A Partnership for Future Information Technology Support at a Community College

Libraries and learning resource centers in community colleges experience challenges and frustrations similar to those of their college and university peers in articulating needed technological changes and negotiating appropriate support levels with the campus computer center. Much has been written about the differences in cultures and values of staff in these two areas that contribute to miscommunication and nonalignment of practices and pursuits. On the community college campus other challenges may exist. For example, at community colleges, four-year colleges, and universities alike, the library as a resource that serves the entire institution generally receives more respect than the computing center. At community colleges, however, that respect frequently does not translate into needed financial resources and technology.

Administrative dependence on the systems provided by computer centers has taken precedence in budget allocation decisions over the less conspicuous dependence of students and faculty on library systems. Library administrators, therefore, have spent inordinate amounts of time and energy on making visible their information system needs, while computer centers often have been free to change costly networks and systems with little review of their plans by others in the organization. This situation existed for some years at Washtenaw Community College (WCC) in Michigan.

WASHTENAW COMMUNITY COLLEGE

Background

Founded in 1965, Washtenaw Community College has a comprehensive mission that includes transfer, career, and occupational courses and programs. The college offers associate degrees and certificates in over seventy disciplines/programs and enrolled more than 16,000 students in credit courses in 1997-1998. Washtenaw County is a generous supporter of the college. Both the quality of the

189

educational experience at WCC and the attractiveness and functionality of most campus facilities demonstrate county taxpayers' commitment to the college's mission.

Organizationally, WCC follows academic tradition. The college library, the learning resource center, is on the instructional side of the house, and the dean of learning resources reports to the vice president of instruction. The information systems department head, the executive director, reported for many years to the vice president of administration. Recently, this reporting relationship changed. The president now supervises the IS executive director.

For several years, faculty and LRC staff expressed dissatisfaction with priorities set by upper administration regarding information systems or services, and they recommended many changes in services and in organizational structure. These communications occurred in the manner common at academic institutions—interoffice memos, committee recommendations and reports, and faculty forums. Neither the climate of discord over information technology issues nor the many proffered recommendations influenced major college computing initiatives or brought about organizational change.

In the mid-1990s circumstances at WCC markedly changed. Many factors contributed to an information systems environment of continuous crises that eventually, in 1997, impacted college mission-critical operations far beyond those of the learning resource center (LRC). In this chapter I offer a case study of the college's response to the breakdown in information systems and services, and to the obstruction of major information technology initiatives. I describe the collaborative processes engaged in by LRC and information systems (IS) stakeholders, faculty users, and an external consultant to create a model for a transformative organizational structure. I also examine the elements of a new three-way partnership among information and learning technology providers and divisional "tech teams" that strengthen communication and user support in a distributed model while retaining the centralized, distinct responsibilities of the LRC and IS units. This chapter is a case study and not a theoretical investigation of ideal structures and models of service. Hence, I address the fiscal realities that affected the implementation of the new model, as well as the unexpected consequences of a new president's arrival at WCC before the implementation of all the model's components.

A Digital Baby Step

In 1991, the learning resource center launched its integrated online library system with Dynix software on an HP platform. The LRC had only minimal, but critical, dependence on the college information systems department. The library system's processor, located in the IS environmentally controlled computer room, was connected to a major data switch. IS staff provided regular system administration routines including system backup. Although the software had high reliability, the annual percentage of library system downtime proved to be unacceptable. This resulted from both the LRC's low-priority ranking on the IS troubleshooting list and IS's inability to assign trained UNIX staff to regular software upgrades and to operating system and hardware maintenance. College executive officers sometimes confused the vigorous efforts of the LRC's dean and other staff to restore service when the system went down with unnecessary interference in IS operations.

The Cost of Connectivity

In 1995, the college, together with industry and community organization partners, sought and received a large federal grant to bring new information technologies to the desktops of community small business owners and to provide
them with instruction and training. The LRC staff and the faculty in computing
and technology disciplines were the primary college players. Accomplishment
of the grant's objectives required the installation of a T-1 line for Internet connectivity and the development of the data wiring infrastructure in the two
buildings where the college partners resided. In fact, the grant funded these installations. IS did not support the grant project. Keeping an older generation of
management information systems software operational consumed most of the
IS staff's time and energy. They often turned down or gave minimal attention to
requests for support of new data-driven projects or curriculum applications.
When the IS director resisted the installation of the new data wire infrastructure, the president ordered that the work proceed according to the grant's calendar. A grant-funded UNIX engineer, under the direction of the LRC as lead
partner, took charge of the project.

Within six months, instructors offered an Internet-based course and consulted with community partners. The librarians in the LRC provided weekly
workshops on searching Netscape and on e-mail fundamentals to small business owners and to college faculty and staff members. The project made the Internet accessible from workstations in the LRC to all college staff. As scores of
college staff members became skilled users of the Internet and became enthusi-
astic about the new possibilities offered by the World Wide Web, they developed expectations for Internet access at their own desktops. Before the year's
end, IS became the target of a groundswell of user demands that could not be
satisfied without significant funding and the development of a campus-wide
infrastructure.

Several other conditions also developed on parallel streams. These converged in 1997. WCC successfully passed a very large bond proposal in 1996 for
new instructional technology and the construction of a new technology education building including a new LRC. When funds became available, departments
immediately began acquiring the computers and systems that they had wanted
for years. Administrators selected and ordered a long needed new telephone
system and a touch-tone registration system. The LRC began discussing the
need for a campus-wide media distribution system. Realizing the lack of year
2000 compliance in the current management and student information systems,
the college rushed to study and select an integrated information system with
multifunctional capabilities. In the meantime, the campus Novell network, on
which much of the instructional computing courseware resided, crashed on a
regular basis. The LRC's CD-ROM network, developed with grant funds and
also using the Novell software, proved unstable as well. IS did not have on staff
any certified Novell engineers or administrators and began outsourcing network repair. Eventually the college turned over the management of the entire
network to an outside vendor. By the summer of 1997, hundreds of new computers were stacked in the warehouse waiting to be placed in labs, classrooms,
and offices before the start of the fall semester. Staff not yet connected to the network demanded connectivity. Staff with network connections demanded desktop support and training. IS postponed installation of new systems. Continuing

network problems halted the installations of software applications for classes starting in the fall. As IS struggled in a crisis management mode, and as the LRC and faculty strove to restore service and courseware to users, campus decision makers became painfully aware of the inadequacy of the current systems, structure, and staffing for information technology. The situation urgently needed corrective action.

Technology Oversight Team

As is customary in academic institutions, WCC initially responded to developing chaos by establishing a team to study and recommend changes. In an atypical departure, however, the president mandated that the team oversee the IS department's decisions and operations. The technology oversight team (TOT) had a threefold function: to guide IS decision making, to take immediate remedial action, and to research and recommend a new information technology structure.

TOT consisted of information and learning technologies stakeholders, providers, and users. Staff representing the LRC, IS, the Executive Panel (the President's cabinet), and instructors made up the small team that set upon a course of action in spring 1997. TOT set priorities for tasks to be completed by the start of the fall semester, organized and recommended resources to accomplish these objectives, established and arranged for staffing of a help desk, and alerted the entire institution to the efforts being put forth to keep initiatives on track. With the assistance of an external consultant, TOT then began serious study of the needs of college student and staff groups and the current organizational capacity to effectively respond to needs. Team members agreed that the primary goal should be to create an organization that provided a premium environment for instruction. TOT understood those traditional boundaries of service and support no longer applied. But TOT did not know yet what the model's configuration might be.

Who Knows Best?

It is de rigueur in community colleges to disparage the administration's use of consultants. Indeed, executive officers at times overly depend on outsiders' expensive advice, ignoring sound proposals or expertise of staff from within the organization. However, during times of near revolutionary change and increasing ambiguity over responsibilities and roles, insularity and dependence on old approaches can be fatal for the organization. Only an outsider can shake loose encrusted mental models and assist insiders in finding creative and strategic solutions, not just incremental adaptations to new environmental challenges. While the study process needed the objectivity and skill of an external consultant for credibility and validity, TOT considered the sensitivity and respect for staff equally important. Therefore, the team agreed on an approach that would respect the dignity of current IS staff members, who were caught in circumstances beyond their control. The college selected a consultant in the fall of 1997 and the process began with exploration of current service issues and projected needs through interviews with providers and users.[1]

The consultant interviewed approximately eighty staff. The consultant also initially assessed over thirty-seven staff providers' current responsibilities, skills, interests, and professional development needs. At this point in the

process, the competence, integrity, and willingness of internal staff to work together complemented the consultant's objectivity and knowledge of successful
models in other institutions. Starting with a powerful collection of assessment
data, TOT and the consultant began the process of restructuring for information
technology support.

A Marriage Made in Heaven or Hell?

Dougherty and McClure, in their examination of reengineering options in the
1997 ACRL publication *Restructuring Academic Libraries*, suggest there are
three forms of reorganization of library and computing organizations in higher
education:

> administrative realignment of reporting and budgetary lines;
>
> collaborative realignment to provide greater working-level linkages; and
>
> blending realignment of the two units into a single, cohesive information
> services division.[2]

At Washtenaw Community College in fall 1997, the circumstances demanded
additional options.

Crises, not limited to those services offered by the LRC and IS, also involved breakdowns in support for information technology initiatives across the
spectrum of instructional and college business activities. The availability of content and courseware on networks changed the teaching and learning process independent of any direction or management of the network environment. Also,
support of instructional labs from a centralized IS proved impossible without
use of distributed divisional staff who had some understanding both of the instructional objectives and of the hardware and software inventory used in the division. Mindful of the complexity of the circumstances and acknowledging that
interdependence had become the norm, TOT went back to the basics and developed the following criteria for evaluating proposed organizational models. They

> will provide quality and timeliness of service,
>
> will be planning-driven,
>
> will empower users,
>
> will include an effective management structure,
>
> will support technological innovation, and
>
> will be cost-effective.

Further goals of the new organization included:

> Design a college-wide, interrelated information technology organization
> based on leadership, intelligent management, and individualized
> service.
>
> Further develop the talents of faculty, staff, and administrators by opti-
> mizing their use of information technology.
>
> Design an environment that will achieve a level of operational excellence.[3]

After TOT and the consultant identified critical success factors, the restructuring process began. It included a participative methodology incorporating analysis of interview and assessment data and review of models at other

organizations. The development of three new models resulted in representing advantages and disadvantages of functional, customer-centered, and discipline-based approaches.

We Are All Client Servers—the New Model

TOT decided on an organizational model for technological support that includes three primary partners and a structure of councils providing strategic planning, monitoring of the implementation of plans and standards, and facilitating essential communication links between providers and users (see figure 1). This model is a modification of the customer-centered approach initially proposed by the consultant. Its prominent feature is that learning resources and enterprise systems and networking (formerly IS) remain centralized, but some responsibilities of the former IS are redistributed. Support of the laboratories and staff desktops is decentralized. Tech teams reside and work in buildings where they provide services. The tech teams, comprising information technology leaders, lab coordinators, and student assistants from various instructional divisions and administrative offices, now provide services that IS previously struggled to provide from a central location with a small technical staff. In brief, the partners in this new organizational structure are the staff in the learning resources division (LR), the staff in the former IS department, now called enterprise systems and networking (ESN), and a distributed group of technical support staff who report to their respective divisional administrators.

The new enterprise systems and networking (ESN) department has a narrower scope than previously. It now focuses on software and hardware management for the new integrated information system, e-mail, and network services. Responsibility for managing the business systems of the college is still the province of ESN. (See lower right quadrant of the organizational chart.) By restricting the scope of information systems services, the model attempts to bolster the department's effectiveness in its remaining service areas. The model strengthens the role of the LR division by both formally recognizing divisional support roles and services and by assigning online library system responsibilities to LR staff. The staff in the LR division already provided a variety of instructional support services, such as multimedia production, instructional design, classroom equipment services, Web services and online information resources. However, annual college budget and staffing decisions did not reflect the division's large increase in number of clients and demands for service. A resulting reliance on part-time staff had undermined seriously the division's service potential. The new model strongly recommends conversion to full-time staffing. It also emphasizes the strong role of LR in designing, developing, and delivering the learning technologies that support instruction. From the library perspective, a very important aspect of the model is the online library system's independence from ESN. Although this change requires moving servers to the LRC and the assumption of new system administration duties by LRC staff, the benefit of direct oversight of these systems is significant.

There are important interrelationships among the three technology support partners that assure that the essential flow of knowledge and collaboration occurs. (The dotted lines on the organizational chart indicate these connections.) Widespread campus dissatisfaction with the prior structure emphasizing an authoritarian IS, the 1980s computer czar model, led to decentralization features in

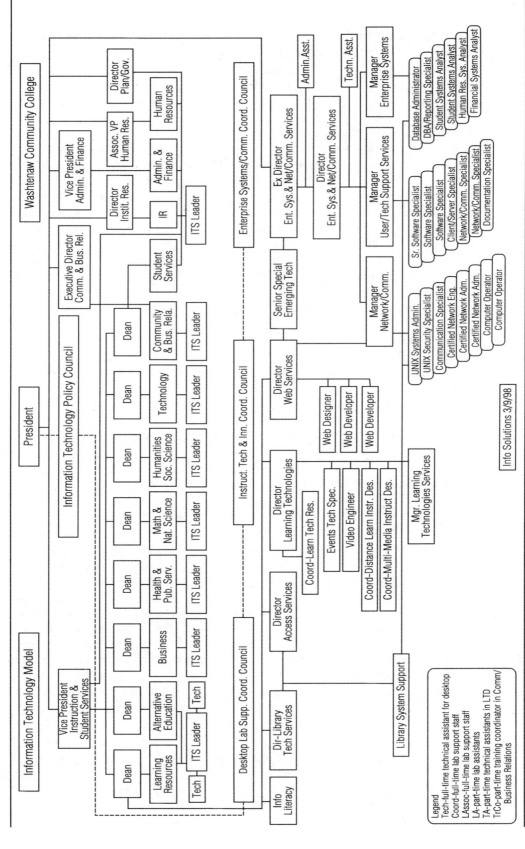

Figure 1 Organizational model for technological support

195

the new model. But planners recognized that with specialized technologies rapidly converging, all information providers need to regularly share skills, knowledge, vision, and services in support of institutional goals.

The Councils

The literature on computing center and library partnerships has given exposure to several different structures. Some moved the units together with a senior executive officer from either the library or the information technology side assuming control. Other partnerships merge certain units only and create a new name and reporting relationship. In reality, success or failure does not appear to depend entirely on the structure. Other variables, such as staff culture, different goals, and varied communication patterns also determine the outcome of mergers and alignments. The model at WCC includes an integrative feature—the role of the councils—that the planners hope will be the key to the success of the structure. The councils link the providers and users together in ongoing collegial relationships that assure the information technology partners collaborate to execute plans and to foster creativity and innovation.

The model requires four councils:

1. The technology policy council, reporting to the president, is the overall umbrella council that receives regular updates from the three coordinating councils on how annual plans are being implemented. The technology policy council members' primary responsibility is to "continuously create and update the college's vision for the future as enabled by information technology resources and formulate strategies to achieve this vision."[4] This council attends to strategic planning and policy making for both information and learning technologies at the college.

2. The desktop/lab support council is a task-focused team that coordinates the use of desktop and lab software. Members are lab and desktop support technicians and faculty and student users. This council recommends standards and operating procedures to facilitate service and increase user satisfaction.

3. The instructional technology and innovation coordinating council is a team that supports creativity and innovative projects. Its members are primarily instructional faculty and staff from the learning resources division. This council focuses on best practices in instruction and on the quality of instructional support.

4. The enterprise systems/networking coordinating council is primarily concerned with the new integrated information system, which is in the process of implementation. Its members are managers from ESN, representatives from the help desk, the student body, department chairs, administrative customers, and the executive panel. They review issues related to security, standards, access, and other policies. These councils work together to operationalize concepts and plans. The goal of the councils is to keep the providers focused on the clients that they serve.

The Implementation—What the Political and Financial Realities Permit

The new model for transforming information technology services at WCC is not inexpensive. Harkening back to the cost-effective criterion that the technology oversight team required from the model, the benefits of consistently high quality services and empowered technology users are worth the cost. Although it might be perceived initially as complex, the model permits a simplicity in communications between providers and users. TOT articulated these and other attributes of the new structure to budget planners in spring 1998.

Although acknowledging the veracity of these principles, the college, due to financial imperatives, halted full implementation of this structure. Executive officers recommended a phased implementation of the entire model over the next two years. They did approve certain aspects of the model for implementation during the current fiscal year, such as LRC staff management of the online library system. A second Web developer position was added to the learning resources division. However, at this time, the other recommended full-time positions are delayed. Only two of the five instructional divisions, business and technology, will have distributed technical staff to handle labs and staff desktops this year. A small technical staff who remain in the enterprise systems and networking department will serve the other divisions and offices. The ESN will be staffed with essential UNIX and CNE networking staff, and will soon hire additional integrated information software support staff.

Of some concern to the planners at this juncture is the future of the councils. With the retirement of a long-serving president and arrival of a new president in summer 1998, the implementation of the council structure is uncertain. Even if the council structure planned in the model is not realized, planners remain optimistic that some organizational representation of this needed dialogue will develop, since all agree that ongoing communication between information technology providers and users is absolutely critical. The planning experience of the last year energized participants and onlookers alike. There is no temptation to regress to familiar but dysfunctional processes or old panaceas. The learning resource center and other information technology partners eagerly seek to realize the full potential of the restructured organization.

What Did the Team Learn?

The technology oversight team learned a lot on the road to organizational excellence. Some of this knowledge is unique to personalities and history in WCC's organization. The following observations may be helpful to other organizations:

There are risks in taking a long time to study and plan change.   Although work with the consultant took less than nine months, the entire process including approval and budget allocation lasted more than a year. During this time, three different persons acted in the position of executive director of information systems. (Two interim directors were hired after the long-serving executive director resigned in fall 1997.) These three directors had different levels of commitment to the new model. This inconsistency weakened the team's advocacy for the model. Also, the frequent change in IS leadership kept alive a climate of disrespect and lack of confidence in IS operations. Changing college presidents before complete implementation of the new model's structure proved even more damaging to the implementation process. As might any new chief executive officer assuming a position in the midst of a major organizational restructuring, WCC's president called a halt to any further implementation to assess first the need for these changes. Planners at other colleges are cautioned not to try to bring about significant organizational change in the last days of a retiring president.

Be a part of the solution.   Most community colleges are unable or unwilling to provide the recommended level of funding for a well-staffed, responsive, information technology environment. Frequently, state and local funding sources for community colleges are not readily available or are insufficient to fund major changes in an institution's software, hardware, or staffing levels. Planners need creativity in finding new funding sources or in developing internal processes to reallocate resources for needed change.

Engaging a consultant gives the team credibility and improves members' effectiveness.   Employees, cynical because of prior failure of college committees to solve information technology problems, will respect a qualified consultant who brings an outsider's perspective and experience and relies on objective data for decision making. Team members more easily find common ground and areas of agreement when an outside expert promotes constructive futuring in place of rehashing previous unsuccessful ventures. In retrospect, WCC's early team efforts were hindered by the president's charge to TOT to oversee IS operations while developing a plan for the future information technology organization. A study team will gain trust and confidence of staff in affected departments more quickly if the study process is conducted independently of the organization's daily operations. Team time will be more efficiently spent as well.

Finding solutions for meeting campus users' information technology support needs is the primary goal of any new process or structure.   Library and information systems staff can easily become lost in a labyrinth of technical justifications for current or desired future structures and methods. Conscientious staff in both professions often delay action by tirelessly seeking perfection. Planning teams need to concentrate continuously on the needs of users when developing a new organization. They need to remember that many models, while imperfect, are workable if all parties are committed to the success of the whole plan. Even if WCC's model is not implemented exactly as designed, the overall goals, nevertheless, should be met. A transformed organization is moving forward.

NOTES

1. The consultant hired by Washtenaw Community College was Judith L. Lyon, Managing Partner of InfoSolutions.edu.
2. Richard M. Dougherty and Lisa McClure, "Repositioning Campus Information Units for the Era of Digital Libraries," in *Restructuring Academic Libraries: Organizational Development in the Wake of Technological Change,* ed. Charles A. Schwartz. ACRL Publications in Librarianship, no. 49 (Chicago: Association of College and Research Libraries, 1997), 67-80.
3. InfoSolutions.edu, "Washtenaw Community College Organizational Analysis Study for Information Technology" (Ann Arbor, Mich., 1998), 4.
4. Ibid., 2.

CHAPTER TWENTY

Creating the New Learning Environment

DAVID W. LEWIS
GEORGIA B. MILLER

Little doubt exists that the academic learning environments ten years from now will be much richer than those today are. Students will have access to powerful computer tools and a wealth of networked information. They will use their resources and the educational experiences created by faculty to learn in new and, one hopes, more effective ways.

The leaders in creating this environment will be the teaching faculty. Librarians and technologists, nevertheless, will be key players. Effectiveness in this endeavor will require both strategic and tactical collaboration. Collaboration is central because of the variety of individuals and units required to work together to create this new learning environment. If the focus is on coordination, which implies tight hierarchies, departments insulated from the outside, and well-constructed chains of command within organizations, success will be difficult to achieve. In the past, universities have been successful largely because they are bottom-up organizations that encourage and reward individual and small-group innovation. They tolerated any resulting disorder and apparent inefficiency. To some, the new communications and computing technologies, and the competitive environment they enable, appear to make obsolete the free-wheeling campus environment of the past. Also, to some, the future development of the university appears to require a choice: campuses may choose either a rich technological environment or they may choose faculty independence. We, however, believe success will come to those campuses that identify strategies that turn this "or" into an "and." Only by combining a rich technology and information environment with an empowered faculty can a campus become the creative learning environment needed to produce quality education in the future.

THE FUTURE OF THE UNIVERSITY

Speculating on the future of the university is a risky, but important, task. Higher education is, by its nature, conservative and slow to change. Therefore, some danger exists in suggesting that we are living in revolutionary times, but we are. The fundamental technological underpinnings of the university are in transition, changing from technologies based on ink on paper and the lecture in front of a chalkboard to technologies that allow information to be communicated over an electronic worldwide network. As Eli M. Noam points out, changes in computer and communications technologies allow information to flow directly to individuals without, as has been the case in the past, these individuals having to come to the university. Noam wonders whether universities can maintain the economic base necessary to support themselves in this environment. Importantly, he notes that the strength of the future university will be in the community it creates and in the role the experts it houses will play in validating knowledge.[1] Donald Langenberg, the chancellor of the University of Maryland system, has estimated that only 100 or so research universities and several hundred liberal arts colleges will survive in their present forms and that the 3,000 remaining institutions of higher education, which serve the vast majority of students, will be profoundly altered by changes in technology.[2]

In examining the effect of technology on the university, some commentators focus on the effect on learning and the ability to replace traditional classroom interactions. They argue that one characteristic of the new technologies is that they are interactive rather than broadcast. This allows the development of learning communities built on complex interactions, much like continuous conversations. Those conversing can be geographically, organizationally, and socially distant from one another. They note that technology also offers the potential to provide customization to accommodate differences in learning styles. The learning experience can be enriched by providing access to large information stores and by creating simulations and visualizations that enlighten and instruct in ways that are impossible using the traditional technologies of the textbook and chalkboard. Accordingly, at the campus and classroom level, the widespread application of technology will require institutions to rethink their approach to teaching and learning. Many consistently conclude that classroom level interactions will change—the lecture will give way to other forms of interaction.

Other commentators focus on dollars. While they hotly debate the details, some contend that the new technologies have the potential to bring to bear significant economies of scale. These commentators make the case that while the initial costs of technology, and the renovations needed to accommodate its use, may be high, the opportunity costs of not moving to the new learning paradigm will be higher. Evolutionary gains may be made by automating current environments, such as providing broader audiences for master lecturers, but revolutionary gains will be possible if there is a rethinking of the full academic endeavor that results in learning and acquiring credentials. John Seely Brown and Paul Duguid, after reviewing these developments, conclude that institutional roles in the new environment will be to provide access, oversight, content, standards, and credentialing. They suggest that there are "three things learners need from an institution of higher education: access to authentic communities of learning, exploration, and knowledge creation; resources to help them work in both distant and local communities; and widely accepted representations for work done."[3]

So what will the future of the university look like? That depends on how academia deals with the opportunities afforded by the technological innovations and the corresponding challenges created by the economics of incorporating those technologies into current structures. Thomas H. Thompson projects, "Higher education delivered asynchronously, targeted precisely at the student's unique learning style and tailored elegantly to exploit his present knowledge and capacity to learn is a radical improvement over the lock-step practices of even today's finest Tier One institutions."[4] Not only is this possible, but successful institutions will be doing this ten years from now. A variety of interactions both face-to-face and virtual will create a sense of community. These interactions will provide students with flexibility not now available both in time and space. Content currently delivered in the classroom and the library will be purchased, in many cases, from national distributors rather than be created and maintained locally. Credentialing will migrate away from course counts and time spent in class, and move toward the use of tests and portfolios.

COMPETITIVE FORCES

The academy no longer has the luxury, as it had in the past, of being able to change at its own pace. As Noam puts it:

> Electronic forms of instruction are inferior to face-to-face teaching (though the latter is often romanticized); rather, they can be provided at dramatically lower cost. At present, private universities charge a tuition of nearly $50 per lecture hour per student. . . . With such Broadway-show sized prices—and without the latter's entertainment value—alternative providers inevitably will enter.[5]

The high fixed costs of providing traditional education, especially faculty labor, coupled with public dissatisfaction with the results of the current system and the potential of new technologies, invites deconstruction of the education value chain. Ted Marchese describes the business view of the potential academic market, as ". . . huge and ripe for the picking . . . an 'addressable market opportunity at the dawn of a new paradigm,' in the breathless words of Morgan Stanley Dean Witter."[6] As has happened in other industries, like health care and banking, the attractiveness of value chain segmentation will allow other education providers to selectively make academic products available to niche markets.

Noam and Marchese make it clear that competition will come to higher education. Philip B. Evans and Thomas S. Wurster provide a good context for exploring this competitive environment through an examination of the effects of technological change on the classic trade-off between richness and reach. Richness has three components: the amount of information conveyed, or bandwidth; the extent to which information can be customized; and its level of interactivity. Reach is the number of people who can receive the information. Universities have been a means of providing rich information services, but their reach has generally been limited. Evans and Wurster wrote:

> The rapid emergence of universal technical standards for communications, allowing everybody to communicate with everybody else at essentially zero cost, is a sea change. . . . Over time, organizations and individuals will be able to extend their reach by orders of magnitude, often with a negligible sacrifice of richness. . . . The changing economics of information threaten virtually every company to rethink its strategy—not incrementally, but fundamentally.[7]

Universities as rich information providers with limited reach are among the institutions that are particularly vulnerable to this change. Organizations that develop strategies that can expand their reach without significant reductions in richness will be at an advantage.

The institutional pressures resulting from the break-down of the traditional trade-off between richness and reach will force universities into a competitive environment unlike any they have seen. This will be especially true for institutions not among the fortunate few elite research universities or highly selective liberal arts colleges. Universities are already being attacked. The success of the University of Phoenix is, at least in part, the result of its successful targeting of the lucrative market for adult business students. The Western Governors University and similar initiatives may peel away the accreditation function, leaving individual institutions to compete to provide courses. However, as Noam argues, textbook publishers who already have in place production teams, marketing capabilities, and distribution channels may ultimately dominate competition in this area.[8] Universities encumbered by inflexible personnel structures, obligations to maintain research infrastructures—particularly the library and the computing center—and traditions that deny the application of market forces to their environment will find the future a challenge.

COMPETITIVE ADVANTAGES OF THE UNIVERSITY

The university does, however, have several competitive advantages. When you can learn anywhere, where you learn may matter more rather than less. First, universities are often attractive and exciting places. They are comfortable communal spaces in a society that is increasingly a fractured community. Second, universities have a culture that may be more adaptable to the information technology revolution than many of its competitors. Evans and Wurster suggest that organizations will evolve a structure that they call "hyperarchy." In a hyperarchy, structures are fluid with amorphous and permeable boundaries. Hyperarchy, as Evans and Wurster state, "Challenges all hierarchies, whether of logic or of power, with the possibility (or the threat) of random access and information symmetry."[9] This sounds in some ways very much like a university, especially that part of it engaged in the core missions of teaching and research. Thomas W. Malone and Robert J. Laubacher argue that technological developments in computing and communication allow individuals to manage issues of coordination in complex projects that once required large hierarchical organizations. This they suggest will lead to what they term an "e-lancy economy" where individuals will work on projects rather than for organizations.[10] This is the way many faculty now work. Unfortunately, most academic administrators, including librarians and technologists, do not find this style of operation comfortable.

The final advantage universities possess is a tradition of being the primary providers of quality education which, when coupled with accreditation, provides a formidable entry barrier to newcomers. Brand names, such as Oxford, Harvard, Michigan, and even the authors' Indiana University Purdue University Indianapolis (or IUPUI), have value.

The advantages cited above mean that universities have an excellent opportunity to succeed if they can manage the transition to the new environment. The pessimists who say that the die is cast and that the university is doomed are probably premature in making that judgment. Universities need to bring their considerable competitive advantages to bear in the near term if they are to enjoy long term success.

AUTOMATING OR "INFORMATING" THE FACULTY

Clearly, the primary advantages the university brings to the table result not from the hierarchies and structures built by administrators, but rather from the culture of inquiry and open and free-wheeling exploration that comes from the faculty. The challenge is to adjust to the new set of technologies without losing the values that make universities special and productive places.

For Plater, faculty time is the key issue. He suggests that the emerging model will be more contractual, with faculty setting group goals and negotiated performance measures. Faculty time will need to focus on institutional needs. He calls for an organization that creates collaborative teams of faculty and other staff who have discretion as teams inside established university goals. His proposals, while challenging to established practice, maintain a central and creative place for faculty in the university. The first item on his agenda for change is to "make faculty and staff development the engine that drives campus mission."[11]

Many have predicted a rise in distributed courses delivered over the Web as an alternative to face-to-face delivery of the same material.[12] Some have seen this as leading to a decline in faculty authority over what is taught and as threatening to faculty employment. Not surprisingly, many faculty members are concerned about their role in the future. A subtitle of an article in the *Chronicle of Higher Education* on technology in the classroom asks, "Will 'unbundling' of tasks give faculty members more time or put them on the sidelines?"[13] David F. Noble, in his article "Digital Diploma Mills," asserts that commercial interests are driving the high-tech transformation of higher education that is being implemented top-down by administrators without concern for faculty or student interests. He further asserts, "As in other industries, the technology is being deployed by management primarily to discipline, deskill, and displace labor."[14] Noble suggests that the impact on faculty will be similar to that on doctors in HMOs.

On the other hand, John Seely Brown and Paul Duguid see similar developments as empowering faculty and providing them opportunities to be more creative in their teaching.[15] Similarly, Stephen DeLong urges faculty to find ways to guide student learners in ways that inspire exploratory self-study. He suggests, "The role of faculty then becomes to facilitate acquisition of knowledge by teaching discernment, which is getting very close to the goal that most of us longingly articulate: we want to teach students to think."[16] Kit Sims Taylor points out that new tools do not necessarily displace the craftsman, but higher education may provide an environment where new tools will magnify the ability of the craftsman to expand and enhance the product.[17]

The conflicting notions of the effect of technology on higher education are familiar. Shoshanna Zuboff described these same tensions in her classic study of computerization in industrial and office settings.[18] She contrasts automation, where systems absorb the skills and knowledge of workers and control remains centralized, with what she calls "informating," where the technology to distribute information is used to enhance the creativity of workers. Whether jobs are automated or informated is a key decision that determines both organizational effectiveness and the levels of satisfaction of those who work in the organization. As these decisions are, or soon will be, made in universities, the results are far from clear. Clearly, the tensions between automating and informating will be present in the university throughout the coming transformations. The productive path is to use the technology to empower faculty, to informate them, rather than developing strategies that automate faculty in an attempt ultimately to replace them.

Critical is the establishment of a new academic model. Creating this model will require universities to review all their structures, including the organization chart, the reward systems, technologies and methods of doing business, facilities and equipment, decision-making customs, communication channels, financial arrangements, and funding streams. The result must provide faculty different, but creative and powerful, roles that will compensate them for the inevitable disruption that change will bring.

LIBRARIES AND COMPUTER CENTERS

In her 1984 article, "The Electronic Library—A Vision for the Future," Patricia Battin proposed the creation of a scholarly information center by merging the computer center and the library. She argued such integration would combine the strengths and expertise of both groups and, "provide one-stop shopping for the university community as well as a stabilizing planning mechanism for effective and flexible response to rapidly changing technologies."[19] In the decade-and-a-half since Battin's article and the merger of libraries and computer center that took place at Columbia University where Battin served as the chief administrator, the debate for and against the administrative combination of libraries and computer centers continues. Though the logic of Battin's argument remains persuasive to some, cultural conflicts, organizational competitiveness, distrust, and simple inertia have limited the integration Battin predicted. Arnold Hirshon's recent study cites only ninety colleges or universities that have consolidated their libraries and computing organizations.[20]

Though perhaps useful in vertical, hierarchical organizations, combining the library and the computer center may no longer be the most sensible solution. Traditionally, computer centers encompassed the bulk of the computing on a university campus. Today, innovations in telecommunications and technology put sufficient computing power on the desktop to handle production and support for many of the critical applications in both teaching and learning as well as research environments. Although the computer center usually manages the network infrastructure, many of the other technology roles are distributed throughout the university. Similarly, the library roles and functions may be changing as large databases are increasingly purchased from external sources. In the new university models, the focus of librarians will be more on teaching students to navigate and evaluate information, and on assisting faculty in using resources effectively in curriculum, rather than on collection building.

Librarians and computing professionals are often excited by current technological developments and see an expansion of their roles. To some, this suggests the need to consolidate to coordinate effectively an increasingly important university function. There are, however, three significant technological trends that, while visible, have not been fully appreciated. As they play out, these trends will make consolidation less likely and alter the roles of libraries and computing organizations. First, bandwidth will expand to the point that it will become essentially free.[21] Second, individuals will own and take responsibility for their own computing devices. These devices will be small, portable, and easy to connect to both campus and commercial networks. Third, the storage and organization of information will move from an activity performed at the local level to one distributed across the network and carried out by national organizations. These three trends, taken together, mean that many of the activities of libraries and computer centers will need to be restructured and may disappear altogether. Geography will become less a constraint, and the local support traditionally provided by libraries and computer centers will be supplied at a distance, or, as is more likely the case, be incorporated into the systems. Information resources will be increasingly bundled into large chunks and licensed at the state or consortia level.

As these changes play out, libraries and computer centers should expect to be radically transformed. What will matter most is not maximization of resource allocations or close coordination of activities, but whether organizational structures and cultures allow librarians and technologists to contribute their expertise in the chaos of the hyperarchy central to the success of the new university. Developing fluid and distributed structures, which encourage individual technologists and librarians to apply their skills to the work of teaching and learning, will be the most productive path.

KEYS TO SUCCESS

There will be several critical success factors for institutions as they move into the next millennium. They include: (a) a faculty committed to a vision based on student learning; (b) a faculty open to determining and implementing new strategies for reaching that vision; (c) an institutional willingness to be organizationally nimble; and (d) alliances with partners that will allow new configurations of the services provided by the university.

When we focus on the relationships between librarians and computer center staff, we are not addressing the critical relationship. While issues of merging organizations and collaboration and coordination between these organizations matter, the central issue is how both organizations relate to faculty. As Battin wrote recently, addressing both librarians and computer professionals:

> We have to look to our scholarly colleagues to contribute, as well. They must work with us in ways that we have not either invited or wanted in the past. . . . We can no longer make those decisions on our own; we have to give up some of this control.[22]

This is the key issue and the key relationship, but it will not be easy. A part of this will require an uncomfortable intrusion of faculty into the workings of both organizations. On most campuses, libraries and computer centers have faculty advisory groups, but they are usually positioned to have little influence on the important decisions of the organizations. Both libraries and computer centers have been comfortably insulated from faculty intrusions into their operating discretion. An empowered faculty committed to transforming the university must have a say in the funding and deployment of the infrastructure.

Budget strategies will also need to be reviewed. Libraries and computer centers are accustomed to operating with resource allocation strategies focused on maintaining infrastructures. Neither organization is comfortable with budgeting that allows much room for discretionary spending. Required is a willingness to consider seriously opportunity costs and an ability to respond to initiatives that will arise from the activities of many diverse groups and individuals. To some, this will appear as an institutional appropriation of funds that rightly "belongs" to the two units. However, the organizational manifestations of the library and the computer center are less important than the overall effectiveness of the university, and that this will require reallocation of resources.[23]

Libraries and computer centers need to reconsider their organizational structures if they are to become nimble themselves and if they are to assist faculty in developing the ability to adapt quickly to opportunities.[24] One approach to this problem, which has been implemented at Indiana University Purdue University Indianapolis, is the use of instructional teams to develop and deliver courses. These teams are led by faculty and include librarians and technologists. They can, if appropriately empowered, provide necessary organizational components for implementing successful learning models. Our experience is that, while this approach requires a considerable allocation of staff resources, it allows for the development of curriculum in ways impossible if faculty worked in isolation.[25]

Central to these efforts is the need to consciously change organizational cultures. Gillian M. McCombs, using ethnographic methods, looked at the culture of an academic computer center. She concluded no longer effective the original values that had shaped the culture of the organization for decades. Nevertheless, these values still shaped the thinking of the organization's leaders, making them unable to help the staff learn new ways of doing things. This resulted in a dissonance in the organization "catastrophic to their [the staff's] personal and professional lives and impacting on their ability to provide adequate service to their users."[26] Unfortunately, this is not an isolated problem. Academic computer centers still often operate with cultures that date from the days of mainframe isolation, and academic libraries often still operate with cultures built over the last century that focused on managing large physical collections and large and complex record structures based on 3x5-card technology. While the technologies used by both organizations have obviously changed radically, cultures have been slower to shift. The dissonance cited by McCombs is a reality in many academic libraries and computer centers. To change demands leadership willing to admit to the cultural impediments to change, and leadership willing to actively push the organization into new modes of behavior. Many of the required changes reduce hierarchical control and lead to more discretion by line professionals. Unfortunately, too often leadership is unwilling to give up control in order to enhance the broader organization's performance.

FINAL THOUGHTS

In an interview with management guru Tom Peters, Thomas Kiely reports Peters' assertion, "Organizations seeking models for success in the years ahead will find them in the work of small, nimble project teams." Peters further predicts that neither "rigid, hierarchical people or rigid, hierarchical companies are going to survive in the next 25 years"; rather that this will be the age of biological models of organizations that recreate or reinvent themselves daily.[27]

If the library and the computing center are spending their time defining the boundaries between the two organizations, then they are not making progress. Unfortunately, most of the players on campus are thinking about what the next step will be for their particular units. We need to envision the academic environment we seek to create and then work backward to today. The conceptual frame needs to be the desired future, not "How will the library contribute?" or "What is the computer center's role?" The key to success will be in having the librarians and technologists and other support professionals on campus, and most importantly the teaching faculty, learning to work together in the increasingly large gray area where all have expertise and responsibilities. The trust required to make this change needs to be built over time. The best strategy is the creation of small fluid teams focusing on course or department level projects.

Major alliances will be formed—among universities, among libraries, with private-sector providers. Some universities will be focused on campuses that create on-site learning environments richly supported by technological innovations; some will coordinate and broker content provided mostly by other providers; some will be providers; and some will be niche players. For librarians and technologists, the key to success is helping our institutions define their role and working, often outside currently existing organizational structures, to make that organization really good at what it has chosen to become.

We are not pessimistic about the future of the university. Though we expect there to be significant change in the academy in the next decade, we are confident in its underlying value to society and the unique role it can play. As Kevin Kelly, the executive editor of *Wired,* said in concluding his review of the networked economy, "The wonderful news about the Network Economy is that it plays right into human strengths. Repetition, sequels, copies, and automation all tend toward the free, while the innovative, original, and the imaginative all soar in value." [28] We believe that ultimately the university is mostly about imagination, and only a little about repetition, and as such its value, too, will soar.

NOTES

1. Eli M. Noam, "Electronics and the Dim Future of the University," *Science* 270 (October 13, 1995): 247-249.
2. Donald N. Langenberg, "Power Plants or Candle Factories?" *Science* 272 (June 21, 1996): 1721.
3. John Seely Brown and Paul Duguid, "Universities in the Digital Age," *Change* 28 (July/August 1996): 18.
4. Thomas H. Thompson, "Three Futures of the Electronic University," *Educom Review* 33 (March/April 1998): 40.
5. Eli M. Noam, "Will Books Become the Dumb Medium?" *Educom Review* 33 (March 1998): 20.
6. Ted Marchese, "Not-So-Distant Competitors: How New Providers Are Remaking the Postsecondary Marketplace," *AAHE Bulletin* 50 (May 1998): 5.
7. Philip B. Evans and Thomas S. Wurster, "Strategy and the New Economics of Information," *Harvard Business Review* 75 (September/October 1997): 74.
8. Noam, "Will Books Become the Dumb Medium?" 20-21.
9. Evans and Wurster, "Strategy and the New Economics of Information," 75.

10. Thomas W. Malone and Robert J. Laubacher, "The Dawn of the E-Lance Economy," *Harvard Business Review* 76 (September/October 1998): 145-152.

11. William M. Plater, "Future Work: Faculty Time in the Twenty-first Century," *Change* 27 (May/June 1995): 32.

12. See, for example, Thompson, "Three Futures of the Electronic University," Stephen E. DeLong, "The Shroud of Lecturing," *First Monday* 2 (May 1997), http://www.firstmonday.dk/issues/issue2_5/delong/index.html (July 21, 1998), or Peter Drucker as quoted in Robert Lenzner and Stephen S. Johnson, "Seeing Things As They Really Are," *Forbes* 159 (March 10, 1997): 126-127.

13. Jeffrey R. Young, "Rethinking the Role of the Professor in an Age of High-Tech Tools: Will Unbundling of Tasks Give Faculty Members More Time or Put Them on the Sidelines?" *Chronicle of Higher Education* (October 3, 1997): A20.

14. David F. Noble, "Digital Diploma Mills: The Automation of Higher Education," *First Monday* 3 (January 1998), http://www.firstmonday.dk/issues/issue3_1/noble/index.html (July 20, 1998). Noble's article is summarized and responded to in *Educom Review* 33 (May/June 1998): 22-34 .

15. Brown and Duguid, "Universities in the Digital Age," 11-19.

16. DeLong, "The Shroud of Lecturing."

17. Kit Sims Taylor, "Higher Education: From Craft-Production to Capitalist Enterprise?" *First Monday* 3 (September 1998), http://www.firstmonday.dk/issues/issue3_9/taylor/index.html (September 8, 1998).

18. Shoshanna Zuboff, *In the Age of the Smart Machine: The Future of Work and Power* (New York: Basic Books, 1988).

19. Patricia Battin, "The Electronic Library: A Vision for the Future," *Educom Bulletin* 19 (summer 1984): 17.

20. Arnold Hirshon, *Integrating Computing and Library Services: An Administrative Planning and Implementation Guide for Information Resources*, CAUSE Professional Paper Series 18 (Boulder, Colo.: CAUSE, 1998), 1.

21. See Kevin Kelly, "New Rules for the New Economy," *Wired* 5.09 (September 1997), http://www.wired.com/wired/5.09/newrules.html (September 8, 1998).

22. Patricia Battin in Brian L. Hawkins and Patricia Battin, "The Changing Role of the Information Resources Professional: A Dialog," *Cause/Effect* 20 (spring 1997), http://www.cause.org/information-resources/ir-library/cem9717.html (July 20, 1998).

23. For an analysis of what this might mean for libraries see David W. Lewis, "What If Libraries Are Artifact Bound Institutions?" *Information Technology and Libraries* 17 (December 1998): 191-197.

24. For one analysis of this issue see David W. Lewis, "An Organizational Paradigm for Effective Academic Libraries," *College & Research Libraries* 47 (July 1986): 337-353.

25. For information on instructional teams at Indiana University Purdue University Indianapolis see http://www-lib.iupui.edu/itt/resource.html (September 8, 1998). For an exploration of the issues raised by this approach see Philip Tompkins, Susan Perry, and Joan K. Lippincott, "New Learning Communities: Collaboration, Networking, and Information Literacy," *Information Technologies and Libraries* 17 (June 1998): 100-106.

26. Gillian M. McCombs, "The Keys to the Kingdom Have Been Distributed: An Organizational Analysis of an Academic Computing Center," *Library Trends* 46 (spring 1998): 695.

27. Thomas Kiely, "Unconventional Wisdom," *CIO* (December 1993/January 1994): 24-28.

28. Kelly, "New Rules for the New Economy."

Contributors

Adella Blain is Dean of Learning Resources at Washtenaw Community College in Ann Arbor, Michigan. Before 1987, she served as director of the Learning Resource Center, the college's library and media services department, and earlier as a faculty reference and instruction librarian. Blain holds an undergraduate degree in English literature and a master's degree in library science from the University of Michigan.

Onadell Bly is the Systems Librarian at the Oliver Ocasek Regional Medical Center at the Northeast Ohio Universities College of Medicine (NEOUCOM). She holds an M.S.L.S. from Kent State University, and, before coming to NEOUCOM, she held a similar position at the University of Akron.

Jennifer Cargill is Dean of Libraries, LSU Libraries, Louisiana State University and A & M College in Baton Rouge, a position she has held since 1991. She also served as Associate University Librarian, Rice University; Associate Director of Libraries, Texas Tech University; and in various positions at Miami University (Ohio) and University of Houston—University Park. Her experience includes technical and public services, collection development, automation, and personnel matters. Her degrees include an M.S. in library science from LSU and an M.Ed. in higher education from Miami of Ohio.

Rhoda K. Channing is the Director of the Z. Smith Reynolds Library of Wake Forest University. She had previous library positions at Boston College and the University of Kentucky. She currently serves on the board of SOLINET, and on the North Carolina State Historical Records Advisory Board, and is chair of the Library Administration and Management Section of NCLA. Channing has an M.S.L.S. from Columbia University and an M.B.A. from Boston College.

Jay L. Dominick is the Assistant Vice President and Chief Information Officer for Information Systems at Wake Forest University. He implemented the first campus network at Wake Forest University after being hired in October 1991. Dominick became the Director of Information Systems in 1995 and Chief Information Officer in 1996. Dominick has an undergraduate degree from the University of North Carolina-Chapel Hill in mathematical sciences, and an M.A. in national security studies.

Connie V. Dowell is Dean of Libraries and Information Access at San Diego State University. She was appointed Vice President for Information Services and Librarian of the College at Connecticut College in 1998. She joined Connecticut College in 1993 from the University of California, Santa Barbara, as Librarian of the

College and Professor. In 1994, she was asked to provide leadership for the college's merger of libraries, computing, and technology planning.

Eugene A. Engeldinger is Vice President for Academic Information Services at Carthage College in Kenosha, Wisconsin. After coming to Carthage as library director in 1990, he was promoted to this new position in 1993. Previously, he held positions at Indiana University and the University of Wisconsin-Eau Claire. At the University of Wisconsin-Eau Claire he served at various times as head of reference, head of public services, and interim director. In 1990, Engeldinger received the Wisconsin Librarian of the Year award.

Robert S. Freeman is an Assistant Professor of library science, Foreign Languages and Literatures Bibliographer, and Reference Librarian at Purdue University. He has an M.A. in Germanic languages and literatures from the University of North Carolina at Chapel Hill and an M.S. in library and information science from the University of Illinois at Urbana-Champaign.

Edward D. Garten is Dean of Libraries and Information Technologies at the University of Dayton. He holds an M.L.S. from Kent State and a Ph.D. in higher education administration from the University of Toledo. Before his tenure at Dayton, he worked at Moorhead State University, Northern State University, and Tennessee Tech University.

Kim Granath is Assistant Professor, Electronic Resources Librarian at the University of Montana's Mansfield Library. She received her B.S. in biology from Illinois State University and her M.L.S. with an emphasis in medical libraries from the University of Oklahoma. She is a Distinguished Member of the Academy of Health Information Professionals.

Larry Hardesty is the College Librarian at Austin College, Sherman, Texas. Previously he held library positions at Eckerd College, DePauw University, and Kearney State College (now the University of Nebraska-Kearney). He received a Ph.D. in library and information science from Indiana University-Bloomington in 1982 and an M.A.L.A. from the University of Wisconsin-Madison in 1974. He has other graduate degrees in instructional systems technology and history, and an undergraduate degree in history and political science from Kearney State College, 1969. He is currently the president of the Association of College and Research Libraries (ACRL).

Jeffry T. Hart is Assistant Director for Management Information Services, Troy State University, Troy, Alabama. He previously held the position of Information Technology Coordinator at Troy State University Library at Troy. Before his career in academe, Hart served as network administrator for Southeast Health Plan, Birmingham, Alabama, and earlier as a computer operator for Bell South. His undergraduate degree is in business administration; he is presently working on a master's in business administration.

Ronald D. Hay has been Executive Director of Computing Services at Louisiana State University and A & M College since 1990. Hay has been at LSU since 1976 and has served in various computing, data processing, and academic positions.

He holds an M.S. in business management from Southern Illinois University-Carbondale. Before coming to LSU, he worked in data processing at Southern Illinois University-Carbondale, Ford Motor Company, and the Federal Bureau of Investigation.

Bernard Hecker is Director of the Learning Technology Project and Director of Academic Computing at Trinity College. His abiding interest in organizational development is supported by his academic training, which includes a doctorate in social psychology.

Kimberly A. Jordan is Director of Computing for the College of Humanities and Social Sciences at Carnegie Mellon University in Pittsburgh. She holds a B.S. in political science from Williams College and an M.S. in applied information management from the University of Oregon. Jordan served previously as Director of Academic Computing at Whitman College and held academic computing positions at Swarthmore and Williams Colleges. She recently served as president of the Social Science Computing Association.

Michael D. Kathman has been Director of Libraries and Media for the College of St. Benedict and St. John's University (Minn.) since 1980; before that he was Director of Libraries for St. John's University, and he served as Director of Academic Computing for both colleges from 1986 to 1992. Kathman has an undergraduate degree from St. Procopius College, and from the University of Michigan an A.M.L.S and an A.M. in American studies.

David W. Lewis is Acting University Librarian, University Libraries, Indiana University Purdue University Indianapolis. He previously held library positions at the University of Connecticut, Columbia University, Franklin and Marshall College, and Hamilton College. He has B.A. from Carleton College, an M.L.S. from Columbia University, and certificates of advance study from the University of Chicago and Columbia University.

Scott B. Mandernack, Associate Professor of Library Science and Undergraduate Reference and Instruction Librarian in the Undergraduate Library at Purdue University, holds an M.L.S. from the University of Wisconsin-Milwaukee.

Edward Meachen has been Associate Vice President for Learning and Information Technology at the University of Wisconsin System Administration since March 1998. He was Associate Vice Chancellor for Information Services at UW-Parkside from 1990 to 1998. He has also served as library director at North Central College in Naperville, Illinois, and as reference librarian at the Newberry Library in Chicago. He received a Ph.D. in history and literature from Emory University and an M.L.S. from the University of Chicago.

Terrence F. Mech is Vice President for Information and Instructional Technologies and Director of the Library at King's College, Pennsylvania. He was Director of the Library at King's College for twelve years before being named vice president of the newly formed division in July 1994. Mech holds graduate degrees from the Pennsylvania State University (higher education), Clarion State University (library science) and Illinois State University (sociology).

Georgia B. Miller is Technology Partnerships Liaison Officer in the Office of the Vice President for Information Technology, Indiana University Purdue University Indianapolis. She served previously as the Executive Director of Integrated Technologies at Indiana University Purdue University Indianapolis, professor and Assistant Dean and Director of Undergraduate Programs for the Indiana University School of Business at Indianapolis, and on the faculty of the College of Business at Western Kentucky University. Miller has a B.S. and an M.A. from Western Kentucky University and an Ed.D. from the University of Kentucky.

Raymond K. Neff has served as Vice President for Information Services at Case Western Reserve University, where he also holds academic appointments as adjunct professor of statistics in the College of Arts and Sciences and adjunct professor of biostatistics in the School of Dentistry. In 1990, he took on additional responsibilities as Director of the University Libraries to coordinate the evolution of the library at Case Western Reserve University. Previously he has served in positions at the University of California-Berkeley, Dartmouth College, and Harvard University.

John N. Olsgaard is an Associate Provost of the University, and is also an associate professor in the College of Library and Information Science at the University of South Carolina. His educational background includes a B.A. from Jamestown College, an M.A. in American history from the University of North Dakota, an M.L.I.S. from the University of Iowa, and a Ph.D. in library and information science from the University of Illinois at Urbana-Champaign.

Vicki Pengelly holds a B.A. in sociology and anthropology from Carleton College, Northfield, Minnesota. Having previously served as trainer, newsletter editor, and help desk supervisor in Computing and Information Services, she is currently Director of Client Services at the University of Montana.

Stephen Peterson is College Professor and Librarian at Trinity College, Hartford, Connecticut—a post he has held since 1991. From 1972 to 1991 he served as Divinity School Librarian at Yale University. He currently is Principal Investigator of Trinity Learning Technology Project. Mr. Peterson holds A.M. degrees in librarianship and Near Eastern languages and literature from the University of Michigan and a Ph.D. from Vanderbilt University.

Donald E. Riggs is Vice President for Information Services and University Librarian at Nova Southeastern University. Prior to his current position, Riggs served as Dean of University Libraries and Professor, University of Michigan, and Dean of University Libraries, Arizona State University, respectively. A prolific author, he has served as editor of *Library Administration & Management, Library Hi Tech*, and is currently editing *College & Research Libraries*. In 1991, Riggs received the Hugh Atkinson Memorial Award for his innovation in library technology.

Sue Samson is Associate Professor, Humanities Librarian, and Library Instruction Coordinator at the University of Montana's Mansfield Library. Previously she served as head of Public Services at the Alaska State Library in Juneau. She received her B.S. in English literature and education from Indiana University, Bloomington, and her M.A. in library and information science from the University of Missouri, Columbia.

Peggy Seiden is the College Librarian at Swarthmore College. Prior to joining Swarthmore in 1998, she was College Librarian at Skidmore College. She previously served as head of the library at Penn State-New Kensington and held various library and computing positions at Carnegie Mellon University. She is currently the president of the Reference and User Services Association (RUSA). Seiden has an undergraduate degree from Colby College, an M.A. in medieval studies from the University of Toronto, and an M.L.S. from Rutgers University.

Paul J. Setze has a Ph.D. in general experimental psychology from DePaul University in Chicago. He has held a number of positions in higher education computing organizations, including Assistant Director for Academic Computing at the University of Illinois at Chicago, Director of Academic Computing at Williams College, and Chief Technology Officer at Whitman College. Setze is currently a project manager with Systems and Computer Technology Corporation (SCT).

George Terry is the Vice Provost and Dean of Libraries and Information Systems at the University of South Carolina. His educational background includes a B.A., M.A., and Ph.D. in American history from the University of South Carolina.

Theresa C. Trawick is automation consultant for the Alabama Public Library Service. Previously, she served as electronic services librarian at Troy State University, Troy, Alabama. In this position from 1994 to 1998, she served as liaison with the university's Management Information Services (computing center) staff. While at Troy, she also served as chairperson of Reference and Collection Management for ten years. She has a master's in library science from the University of Alabama and additional credited course work in computer science.

John Mark Tucker is Humanities, Social Science and Education Librarian and Professor of Library Science at Purdue University. He earned a Ph.D. from the University of Illinois, M.L.S. and Ed.S. degrees from George Peabody College for Teachers of Vanderbilt University, and a B.A. from Lipscomb University.

Robin Wagner is Director of Library of Services at Gettysburg College. From 1994 to 1997 she served on the Planning, Training, and Delivery Teams in Information Resources and later was Delivery Team Leader. Before coming to Gettysburg College, Wagner served as Associate Librarian for Systems and Access at Franklin & Marshall College and as a Reference Librarian at Dartmouth College. Robin began her library career in Manuscripts and Archives at the University of Virginia. Robin's academic background is in history and anthropology. She earned a B.A. from Dickinson College, an M.L.S. from the University of Kentucky, and an M.A. from Dartmouth College.

Andrew W. White is Systems Librarian, Bates College, Lewiston, Maine. He has served as Project Manager and Information Fellow for Information Services at Connecticut College. Prior to coming to Connecticut, White served as Electronic Services Coordinator for the Indiana University undergraduate library. White holds an M.L.S and M.A. in literature from Indiana University.

Delmus E. Williams is Dean of University Libraries at the University of Akron in Ohio. He holds an M.S.L.S. from the University of Kentucky and a Ph.D. in library science from the University of North Carolina. Prior to his tenure at Akron, he worked at Washington and Lee University, Western Illinois University, and the University of Alabama in Huntsville.

Index